Microeconomics

FOR

DUMMIES

A Wiley Brand

U.S. Edition

**by Lynne Pepall, PhD, Peter Antonioni,
and Manzur Rashid, PhD**

FOR

DUMMIES

A Wiley Brand

Microeconomics For Dummies®, U.S. Edition

Published by: **John Wiley & Sons, Inc.,** 111 River Street, Hoboken, NJ 07030-5774, www.wiley.com

Copyright © 2016 by John Wiley & Sons, Inc., Hoboken, New Jersey

Adapted from *Microeconomics For Dummies,* U.K. Edition (978-1-119-02662-4) © 2016 by John Wiley & Sons, Ltd., Chichester, West Sussex, UK

Published simultaneously in Canada

For general information on our other products and services, please contact our Customer Care Department within the U.S. at 877-762-2974, outside the U.S. at 317-572-3993, or fax 317-572-4002. For technical support, please visit www.wiley.com/techsupport.

Wiley publishes in a variety of print and electronic formats and by print-on-demand. Some material included with standard print versions of this book may not be included in e-books or in print-on-demand. If this book refers to media such as a CD or DVD that is not included in the version you purchased, you may download this material at http://booksupport.wiley.com. For more information about Wiley products, visit www.wiley.com.

Library of Congress Control Number: 2015960129

ISBN 978-1-119-18439-3 (pbk); ISBN 978-1-119-18440-9 (ePub); ISBN 978-1-119-18441-6 (ePDF)

Manufactured in the United States of America

10 9 8 7 6 5 4 3 2 1

Contents at a Glance

Table of Contents

Introduction

Economics is about many things. On one level, it's concerned with humanity's struggle to cope with scarcity and how this leads individuals to make choices about the things that should have priority. On another level, it's about the human quest for happiness in an uncertain world, and the ways people have found to achieve it. On yet another level, economics is about how societies organize themselves from the bottom up, using markets as a way of trading with each other. However you look at it, economics is a huge subject.

Microeconomics looks at economics on the smallest scales — at the level of individual consumers and firms — and builds up to an understanding of how markets and industries work. Microeconomics has become a very big subject too, taking in everything from what kinds of decisions people make to the right way to measure and analyze those decisions. It's the part of economics that's like looking through a microscope as small creatures go about their business.

So that's what microeconomists do. The microscope, though, is a bit unusual. It's not made of glass, but of tools, called models, which are ways of representing the world that you can use to examine real life. They're not real life itself. Making a model of real life that was accurate in every way would be akin to the perfect global map in a Lewis Carroll story that ended up being the size of the entire world. Instead, models are guides to help you when you need to know what's going on in a particular situation.

Maybe you're thinking about starting a business. Microeconomics can help with everything from working out how much to pay staff to knowing which markets to avoid. Maybe you're wondering whether a company is a good place to invest in. Microeconomics can help you figure out whether the company is profitable in the market it's competing in. Maybe you want to figure out how to get the best price for something you want to sell. Microeconomics can help you work out how to auction it off to get the highest price. In all these places in life, microeconomics can help you figure out an answer.

About This Book

This book takes you through the most common tools and models that micro-economists use to make sense of a complicated world. The aspects that we cover include the following:

- ✔ What utility is and why microeconomists assume people maximize it.
- ✔ What a firm is and what it does.
- ✔ What happens when firms and consumers interact in a market.
- ✔ Why competition is usually better than monopoly.
- ✔ How to understand competition among firms, and how the outcome depends on the way firms compete.
- ✔ What happens when some people in a marketplace know more about the trade than others.
- ✔ How you can generalize — to some extent — the results from one market to all markets, and how that informs decisions you may make about distributing resources.
- ✔ How you can figure out which options a firm will choose to take when it has competitors who also want to do the best for themselves.
- ✔ How and why markets fail, and some of the things you can do about it.

Foolish Assumptions

Economists often make assumptions — they have to make models when they don't know exactly how things work in a specific case. Sometimes those assumptions can be foolish, something we learned from Samuel L. Jackson in *The Long Kiss Goodnight* and Eric Bogosian in *Under Siege 2: Dark Territory*. In writing this book, we make some foolish assumptions about you:

- ✔ You're interested in putting together a picture of why the world is as it is.
- ✔ You're smart and you don't just accept a glib and easy answer — like us.
- ✔ You're interested in learning more about economics and are looking for a good place to start. Maybe you're considering studying more at school or university, or adding to your impressive portfolio of professional skills.

✔ You're a citizen bemused by discussion of business news and want to know how anyone arrives at the opinions they do.

✔ You're not frightened about using the odd number or bit of simple math — we try to do nearly everything in words, but economics deals with money, and money comes in numbers and that's not something we can do anything about.

✔ You're sure, from the book's branding and its fun, accessible style and easy-to-read layout, that you'll gain more utility from reading it than from other activities, such as archaeology or knitting.

Some of or all these assumptions may turn out to be true. Whichever are, we hope that this book jibes with your desire to understand the wild world of microeconomics.

Icons Used in This book

To help you get the most out of this book, we use a few icons to flag particularly noteworthy items.

This icon highlights handy hints for smoothing out your microeconomics journey.

Some of the ideas in this book are so important for understanding microeconomics that they need special emphasis — often because they're easy to get wrong. When you see this icon, you know that the associated text is something economists really want you to understand.

The world is full of pitfalls for the unwary. Here we stress areas for which you need to watch out.

Economists use technical terms to speak to each other — it's just shorthand usually, so that no one needs to go through pages and pages of the same things. When you see this icon, you know that you're being let into the clubhouse — economics is an inclusive science — and picking up a piece of lingo that economists use to cut long stories short.

Theories are great, but ultimately economics is about the real world, and the best way to see what microeconomics can do is to see it in action. This icon tells you that you're getting something from real-life practice to help you get the idea.

Beyond the Book

But wait! There's more! A handy e-cheat sheet (at www.dummies.com/cheatsheet/microeconomics) to keep important info handy at all times.

Where to Go from Here

The great thing about a reference book like this one is that you don't have to worry about spoilers and can dive straight in anywhere you choose. If you've just seen the film *Dr. Strangelove* and you want to jump further into the wacky world of game theory, be our guest (check out Part V). If you want to figure out why someone wants to break up a monopoly, move straight to Chapter 13 without passing Go. To see how economists think about pollution, check out Chapter 14. Feel free to peruse the table of contents and index to look up whatever may interest you and flip right to that page.

Economists are fine with choice — trust us, we make a living *because* people are able to choose. A common choice with books is to start at the beginning. That way you get to see how the whole subject unfolds, from simple ideas to more complex levels.

However you choose to use it, we hope you enjoy — and get lots of utility from — this book. With that, we wish you good luck and happy reading!

Part I
Getting Started with Microeconomics

In this part . . .

- ✔ See how microeconomics looks at firms and individuals.
- ✔ Discover how microeconomics builds on people's choices.
- ✔ Understand how consumers choose.
- ✔ Look at the ways firms make their decisions.

Chapter 1

Discovering Why Microeconomics Is a Big Deal

In This Chapter

▶ Introducing the areas that are the focus of microeconomics

▶ Understanding the key roles of rational decision-making, competition, and cooperation

▶ Seeing that markets don't always work

A s we're sure you know, *micro* as a prefix often indicates something very small, such as a microchip or a microcosm. *Micro* can also mean something that isn't small itself but that is used to examine small things, such as a microscope.

Microeconomics is the area of economics that studies the decisions of individual consumers and producers and how they come together to make markets. It explores how people decide to do what they do and what happens when interests conflict. It also considers how people can improve markets through their actions, the effects of laws, and other outside interventions. So despite the name, microeconomics is in fact a huge subject.

Traditionally, people contrasted microeconomics with *macroeconomics* — the study of national economies and weighty topics such as growth, unemployment, inflation, national debt, and investments. But over the years, the scope of microeconomics has grown; today economists analyze topics in macroeconomics using microeconomic tools.

Microeconomists employ those tools to look at things that form from the bottom up, because markets build on the actions of individual companies and consumers. This approach involves starting with an account of how companies and consumers make decisions and building on that to investigate more complex things that "emerge" from those decisions — such as how a market is structured.

In general, microeconomics works by building models of these situations. *Models* are mathematical — or graphical — pictures of how the world works given some basic assumptions. Models aren't reality; they're a description of something that resembles reality. Like an architect's model of a house, models don't have to stand up to reality; they just have to provide a feeling for what the real world looks like. Microeconomists also test models against real data to see how well the models work — the answer is often *variably*.

This chapter introduces you to microeconomics and its core areas of interest, and we touch on the fact that markets don't always work.

Peering into the Economics of Smaller Units

Microeconomics is fundamentally about what happens when individuals and companies make decisions. The idea is to understand how those decisions are made and explore their consequences.

What happens, for example, when prices of houses go up? Well, on the one hand, people are likely to buy fewer or smaller houses. On the other hand, developers may want to build more houses so that they can get more revenue. The result could be a lot of unsold houses! Then there will be pressure to get rid of those stocks of unsold houses, and that leads to lower prices.

When does that process stop? At the limit, the only logical place to stop cutting the price is when exactly as much is sold as is available to sell. This point is called an *equilibrium* in the housing market — a place where supply and demand are equal. Chapter 9 discusses equilibria more fully.

When people talk about *market forces,* they're talking about the outcome of all these decisions taken together. No vast impersonal power called "market forces" exists, just a lot of smaller entities — consumers and companies — making a lot of simple decisions based on signals that come from prices. That's really all market forces means.

The way markets work seems so impersonal because every one of the smallest units — small companies and individuals — makes up just a tiny fraction of all the decisions taken. Even the biggest corporations or most powerful governments have limitations on their ability to influence the world. Microeconomics also looks at the exception to the rule when a decision-maker — a buyer or seller — is not so small and *can* influence market forces.

All these small decision-makers do the best they can, given that ultimately they're acting with imperfect knowledge of a complicated world. People and companies can't know *exactly* how much they'll be earning next year or exactly how much they'll sell. They just look for ways of making decisions that give them the best chance of doing the best they can — which is about all anyone can ask for in an uncertain world.

Making Decisions, Decisions, and More Decisions!

One word that's central to microeconomics is *decision*. Microeconomics is ultimately about making decisions: whether to buy a house, how much ice cream to make, what price to sell a bicycle at, or whether to offer a product to this or that market, and so on.

This is one reason why economists center their models on choice. After all, when you don't have options to choose from, you can't make a decision. Deciding to make something or to buy something is the starting point for microeconomics.

To a microeconomist, decisions aren't right or wrong. Instead, they're one of the following:

- ✔ **Optimal:** Getting the best of what you want, given what's available.
- ✔ **Sub-optimal:** Getting less than the best.

Of course, a model of decisions needs two sides:

- ✔ **Consumers** base their decisions on the value they get from choosing one option as opposed to another.
- ✔ **Companies** base their decisions on a measure of monetary benefit — revenue against costs.

This book presents a few ways that microeconomists look at these decisions. Chapters 2–8 use a framework for making the best decision given some kind of constraint — budget, time, or whatever else constrains you — to show you how microeconomists look at individuals and companies separately. In Chapters 9–15, the famous supply and demand model shows you how different types of markets lead to different results. And Chapters 16–19 introduce you to *game theory,* which looks at how individuals or companies (or even other entities, such as governments) strategically interact with each other.

Addressing how individuals and companies make decisions

Economists look at decisions in a slightly different way from how you might expect. They don't have a model of all the things that you as a consumer would use to inform your decisions. They don't know, for example, who you are, or more precisely what all your values are. They make no assumptions about gender, ethnicity, sexuality, or anything else. They just know that you need to make choices and they explore how you may do so.

Starting simply

Economists make the least possible number of assumptions about the decision-making process and ask what you'd do if you cared about getting the best possible outcome. Here are the two basic assumptions:

- **The consumer is utility-maximizing:** She seeks to maximize her *utility*, which is the value to the consumer of her choice (see Chapters 2 and 4 for more details).

- **The company is profit-maximizing:** It wants to maximize its profit — see Chapters 3 and 8.

These choices don't necessarily involve selfishness. A utility-maximizing consumer can get benefit from helping other people, and a profit-maximizing company may want to redistribute surplus profits to charitable causes.

Growing more complex

To begin with, these models are quite simple. If Bob has $10 in his pocket and he wants to decide between having a burrito or a pizza, he'll get the meal that gives him the most value or utility, given that it costs less than $10. Simple!

But later on, the models start to incorporate all kinds of other factors, such as budget constraints (discussed in Chapter 5): If Bob's income goes up, will he buy more or less pizza? Or what about the utility of other people? If Bob's friends won't eat pizza with him (perhaps he chews with his mouth open), he may get less utility from the pizza. Eventually, even with simple assumptions, models can end up incorporating some pretty complicated reasoning.

When you look at this example from the perspective of the pizza restaurant, things also start off simple: The restaurant just wants to make as much profit as possible, working to reduce its costs to do so. But what if you factor in competitors? What if the shareholders of the pizza company — the company has grown, adding layer on tasty layer — have different interests than the managers? What if the managers don't just want to get costs down, but want to keep competitors out? Again, the key is to start from the fewest justifiable assumptions and then build up as you get more familiar with models.

Even at the simplest level, models tell you plenty about reality. They can give you an account of how people and companies react to prices, and how this reaction changes as industries get more competitive or as companies get bigger.

Seeing how decisions come together to make markets

Markets are places, real or virtual, where consumers and producers come together to trade. In theory, the trades make both sides better off, though not necessarily to the same extent.

Markets coordinate people's desire for "stuff" with producers' ability to make "stuff," but importantly with no one being in charge of the process. The only thing you need is that both sides respond to a price signal. That's it.

Microeconomists say that markets are *equilibrium-seeking,* which means that trading in a market ultimately leads to a point where as much is supplied as consumers demand (and no more or less). The concept of equilibrium is much used in microeconomics, especially in the supply and demand model that we introduce in Chapter 9. This model looks at *partial equilibrium* or an equilibrium in one given market (for example, the market for canned tuna, or the market for books). We also want to understand how a partial equilibrium is related to the following:

- ✔ **Nash equilibrium:** A point where two people or entities are competing for something and arrive separately at a point where no one has an incentive to change their behavior. (Chapters 16–19 explore this situation.)

- ✔ **General equilibrium:** An equilibrium state exists across a whole economy given certain conditions. This is used for the analysis of welfare, and Chapter 12 talks more about it.

Of course, reality can get very complicated, and there are situations where someone — often government, but sometimes private monopolists or property owners — wants to control the price, which is often not desirable. Take rent control, for example. Introduce too low a maximum rent, and more people will want to rent than there are people who are willing to put their house up for rent. As a result, setting a rent control at a very low level just creates homelessness — more people trying to rent, but landlords withdrawing their properties from the market because the price is too low for them to bother.

What if you set the rents too high? Well, if the maximum rent is above the equilibrium in the market, landlords are more willing to rent at that price and so more enter the market. But fewer renters are willing to rent at that price, so the result is an excess supply of rentable properties. As a result, some landlords drop out — those that need the highest level of rent to make a profit — and the price falls until it reaches market equilibrium.

Controlling prices can have other consequences, too. The price isn't just an absolute number — say, a price of $5 — it's also a *relative* measure. For example, a car costs far more in terms of other things you can do with your money than a sofa does. Our model of consumer behavior eventually tells you that the relative price of goods encapsulates what consumers value. When you affect the relative price, you affect choices *everywhere*. That's one reason why economists prefer almost any intervention to one that affects relative prices.

Markets are themselves complex things in reality and vary widely from type to type. For example, financial markets are different from labor markets in their scope, participants, and trading outcomes. Microeconomists look at all these types of markets, starting with the simplest model, and then try to incorporate distinctive differences in these markets into the models.

The great economist Alfred Marshall was the first to make a key point, though: A big difference exists between the practical results of *markets* in reality and the simulation that economists use, which he called *The Market*. When you encounter a type of market you don't understand, starting to analyze it using the simulation is a good starting point. If you know more about the market, you will see the limitations of a simple simulation.

Understanding the Problems of Competition and Cooperation

The situation of many companies following their own interests leads to competition (we discuss perfect competition, which consumers usually love, in Chapter 10, and imperfect competition in Chapter 11). In almost all circumstances, competition is a pretty good thing, because it can lead to lower costs or more innovation. For example, if only one store operates in your area, it may be able to get away with selling milk for $5 a gallon. But if other stores get in on the act, the competition leads to the price falling and stores trying to keep their costs low.

Businesses typically face a competitive environment, but inside the business people cooperate and work together to achieve common goals. Microeconomics studies cooperation as often as it studies competition. The desire is to understand what type of circumstances lead people to choose to cooperate or compete and what are the pitfalls of competition and cooperation.

Even businesses that are competitors in one area sometimes form alliances in others — Apple's relationship with Motorola in the early 2000s being just one example.

Microeconomists are often accused of overselling the benefits of competition, but they also point out that cooperation can be perilous too. When a group of companies with large shares of a relevant market work together, the result is often harmful to the public, as Adam Smith pointed out. Working together in that way is illegal, not surprisingly. Similarly, a trade union where a lot of people work together to get the best bargain with their industry can have negative effects on anyone not a member of that union. Microeconomists go on to investigate all these possibilities.

Realizing why authorities regulate competition

At some point, no matter where they operate in the world, businesses have to deal with the legal institutions that govern the region where they operate. In general, a lot of basic rules restricting how business is conducted underpin every legal market, from ensuring that products are what businesses say they are to not allowing companies to exploit market dominance. But if a basic tenet of microeconomics is that trades and markets emerge with no one in charge, why do we need such governance?

Because markets in reality are far from perfect. Sometimes market trades impose costs, such as environmental costs, upon people who aren't involved in that particular market. Sometimes restricting trade or conduct in a given market leads to better behavior. But perhaps the most interesting reason for regulation is because of what happens when a competitor gets too successful. When that happens, the company makes larger profits, which is good for shareholders. But suppose market conditions are such that no company can set up as a rival — maybe the costs involved in being in that market are too high, or the successful competitor holds the entire supply of a key resource.

The idea is that you don't want a company to exploit its advantage in a way that leads to too many losses for everyone else. At this point, competition law can step in and place restrictions on what a company can and can't do (see the next section), because the costs of runaway success can be very large indeed.

Considering antitrust law

Antitrust law is at the very top of things that a society can do to make sure that markets don't hurt the public good. The purpose is to ensure that if a market isn't competitive, at least the costs can be minimized. Antitrust law is the last line of defense against the worst kinds of behavior, preventing the biggest companies from prejudicing competition.

The idea is that competition is good, so stopping the biggest companies from subverting competition requires constant vigilance. In practice, it means that part of the legal system switches from treating everyone equally to treating those companies with the biggest market shares differently from smaller ones.

Many rules are in place to stop large companies from subverting competition:

- ✔ **Predatory pricing** makes it illegal for a company to drop its prices below cost to deter or drive out potential rivals.

- ✔ **Merger rules** prevent a large company from buying out its competitors and ensure that competition is achieved where possible.

- ✔ **Behavioral remedies** stop the largest competitor from owning a key resource. For instance, if you own a network, you aren't allowed to offer your own content providers preferential prices to access the network.

In all these cases, companies are treated differently because everyone recognizes that if competition fails, everyone loses out in the long run — ultimately getting poorer quality goods at higher prices.

Microeconomists examine all these cases with models that compare competitive outcomes to those achieved by noncompetitive organizations. In most situations, the intuition microeconomists form is that competition is good. But not always. In some cases, competitive markets just don't produce a good, and in others the diversity of products isn't as good in a competitive market, and so unlike many political partisans on the right and left, economists — as a whole — aren't ideologues about this idea.

Investigating Why Markets Can Fail

If you look around the world, you find almost no examples of countries where absolutely everything gets produced through markets alone. Almost everywhere, markets co-exist with other systems: the government, philanthropy, sometimes even the "command and control": structure of a military.

The ultimate reason for this situation is that markets, like anything else, sometimes fail. For example, markets may fail where monopolies exist (see Chapter 13) or where adverse selection problems (Chapter 15) can result in people who need health insurance not getting it. Or where you sell your land to a company that builds a polluting factory, making you and the company happier — but certainly not all the residents living around you, who have to put up with the factory belching fumes (see Chapter 14).

Economists tend to take a practical attitude to markets, perhaps more so than the general public suspects. Economists certainly don't assume that markets can inevitably produce everything that everyone wants with no drawbacks. They believe that in some cases market-based prices would help improve decision-making, and that choice is valuable in and of itself. But that doesn't mean economists want to introduce markets in absolutely everything.

Most economists believe that markets sometimes need a helping hand, especially in two situations: when they don't produce what people want, and when they cost too much. This is because markets have trouble pricing goods when all the costs of making those goods are up front and unrelated to consumption of those goods. You can read more about these situations, along with the instance of markets producing what people don't want, in Chapter 14.

Chapter 2

Considering Consumer Choice: Why Economists Find You Fascinating

Consumer choice is the backbone of market economies. Today you can choose to buy from among more items than at any time in the past, and people are certainly taking advantage of the opportunity. In the United States, consumer spending accounts for roughly 70 percent of Gross Domestic Product, which is a hefty $12.4 trillion expenditure. When you look at the importance of consumer spending in our economy, you quickly see why economists want to understand the consumer as much as possible.

Consumers are people with individual preferences, ideas, backgrounds, histories, identities, and all manner of complicated personalities that can make understanding what they like and don't like difficult. This could be a problem if you want to understand what makes a person tick, but what we want to understand is how people, given those tastes and preferences, decide what to buy and how markets respond to consumers' choices.

As a result, economists have developed their tools so that an analysis of markets can make sense, even when they know very little about the psychology of the consumer. These tools don't attempt to understand people in all their complexities, but instead represent how consumers behave. The economic model of a consumer that we describe in this chapter may appear to be a very simplistic view of a person, but it's a view that's adapted for a specific way of looking at a specific type of interaction.

Ultimately, microeconomists want to lay out a set of conditions that explain how consumers come to their decisions in a way that makes sense — we describe what we specifically mean by "makes sense" in this chapter — and how that then affects their behavior in the marketplace. This chapter shows you how to set the foundations of the microeconomist's view of consumers — how they behave and why — which you can use when building more complicated models (such as the ones in Chapters 4 through 6).

Studying Utility: Why People Choose What They Choose

There are many views about why people choose what they do, with psychologists and sociologists approaching the question in their own ways. In turn, microeconomists focus on one explanation for people making a given choice over another one: that the choice delivers more utility.

Introducing the idea of utility

Utility is a tricky term to pin down in concrete terms (see the nearby sidebar "The complex history of utility" for a discussion of the philosophical issues involved). Economists view *utility* as the value of someone's choice, whether that value derives from their happiness or whatever their motivation. Utility is not measurable directly in any particular set of units, but it is *revealed* when someone makes a choice between options. If a person chooses tea over coffee, then to an economist the person must have gained a greater amount of utility as a result of that choice.

Contrasting two ways of approaching utility: Cardinal and ordinal

In general, you can look at utility in two ways:

- ✔ **Cardinal utility:** The less often used of the two options, cardinal utility attempts to *measure* utility and so requires a unique level of utility associated with each possible choice of a bundle of goods (called the *consumption bundle*). Often that utility is measured in an invented unit called *utils*.

- ✔ **Ordinal utility:** Ordinal utility establishes a *ranking* from the ordering of choices, so that it tells you the order in which things are preferred. To see how this approach can affect the way an economist chooses to use utility in models, we walk you through an example.

The complex history of utility

The meaning of the term *utility has* changed over time. Philosophers in the 18th century were the first to use the term utility. These philosophers were concerned with understanding the nature of *good,* in the sense of moral goodness. One group, often associated with the English reformer and thinker Jeremy Bentham, proposed an answer based on the consequences of actions: good actions tend to promote good consequences, and bad ones, bad consequences. This philosophy is called *utilitarianism*, and in its early versions, as laid out by Bentham, it attempted to refine the concept so that a formula could be used to determine how much of a good thing any given item was, from a cup of tea to a decision on making something. Later, John Stuart Mill identified utility with happiness and went on to argue that the ultimate guiding principle of goodness was whether it produces a greater happiness for a greater number.

Thinking about utility as aligned with happiness is a decent start, but other thinkers had some objections that modern economics has accepted. The first objection comes from George Edward ("G.E.") Moore, who pointed out that *happiness* and *good* have a more complex relationship than Mill would've liked. The second is that even if you take the moral position out of the equation, it's not hard to think up situations where someone may make a choice that yields less "happiness," because different things may make different people happy in different ways. A dishwashing machine may reduce the time and labor of washing dishes, but some people may find something intrinsically good in the act of washing dishes by hand, whether it's quiet time for reflection or a kind of satisfaction in observing the progress of the dishes becoming cleaner.

Consider the following example of a consumer to illustrate the two utility options in practice. Allan has three possible goods (tea, coffee, and cocoa) and has measured (in his own way) the utility he receives from consuming a unit of the three delicious hot beverages available (see Table 2-1). For a system of cardinal utility, you need to be able to ascribe a level of utility to each unit consumed, just as Allan does.

Table 2-1	Example of Cardinal Utility
Good	*Utility from Consuming the Good*
Tea	10
Coffee	7
Cocoa	5

As the table shows, Allan prefers tea to coffee, and coffee to cocoa. Therefore, you can rewrite the table so that Allan's preferences are expressed as ranks to provide the ordinal utility (see Table 2-2).

Table 2-2	Example of Ordinal Utility	
Good	*Utility from Consuming the Good*	*Rank of Choice*
Tea	10	1
Coffee	7	2
Cocoa	5	3

As you can see, the ordinal utility preferences preserve the ranking of the preferences without using a particular value for utility. Crucially, therefore, you can easily transfer any representation of utility that's cardinal into an ordinal representation — just by writing down the numbers in order. For cardinal utility, you need to know something more exact about what a person values than economists usually know about a person, and so by the principle of fewest assumptions, you encounter ordinal utility more often than cardinal.

Modeling Consumer Behavior: Economic Agents

Economists call a person who makes a decision or takes an action an *agent*. Economists begin their understanding of how an agent acts by building a generalized picture of the agent, often called *homo economicus,* meaning "the economic person." Instead of being a particular person, the agent is an abstract representation based on making the fewest possible reasonable assumptions about what a person may do.

Making assumptions is necessary as a first stage of modeling anything. A model doesn't attempt to replicate everything in the world, but represents a simplified view of the world so that you can draw enough conclusions to make a reasoned argument. As a result, modeling begins by making some restrictions and looks at the small picture where those restrictions are binding (some of them can be relaxed later, after you develop an intuitive feeling for what's going on in the model, and some of them hold throughout most models).

The restrictions that economists place on a completely generic and abstract person are often things that non-economists find funny. However, the reasons for doing so make sense when you're trying to create a model. In essence, what economists demand isn't that the representative agent is a type of psychological makeup, but is logically consistent so that a model isn't internally contradictory.

Acting rationally in economic terms: A mathematical tool

Economists begin with a model that has *rational* agents — in the sense that they are logically consistent in their behavior — and they make the fewest assumptions about the tastes or preferences of these agents. Because economists don't know very much about the people they're modeling — there are 7 billion people on Earth, after all — starting with what you think is common to them all makes sense.

We describe the assumptions here so that you can see what lies behind all the models that economists build from those foundations:

- **(Local) Non-satiation:** In general, a person prefers more of something to less of it. The local aspect acknowledges that the assumption holds at times. For instance, after the 10th slice of chocolate cake, people don't prefer more to less (something we discuss more in Chapter 4); but up to a certain point, they generally do.

- **Completeness:** You can take a list of the possible choices or actions that can be made in a situation and rank them from best to worst, even if some of them may be choices of equal rank. This means that you can associate with that ranking a *utility function* (a mathematical representation of the consumer's preferences) that incorporates all those choices.

- **Transitivity:** If an agent prefers one thing to a second thing, and the second thing to a third thing, it must follow that the agent prefers the first thing to the third. So, if you prefer tea to coffee and coffee to cocoa, you prefer tea to cocoa. Again, if preferences aren't transitive, the ranking or the utility function would be inconsistent, and you wouldn't be able to use it to build models.

- **Reflexivity:** Any bundle of goods is at least as good as itself, so that the utility associated with a bundle isn't surpassed when the same bundle is offered in a different way.

When these conditions are satisfied, economists say that a person's preferences are *well-behaved*. This term means that they satisfy all the mathematical conditions that ensure consistent behavior and therefore it's a suitable tool for modeling choices in the context of a market. More exactly, it means that you can construct a utility function to represent the consumer's preferences.

Addressing an objection to the representative economic agent

A criticism sometimes leveled at the economists' view of a representative "person" is that such a construction could describe a psychopath, in the sense that representative consumers follow their own interests and make a rational choice between options that allows them to maximize their own utility.

We aren't psychiatrists and so can't give a medical view on whether this description satisfies the conditions for diagnosing a psychopath, but we do want to point out a couple of flaws in this view of what economists think of as a representative agent:

- ✔ **This criticism is rooted in what we can call a *framing* problem.** Suppose a person says he prefers a treatment with a 70 percent success rate over one with a 30 percent rate of failure. To an economist, this is inconsistent or illogical because a success rate of 70 percent is the same as a 30 percent rate of failure. But *framing* the example of the choice in two different ways tends to affect how the choice is perceived. Advertisers understand this aspect of human behavior. Political marketers are experts in framing — saying that an incumbent congressman "was absent 16 times to vote on matters of national importance" sounds very different from saying that "the congressman had a 99% voting record." Both statements are true but framed differently.

- ✔ **Economists make no assertions about people's motivations beyond that they like doing certain things.** Some people are interested in which charitable activities they should engage in — others are choosing whether to buy a Ferrari or a Lamborghini. Some people are more selfish than others. But an economist does not look at these choices from a moral perspective. Economists are interested in the process of choosing and not in the reasons why a person chooses one thing or another.

We don't mean to imply that the way economists model preferences has no issues. In fact, in the later section "Noting issues with the preference model," we introduce a few points of criticism. We only mean that the psychopath objection isn't really one of them.

Pursuing Preferences and Investigating Indifferences

Microeconomists want to look at the different ways in which a consumer may prefer one bundle of goods over another. This requires them to examine people's preferences.

Mathematically, economists use three different ways of expressing a relation between two consumption bundles:

- ✔ **Strong preference:** A consumer gets more utility from a good that's strongly preferred to another.

- ✔ **Weak preference:** A consumer gets at least as much utility from one good as another.

- ✔ **Indifference:** A consumer gets exactly as much utility from any one option as from another; that is, the consumption bundles yield exactly the same level of utility.

To illustrate how economists use these relations, let's consider Allan's preferences in hot beverages. In both the cardinal or the ordinal model, Allan prefers tea to coffee (see the earlier section "Contrasting two ways of approaching utility: Cardinal and ordinal"). In fact, Allan gets more utility from tea than from coffee, and so in this case Allan strongly prefers tea to coffee. Economists express this preference as follows:

Tea ≻ Coffee

If Allan were to get at least as much utility from tea (and possibly more) as he does from coffee, you'd say that the preference was *weak* and write:

Tea ≽ Coffee

If he were indifferent between the two, you'd write:

Tea ~ Coffee

The key point is that you can use these relations to picture choice and utility for Allan. Economists construct a tool called an *indifference curve* to describe these preferences. In this section, we use the curve to look at how to represent some different situations in terms of choice.

Becoming bothered with indifference curves

Indifference curves are a popular tool among economists for analyzing why consumers choose one option over another (Chapters 4 through 6 use them to look at how consumers choose, given a budget constraint). Here we explain the concept briefly and describe what these curves can tell you.

An *indifference curve* plots all the consumption bundles for which a consumer gets the same level of utility — that is, all the possible consumption bundles between which a consumer with well-behaved preferences is indifferent. Any given indifference curve yields the same amount of utility along that curve. In order to move up to a higher level of utility, you have to be on a different — higher — indifference curve.

We plot a simple indifference curve in Figure 2-1: here are a few things you're looking at. We imagine that over the course of a week, Allan allocates his consumption to tea and coffee so that each point of the indifference curve is a combination of a week's tea and coffee usage that yields Allan exactly the same utility.

Figure 2-1 shows that if he wants to maintain the same utility while increasing his consumption of tea, he can only do so by reducing his consumption of coffee. An indifference curve tells you that the total utility from achieving coffee *and* tea must be a constant, so if tea goes up, coffee must come down. The slope of the indifference curve at any given point expresses this as the economic concept called the *marginal rate of substitution* (MRS). All points on the curve yield the same amount of utility, but the combinations of tea and coffee must yield a constant level of utility along the curve.

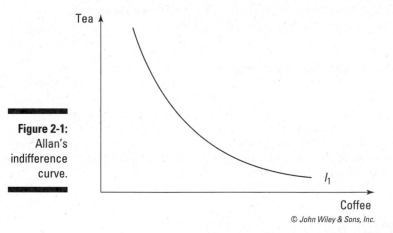

Figure 2-1:
Allan's
indifference
curve.

© *John Wiley & Sons, Inc.*

Figure 2-2 draws the MRS and annotates the original indifference curve to show how you depict it on a graph. Mathematically, the slope of the indifference curve at any given point is the MRS of Good 1 for Good 2 at that point. The tangent is a straight line with the same slope as the indifference curve at the point or at the number of cups of tea and coffee you're evaluating. Both the tangent and the indifference curve have the same slope — which equals the marginal rate of substitution of tea for coffee at that point:

$$\text{MRS} = (\Delta \ Good \ 2)/(\Delta \ Good \ 1)$$

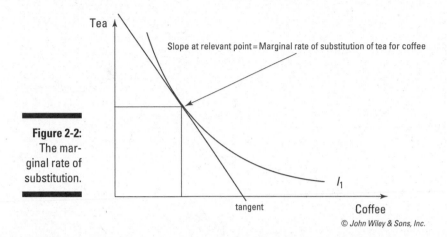

Figure 2-2:
The marginal rate of substitution.

Indifference curves have to slope downwards, because the distance from the origin is reflective of the degree of utility gained by consuming a bundle on the indifference curve. Thus if the indifference curve sloped upwards, the consumer would be indifferent between consuming a lower level of utility and a higher one. To an economist this is absurd, and so a restriction gets placed on the curves so that they don't. (One exception, though, is when one of the goods is *a bad,* which is a good that gives disutility when consumed, for example, broccoli (if you're George H.W. Bush).

Indifference curves cannot cross. Figure 2-3 shows two indifference curves, which theoretically show the same level of utility along each curve. Bundles X and Y are along the same curve, I_1. However, look at Bundle Z: It delivers a higher level of utility than Bundle Y and therefore can't lie on the same line as Bundles X and Y. And yet, because the two curves cross, where they cross they *must* yield the same level of utility as each other. Thus, Bundle Z can't be on the same indifference curve as both X and Y, and therefore can't be on a curve that crosses I_1.

Bowing to convex curves

Indifference curves tend to be *convex,* which means they have the scooped bow shape shown in Figures 2-1 through 2-3, where the marginal rate of substitution is negative along the entire curve. At any given point, getting more of Good 2 requires a greater sacrifice of Good 1, and the more of Good 2 you desire, the more of Good 1 you have to give up.

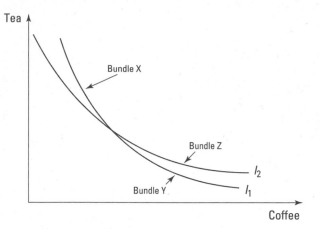

Figure 2-3:
Indifference
curves can't
cross.

Two limiting cases apply (see Figure 2-4):

✔ **Perfect substitutes:** Any consumption bundle along the line is equivalent to any other, and giving up Good 1 just means getting the same corresponding amount of Good 2. Consider yellow and white tennis balls as an example. For these two goods, the indifference curves are straight lines. For some people, Diet Coke and Diet Pepsi are perfect substitutes — they can't tell the difference.

✔ **Perfect complements:** These must be consumed in fixed proportions of each, and only one unique way of allocating your spending exists between bundles. So, only one point on the curve is useful, and the curve has an L shape, reflecting the fact that when a consumer is away from the ideal combination, adding more of Good 1 or of Good 2 is of no use on its own. A recipe mixes ingredients in fixed proportions — you can't substitute flour for milk when making a cake.

Mostly, though, unless disutility is involved, as may be in the case of goods that economists call *bads,* indifference curves are convex. In fact, in some cases they can be *strictly convex,* which means that the weighted average of a bundle of goods is preferred to an extreme bundle where only one of the two goods is consumed. For example, if the goods are health care and housing, it is not unreasonable to assume that people want some amount of both goods — they can't live on health care or housing alone.

If indifference curves don't at least have the feature of being convex, drawing implications is difficult for the functioning of a market (the way Chapter 9 does), and so this general restriction on "goods" gets imposed to prevent badly behaved results later.

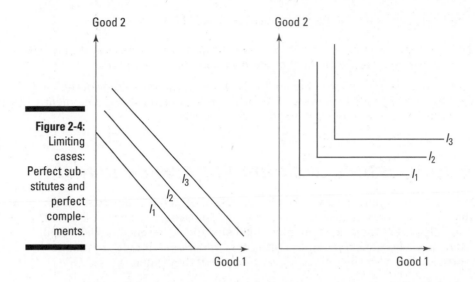

Figure 2-4:
Limiting
cases:
Perfect sub-
stitutes and
perfect
comple-
ments.

Staying interesting with monotonicity

If you are sitting in on a seminar of economists, you may hear utility functions described as *monotonic* (note, not monotonous).

Monotonicity, a key feature of well-behaved indifference curves, means that if you were to increase a person's capability to consume both goods at the same time, the new bundle must be preferred to the old. This means that if our hot-beverage consumer Allan has the wherewithal to buy more tea and more coffee (for instance, if random circumstances make his income go up or both goods cheaper), he must prefer this bundle to his old bundle.

Relatedly, a *monotonic transformation* of an indifference curve or utility function is one that preserves the order of any particular ranking of utility of any bundles consumed. Table 2-3 shows Allan's original utility (from Table 2-1) under three possible monotonic transformations: adding a number, multiplying by two, or cubing the number, and as you can see, the rank order is preserved.

Table 2-3   Example Utility after Three Monotonic Transformations

Good	Utility from Consuming the Good	Transformation (Adding 1)	Transformation (Multiplying by 2)	Transformation (Cubing)
Tea	10	11	20	1,000
Coffee	7	8	16	343
Cocoa	5	6	10	125

Together, convexity and monotonicity mean two things:

✔ Indifference curves can't slope upwards, for the reasons indicated in the earlier section "Becoming bothered with indifference curves."

✔ When you move out to higher levels of utility, the rank order of the bundle of goods is preserved. We ask you to accept this for a moment, but we make use of it in Chapters 4 through 6.

Noting issues with the preference model

We want to examine briefly a couple of issues that people have raised with the model of consumer preferences. For now, please note them, and even if you fully accept them, keep in mind that using the preference model is still useful as a yardstick to compare with other versions — it may after all be worth knowing *how* models differ and *from what* they differ.

✔ **Lack of rationality:** Experiments tend to confirm that when uncertainty is introduced into the choices, an individual's weighting of utility may not be rational (as we describe *rational* in the earlier section "Acting rationally in economic terms: A mathematical tool"). For instance, take an offer of $10 now versus entry in a lottery where you have a 1 in 10 chance of earning $100. The expected gain from both offers is $10. The first offer gives $10 with a probability of 1, whereas the expected outcome of the second is 0.1 (that is, 1 in 10) times 100, which equals, yes that's right, $10. If someone is strictly *rational,* as we have described rationality, that person will be indifferent between the two offers. But relatively few people would accept that the offer of $10 with certainty is the same as the option of $100 with a one in ten chance. So, people faced with uncertainty in their choices may not be rational in the way we have described.

A number of similar experiments show some quite consistent biases. One, for instance, is that people tend to value the prospect of losses more negatively than they value the prospect of gains positively, which means that they tend to do irrational things such as throwing money at a losing position rather than doing as rationality suggests and closing down their trading book and walking away.

✔ **Bounded rationality:** People can be *bounded* by a number of constraints in their lives, including time, which may mean they can't figure out their preferences and so they can't optimize their utility. Instead, they go for "good enough," because the time taken to make a decision, or their resources or their ability to think is constrained. Bounded rationality is becoming more widely used in economics, particularly in complex systems models. The key implication of the bounded rationality approach is that the inference economists make from applying utility and preference theory to markets isn't always correct. Chapter 5 talks more about constraints.

By contrast, the *behavioral economics* approach seeks to map and explore the differences between the results the utility and preference models predict and what happens in reality. It does so by using lab experiments and real-world data and testing how preferences really work in people. Some results already show the existence of persistent biases in people's reasoning. The example where people attach more weight to losses than their potential gains is one such bias.

Both these approaches — the behavioral and the bounded rationality approach — make some specific challenges to the model that we present. The key one is that people may not have such well-behaved preferences as economists like to ascribe to them, and therefore the results of such preferences may be less robust than economists would like them to be.

Getting the "standard" utility model under your belt is a good idea, however, before jumping in to questioning the results. Even if consumers don't reason like *homo economicus,* they may behave *as if* they do, and even if they don't behave exactly like that, you're best off exploring how they might before making changes to the model. Either way, a microeconomics course probably won't feature much of these approaches at first, but will introduce them in later modules.

Chapter 3

Looking at the Behavior of Firms: What They Are and What They Do

In This Chapter

▶ Understanding the firm as an economic organization

▶ Understanding how microeconomists view firms

▶ Thinking about why people form companies

One of the key insights into how a market economy organizes production is the concept in microeconomics of *a firm:* an entity or agent that produces things. This description is very general, necessarily, because in the real world many different types of organization can be called a firm. For simplicity, we start from an assumption that all these firms are of the same type — even if we give them many different names in reality — and share similar essential features.

In this chapter, we expand on the general description and then firm up (sorry!) a few of the concepts that underlie the production that firms undertake. We look at some of the different structures of firms and some of the critical problems associated with organization. After reading this chapter you'll have a firm (oh no, not again!) grasp of how firms form the backbone of production in a market economy.

Delving into Firms and What They Do

The best approach to start thinking about the firm is in a simple way, by considering the smallest possible unit of production: a single-person-operated firm such as a market stall (in the U.S., this is called sole proprietor). This section also introduces you briefly to other types of firms.

Looking at this sole proprietor firm, an economist would want to make some general statements about what it does, and why it does it. Therefore, microeconomists abstract away any particular features such as special features about its operation that aren't generalizable across industries or markets unless they're absolutely necessary. The simplest way to do this is to turn to the foundation of business and accounting and make some general statements about the costs and benefits that accrue. (To find out why economists think of firms this way, check out the later section "Considering How Economists View Firms: The Black Box.")

Recognizing the importance of profit

At its most basic, a firm takes some things in, transforms them in some way, and places what it produced on the market hoping that the difference between what it receives (*revenues*) is bigger than the costs of taking those things in and transforming them (*costs*). That difference is called *profit* (or if you're unfortunate in running your firm, *loss,* which economists write as a negative profit). The Greek symbol pi, Π, denotes profit so that you can write the following simple equation:

$$\Pi = TR - TC$$

The equation says that the total profit the firm makes is the difference between all revenues that the firm takes in and all costs that the firm incurs to conduct its activities.

At this stage, you haven't done anything to break down those costs into corresponding production activities (we do so in Chapter 7), and so for the moment we suggest that the sole proprietor's costs include not only the cost of goods bought in and the cost of labor, but also the fixed costs of its operation, that is, the rent due on the stall irrespective of how many things are sold individually.

At heart, economists treat every firm in this way. Of course, firms vary considerably in size and complexity, and comparing the activities of a transnational corporation to a market stall trader would be a little simplistic. But all firms share in common the profit motivation, and profit is the indicator of revenues being in excess of costs. A *rational* firm (in economic terms) seeks to maximize it.

Chapter 7 talks more about profit, revenue, and costs, but we want to make one very important point about profits here: Profits accrue after all relevant costs have been paid, including what the sole proprietor gave up in terms of alternative use of their time in order to open up the stall. This approach is slightly different from an accountant's point of view, where several different accounting measures and accounting terms are used to indicate firm profitability. Typically, these terms include *income, earnings,* or *net* or *gross profit,* depending on which part of the firm's accounts you're looking at.

Economists take a more general view on profit than accountants, and to an economist there is only one way to measure profit.

Discovering types of firms

Many firms are of course significantly more complex than the sole proprietor mentioned in the preceding section.

Company law distinguishes a few types of firms according to how profits or losses earned by the firm are distributed, including:

- ✔ **Partnership:** There are several owners of the firm that are permitted to share in any profits generated by its business and are equally liable for all its losses.

- ✔ **Limited liability company (LLC):** An entity that the law defines as owning the profits which may then be redistributed to those who own the company, called *shareholders.* In a limited liability company, shareholders are only liable for losses up to the stake they hold in the company.

- ✔ **Co-operative:** Owned and operated by its members. Typically, it redistributes profits to those members.

Each of these types of firm has legal advantages in certain situations and drawbacks in other situations. For instance, the limited liability company has advantages in its ability to raise capital but disadvantages in terms of the ability of the shareholders to run the company or to observe and control the activities of managers. For much more on companies, flip to the later section "From Firm to Company: Why People Form Limited Liability Companies."

Considering How Economists View Firms: The Black Box

Economists are often accused of treating firms too simply. By disregarding differences in organizational behavior, technology, or place, and by treating firms more simply as a kind of black box that takes inputs in and creates outputs from them, are economists painting a misleading picture that makes firms interchangeable and ignores important differences between them?

Economists have faced this accusation many times, and so in this section we describe why economists view firms as they do.

Seeing why economists think as they do

Economists are interested in how the profit motive affects what a firm _would do_, first and foremost. When they understand that, they can start to look at how firm behavior differs across different industries or markets.

The economist looking at a firm makes simplifications for two reasons:

- ✔ You can't build a model without placing some restrictions on your model. If you rule nothing out, you rule anything in, and before you know it you've reenacted the Lewis Carroll story about the map so accurate that it has to be as big as the kingdom it maps.

- ✔ You want to compare common features of firms, without focusing on all those details, so that you can zero in on the ones that are most important to building a model of a market.

Peering inside the Black Box: Technologies

The preceding section's rationale doesn't mean that economists take the nature of changing inputs into outputs for granted. Since Adam Smith, economists have been describing in various ways the methods a firm can use to transform inputs into outputs, which they call _technologies_.

A _technology_ is a description of the way a firm transforms inputs into outputs (see Figure 3-1). Economists aren't restrictive about what makes a technology. Rather than take a narrow definition or restrict the meaning of _technology_ to a particular kind of machine, they take a wider view and say that any method of turning inputs into outputs fits the bill. Whether it involves buying wood and carpentering wood into furniture, or employing people to help clients understand financial planning, it doesn't matter: Those are both descriptions of a technology.

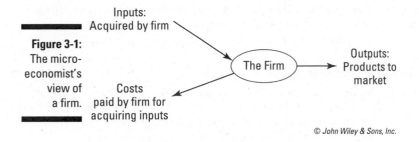

Figure 3-1: The micro-economist's view of a firm.

The inputs that go into a technology are called the factors of production. The three most common factors of production are

- ✔ Land
- ✔ Labor
- ✔ Capital

Let's take a closer look at each factor in turn.

Land: They ain't makin' any more of it

Land is without doubt an important factor of production, but it tends to be studied apart from other inputs. Land costs can be significant and important to the firm, taking up the greater fraction of operating costs for businesses in some places. Land costs can be made worse by restrictions on bringing new land into use or preventing new uses for old land — for instance, in turning former agricultural land into housing.

When economists consider the inputs available to a firm, land is generally held constant and looked at in specific contexts of urban growth rather than considered as part of a technology.

Labor: Getting the job done

The human element of production is labor, usually denoted by L and typically measured in man-hours per week. The firm hires labor by paying wages, w, per man-hour to the workers who are hired to do the work. Thus the total a firm pays out in labor costs is w times L, or wL.

To begin with, economists assume that workers are indistinguishable and undifferentiated so that each worker makes the same contribution to output. This is only where things begin, though, because later, when you've got the hang of the general picture, you can use a variety of more advanced tools to look at various differences between or among workers and how these differences affect output or costs. But for the moment, assume that workers are the same and that each one is neither harder working nor shirking.

Capital: Tangible and intangible

Labor is important, but workers can't create an output on their own without at least *some* equipment. Carpenters need woodworking tools, and authors need nice flashy laptops, or at least yellow legal pads and pens. Therefore, labor has to be combined with the other factor of production: capital.

There are two types of capital:

- ✔ **Tangible capital:** Includes physical capital such as tools, machines, and plant equipment, often measured in machine-hours. A machine is durable and is able to yield a certain number of machine-hours before it breaks down and has to be replaced.

- ✔ **Intangible capital:** Includes such assets as brand value and the knowledge and skills embodied in the firm. (Skills embodied in labor are often called *human capital*.)

In each case, the capital plus labor combine to make the *output,* and so capital is generally held to be useless on its own. The cost of a unit of capital is denoted by r. This isn't quite the same as the interest rate, because it has to cover the *opportunity cost* of doing something else with your money rather than buying or investing in capital. If r goes up, then the purchase of capital or investment by firms falls because of the following:

- ✔ If the firm has to borrow money to increase its use of capital at a higher cost of borrowing, the firm has to borrow more money to invest in the capital it wants.

- ✔ If the firm is investing its own money, then a higher cost of capital implies that the opportunity cost of investing is higher and that a firm wants higher returns to capital to compare with other opportunities. Therefore, the firm is likely to use less capital.

You can use a number of techniques to evaluate the costs of using and deploying capital, most of which are based on how investors discount the receipt of revenue earned in the future or discounting the value of future earnings and costs so that future and present costs and benefits can be compared.

Entrepreneurship: The alchemy of factors

Some economists like to think of entrepreneurship as a factor of production. *Talent* differs from the other factors of production (land, labor, and capital) by being concerned more with seeing the opportunity to create a firm or a product or somehow finding a way of creating value in the marketplace.

A firm may need to buy entrepreneurship at great expense, particularly if it's rare. But entrepreneurship can also be a collective phenomenon, something that comes from a great number of people working together or embodied in one entrepreneur who has the gift of this insight. Research into entrepreneurship tends to be an enterprise of its own, using somewhat different sets of tools than those in this book.

Minimizing costs

A firm with a given technology makes a choice about how much of each of the factors of production to use to make how much output — and pays the cost for doing so. The question for the firm is how to use its technology and choose its inputs in order to make its profits as large as possible. The way it does so is to choose its inputs in order to make the costs as small as possible (see Figure 3-2). The technology shown in the figure is a specific form known as a Cobb-Douglas production function.

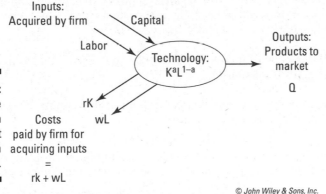

Figure 3-2:
An example of how an economist looks at a technology.

If you're wondering why economists think this way, consider profit maximization (discussed in detail in Chapter 8). In the following equation (introduced in the earlier section "Recognizing the importance of profit"), profit equals the difference between total revenue and total cost:

$$\Pi = TR - TC$$

A firm can determine what to make and how much to make, but it doesn't have any control over what consumers choose to buy. Therefore, it makes sense that economists model the things that the firm does control — its own costs — and so they assume that profit maximization is the same thing as cost minimization. (Chapter 4 looks inside the costs of production at how a firm actually makes its decisions.)

Maximizing profits

When discussing a firm, economists generally assume that the firm wants to maximize profits — in other words, that the difference between total revenue and total costs is positive and as large as possible. Economists don't think there's anything immoral about profit maximization. Rather, they believe that profit maximization is a goal that helps a firm be efficient, and firms that don't make profits tend not to operate as firms for very long.

Of course, some nuances apply to this view of profit. For one, the existence of profits in the economist's sense says nothing about how those profits may be distributed. For example, an LLC may want to retain some profits for future investment and return some to shareholders as dividends. But although a nonprofit company still intends to make a *surplus* (as it would be called in the accounts, reflecting the different *legal* as opposed to *economic* definition of the company), it does different things with that surplus, which may include distribution to workers or to chosen worthy causes.

But beyond this consideration, other reasons may exist why a firm may not be acting as a profit maximizer:

- Tax systems where company taxes fall on profits can provide an incentive to declare lower levels of profit.

- Managers may have different incentives than shareholders and prefer to generate higher salaries for themselves than higher profits for the company (managers' wages here would be a cost to the company).

- A company may prefer to evaluate its performance using some other measure, such as sales or market share, at least in the short run. Some examples include companies in online markets where interim measures commonly used include market share or number of users.

Is this a problem for microeconomists? Not necessarily. In most situations, they want to make a simplification that helps them understand the world instead of covering every possible case. So, when considering different types of markets the benchmark of the profit-maximizing firm helps economists consider how they may be similar or different.

Economists also want to compare their models to real-world situations. In order to do that, they can start from a simple assumption and then, as things become more complicated, refine it in the light of real-world events.

From Firm to Company: Why People Form Limited Liability Companies

Many economic activities require rather more than simply buying something and selling it on. These stages of creating the product involve more complex forms of organization than our example of the sole trader. Consider, for example, the set of production processes involved in making the computers we're using to write and publish this book: dealing with contractors; managing international product development; creating the complementary products (software and operating systems); and managing the people and processes involved. As a result, a structure that places all these activities into one entity can bring a number of advantages.

Also, the LLC is only one potential structure among many in which people could do this. Over human history, people have used a number of other organizations to arrange production: armies, hierarchies — literally a rule of priests — and various kinds of state actors have all been involved in the production process. Some key advantages, however, apply to arranging production in an LLC:

- ✔ Shareholders are liable only for losses up to the extent of their ownership stakes. By having many shareholders, the limited liability company structure allows for the spreading of risk among shareholders, which in turn allows the company to raise capital more easily.

- ✔ Having a pool of capital sources for a company to draw upon is important to understanding how firms grow.

Although reasonably compelling reasons exist for some types of investor to favor the LLC structure, pooling activities into a single entity also provides an additional advantage. The eminent economist Ronald Coase first pointed out in the 1960s that in reality, using the market might not be free and costless, especially if you have to search for and transact with many different people in order to do business — which is, in itself, a cost.

Putting all your bows in one basket

In the Middle Ages, demarcation of jobs by guilds was a fact of life. However, these guilds often had very narrow boundaries. Buying a bow and arrow — and bear in mind, all English adult males were required to practice archery — involved a visit to a bowyer to make the bow, a stringer to string it, and a fletcher to make the arrows. If you had to search for all these suppliers in town one by one, you'd encounter three sets of *transactions,* and the costs of making these transactions is the cost of using the market itself.

But if someone merged all those activities into one company, Ye Olde Archery Supplies Store ("We bow to all our customers' needs!"), you'd incur those costs just once. Thus a structure that permits this consolidation of costs is preferable to one that doesn't, on the grounds of efficiency for the buyer if nothing else. Thus, transaction costs lead to people finding a way to minimize those costs by putting them in one consolidated entity.

 Putting all these costs in one place has the advantage of ensuring that you incur them once only. Check out the nearby sidebar "Putting all your bows in one basket" for an example.

 A limited liability company structure has one key implication: Owners are typically not the same people as managers. Instead, economists describe owners (that is, shareholders) as *principals,* and the managers as their *agents.* This distinction is important when you start to think about firms in the real world and how they behave in a marketplace.

Why would anyone want to separate ownership from management? Aside from the advantages of diffusing ownership in an LLC (which includes greater sources of capital for a company and some protection against losses for an owner), a shareholder may have shares in many different companies. Could such a shareholder be able to manage all those companies full time? Not unless the person was some type of shareholding superhero. So in each venture, companies need to appoint professional managers.

But this arrangement doesn't work perfectly, in all situations. The *principal-agent problem* is how we describe the kinds of problems that can arise.

 Companies, which shareholders own but professional managers manage, feature two sets of interests. The shareholders' interest is for the firm to make as much profit as possible. The managers' interests, however, may include having as big an office as possible or as great a chance of staying in the job as possible. How do shareholders manage this problem?

Commonly, they choose to reward management with shares in the company, which has the advantage of *aligning* the interests of shareholders and managers. Steve Jobs, famously, was only paid $1 in salary when he returned to Apple as CEO in 1997 — the rest of his salary was paid in shares.

The evidence on management share schemes or employee share schemes is mixed, with the variation in schemes making it hard to draw an overall conclusion on whether or how these incentive schemes benefit firms.

Another, subtler aspect to this debate is that shareholders and managers aren't the only people with an interest in a company: Customers, civil society groups, unions, government, and others can all claim some degree of ownership of the company. This situation results in two competing views of companies:

 ✔ **The stakeholder model** sees the firm as being the nexus of all societal interests.

 ✔ **The shareholder model** sees only shareholders as being relevant or important.

Fashions for describing firms have changed several times in recent history. The American Academy of Management, for instance, pronounced in favor of the stakeholder model in the 1970s, changed to the shareholder model in the 1980s, and then back to the stakeholder model in the late 1990s.

Currently, management and firm theorists prefer the stakeholder model. However, to begin analyzing the firm and for quite a long way on the journey to understanding the firm, the shareholder model is likely to be what you will encounter in microeconomics. Consumers are the key stakeholders in microeconomics as they decide whether to buy goods or not, and at the same time they are also the shareholders in that they hold their savings in funds that provide capital to firms. In microeconomics, we have a saying: *Consumer is sovereignty.*

Part II
Doing the Best You Can: Consumer Theory

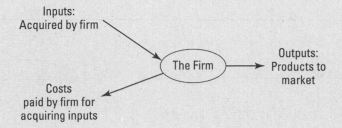

In this part . . .

- ✔ See how economists use utility to investigate consumer behavior.

- ✔ Understand how budget constraints affect people's best options.

- ✔ Appreciate how price changes make consumers reevaluate their choices.

Chapter 4

Living a Life without Limits

Sometimes you just can't seem to choose what you want — limits are everywhere: speed limits, calorie limits, age limits, height limits on rollercoasters that drive the child who's just an inch short of the restriction wild with frustration. Well, no limits in this chapter. Here we look at unconstrained consumer choice. This situation may not be very realistic, but it allows economists to examine consumer behavior with no nasty intrusions to get in the way of what people want, such as lack of time or money (don't worry, Chapter 5 covers constraints).

Chapter 2 looks at the consumer choice model that economists use to investigate people's preferences and introduces some of the key tools of analysis — for example, indifference curves and the concept of *utility* (the value a representative consumer gets from consuming something). This chapter looks at utility in a more mathematical way, in particular in terms of something called the *utility function*. This tool occurs frequently in economics and is helpful for understanding what lies behind demand and supply in a given market, and so it's a tool with much utility (groan).

We build up a mathematical picture of the way in which utility motivates the choices of a representative consumer, and for that we need to build up a picture of how people choose when they don't have constraints (see Chapter 5 for more on constraints and Chapter 6 for how the picture in this chapter changes when you introduce them). We look at how to evaluate the amount of utility consumers get from their choices, including *marginal utility,* which is the amount of utility gained by consuming an extra unit of something. To keep things straightforward, we suppose that these choices aren't constrained.

Eating Until You're Sick: Assuming that More Is Always Better

In general, economists assume that, given the choice, people prefer more goods to less. This assumption holds, up to a limit, because at some point people get satiated by their consumption of a good and don't want to consume any more of it.

If you've ever been unable to consume a tenth bar of chocolate, you've experienced this phenomenon. Economists call it *diminishing marginal utility*, meaning that as you consume increasing amounts of the same thing, the utility gained from each additional amount is smaller, as you add more and more. At some point, the marginal utility can fall to zero and you desire no more of the good — it can even turn negative afterwards (yes, it's true, you can eat so much chocolate that eating any more causes displeasure rather than pleasure).

However — and this is quite a big however — up to that point, the more-over-less assumption operates. The later section "Deciding How Low You'll Go: Marginal Utility" looks more closely at this issue. But here we begin from the assumption that more is better and define some terms that economists commonly use "in the field." The key starting point is the concept of a consumption bundle, something touched on in Chapter 2 but examined in more detail in this section.

Once you get the idea of what utility is to the economist, you can start putting together the building blocks that economists use for modelling. In this section, we go through the terminology, showing you how economists represent preferences in a special shorthand that you can then use to ensure that models are consistent.

Making your choice: The consumption bundle

A *consumption bundle* is a set of goods that a consumer may choose to consume. Suppose the only goods available in the world are tea and coffee. Then a consumption bundle is any combination of cups of tea and coffee that the person could choose, and you can write

(tea, coffee)

For the bundle containing one cup of tea and one cup of coffee, the bundle would be written as

$$(1 \text{ tea}, 1 \text{ coffee})$$

Now imagine that the items in the brackets can represent any goods whatsoever. We call them x_i, where i is an index identifying the good in which you're interested. You can then rewrite the bundle as follows:

$$(x_1, x_2, \ldots x_n)$$

Here n denotes the number of all goods possible to consume.

Although this bundle of n goods is realistic (in that at some level, every good competes for your wallet with every other good), it's also cumbersome. Instead, for simplicity economists often use two goods: the one they're interested in and everything else, which you can think of as money. We follow this two-good layout for now, but if you're interested in doing so, you can eventually generalize the simple model to all goods.

The two-good layout leaves the consumption bundle as being the following:

$$(x_1, x_2)$$

Here x_1 is usually plotted on the horizontal axis of any graph or space, and x_2 on the vertical axis.

Consumption bundles have to follow the normal rules of preference (discussed in Chapter 2), which means that, for instance, with three bundles, A, B, and C, and where A is preferred to B, and B to C, A must be preferred to C.

Provided that your tastes satisfy the rules for well-behaved preferences (completeness, reflexivity, and transitivity — see Chapter 2), any consumption bundle can be associated with an *indifference curve,* and an indifference curve describes all the consumption bundles that yield an identical level of utility. If you were to take any bundles on the curve (call them P and Q for the moment), you'd be indifferent between them and can write, as Chapter 2 does, the following:

$$P \sim Q$$

Thinking about utility in another way: Possible sets

Another way to think about consumption bundles and preferences is to think about all the possible choices. If we describe the set of possible choices in a diagram, we can see pretty easily which choices the consumer would prefer. For instance, Figure 4-1 draws an indifference curve for all the consumption bundles for which Bob gets the same amount of utility. We mark on it two equivalent bundles, A and B. The shaded area shows the set of all possible points yielding higher utility than bundles A and B. He's now offered a bundle that offers more utility than these two — call it bundle C — and we translate this into microeconomist speak as follows:

$$C \succ B, C \succ A$$

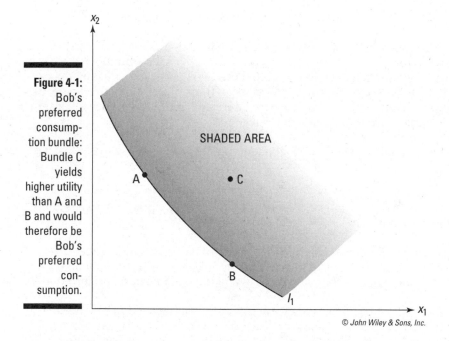

Figure 4-1:
Bob's preferred consumption bundle: Bundle C yields higher utility than A and B and would therefore be Bob's preferred consumption.

This expression confirms that C is strictly preferred to B and A. In Figure 4-1 we picture C as being a member of the set of points that are strictly preferred to A and B, and we shade the area covered by that set. Because we specify that that relationship is *strict preference* (see Chapter 2), it can't include the indifference curve itself, because that would mean Bob gets at least as much utility from something we've already said yields *more* utility.

Drawing a utility function

In the preceding section, we draw indifference curves corresponding to different levels of utility, and that level of utility is the same along all the points of the curve. But suppose you want to compare bundles that are on different levels of utility. Easy! You draw a set of indifference curves moving away from the origin. Each individual curve has the same level of utility along the curves, and each curve expresses a higher level of utility the further away from the origin it is! Check out Figure 4-2.

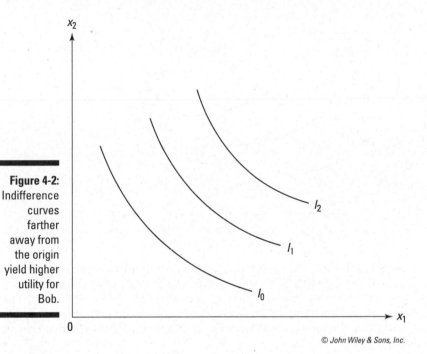

Figure 4-2:
Indifference
curves
farther
away from
the origin
yield higher
utility for
Bob.

© *John Wiley & Sons, Inc.*

The great thing about this depiction is that if you connect a line going through the indifference curves, and the indifference curves are derived from well-behaved preferences, any point on the new line is part of a nice, well-behaved utility function. Figure 4-3 shows this, where the new line goes from the origin through the indifference curves.

But, you may ask, what if all those points are different combinations of goods? After all, imagine that you've shown that for indifference curve 1, Bob will be indifferent between the bundle of three cups of tea and four cups of coffee and the bundle of five cups of tea and two cups of coffee, but prefers the bundle on indifference curve 2 of six cups of tea and two cups of coffee. What is this telling you?

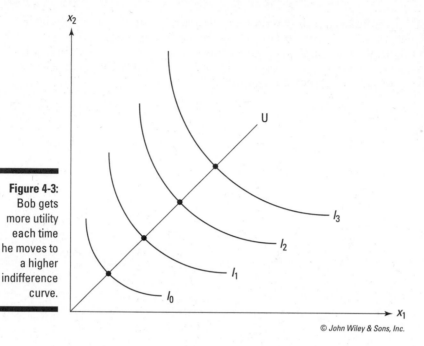

Figure 4-3: Bob gets more utility each time he moves to a higher indifference curve.

The answer is something very important about utility functions, which is that if preferences are well-behaved, almost anything that satisfies those rules could be part of a utility function! (In fact, a near infinite number of possible, consistent, utility functions could satisfy those rules. You just wouldn't know which particular one any individual consumer is on until his behavior reveals it in some way.)

The absolutely crucial point to take away is that *well-behaved preferences make well-behaved utility functions*.

Deciding How Low You'll Go: Marginal Utility

One really big thing to get clear is the difference between total and marginal utility. *Total utility* (the amount of utility gained in total from consuming something) is a useful concept, but economists far more commonly look at how utility changes as consumption at the margin changes. For that, they use the concept of *marginal utility:* the utility that is gained from consuming one extra unit of a good.

Considering the last in line: The marginal unit

The concept of the marginal unit is one of the most important concepts in the economics toolkit. Economists use it to analyze pretty much all production and consumption decisions. For instance, as Chapter 7 shows, firms optimize their production based on the relationship between marginal revenue and marginal cost. For a consumer, the concept of marginal utility is key in looking at consumption decisions. But what is this mysterious marginal unit of which we speak? We're glad you asked.

The *marginal unit* is defined as only the last, incremental unit of something, whether that be cost, benefit, utility, or revenue.

Suppose that chocoholic Ray is looking at six bundles of chocolate bars, each containing one more chocolate bar than the preceding bundle. Table 4-1 describes the utility gained by Ray from consuming the different bundles. As in the preceding section, Ray's preferences can be described by the points on this utility function, and we now add an extra column, which tells only the gain (or loss!) in utility from consuming an extra bar of chocolate. This is the marginal utility obtained from only the incremental last extra unit of chocolate, which does not include the utility from the consumption of the other bars in favor of looking just at what happens to Ray's utility as he consumes that last extra unit.

Table 4-1 uses cardinal measures of utility (flip to Chapter 2 for an explanation), so you can see what happens with some simple numbers. Suppose Ray gets 5 units of utility from his first bar. The second bar is even more enjoyable than the first and he gets 6 units of utility from it. The third, however, is starting to cause icky chocolate tummy and he gets less utility from that, and the fourth is really not giving all that much more utility. By the time he's on to the fifth he's feeling queasy and not so much enjoying it as suffering it.

Quantifying all the utility, we draw up a table for Ray in Table 4-1.

Figure 4-4 plots the table, and, as you can see, utility rises to a peak level — what economists call *satiation* — and then becomes disutility. Peak utility is found somewhere between the fourth and fifth bars (and we hope that these are fun-sized rather than full-sized bars). Assuming Ray is economically rational (and doesn't have any other constraints), he stops eating there.

Table 4-1	Ray's Total and Marginal Utility from Consuming Chocolate Bars	
Bar of Chocolate	*Total Utility*	*Marginal Utility*
1	5	5
2	11	6
3	16	5
4	19	3
5	19	0
6	17	−2

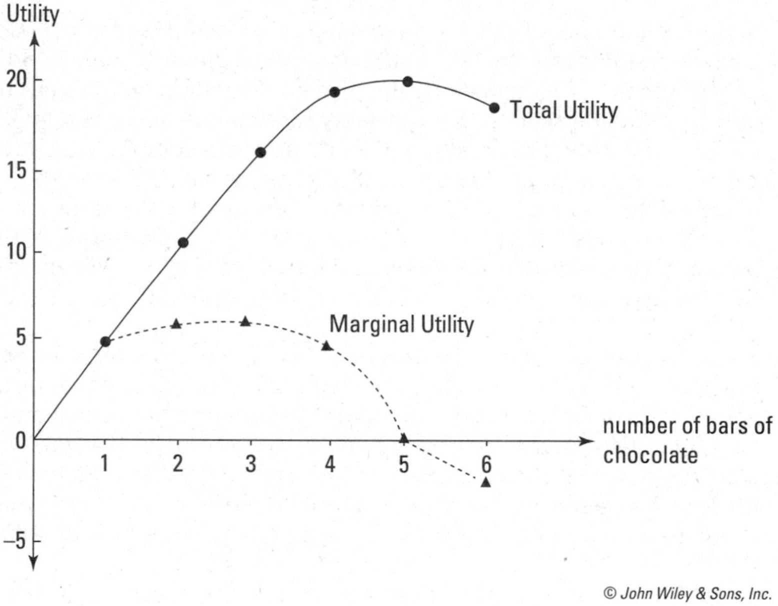

Figure 4-4:
Ray's total and marginal utility functions for chocolate.

© John Wiley & Sons, Inc.

Don't confuse marginal utility with the marginal rate of substitution (MRS is the slope of the indifference curve — see Chapter 2). Marginal utility is the gain in utility associated with an extra unit of something, whereas MRS tells you how much of one thing you have to give up in order to get an extra unit of something else.

Creating a formula to model utility

Chapter 2 says that utility gets revealed from behavior rather than measured up front. Well, if you know how a person exchanges one good for another along the indifference curve (which you can infer from behavior), you can use the formula we present in this section to learn something about the marginal utility gained from consumption of an extra unit.

You can write the formula for the marginal utility of a good when the quantity of the good changes. Start by writing a utility function (U) for the utility gained from consuming quantities of two goods, x_1 and x_2:

$$U(x_1, x_2)$$

Note that if you write $U(x_1, x_2)$ equals a constant — that is, $U(x_1, x_2) = K$ — you've written a mathematical description of an individual indifference curve, that is, you've described all the consumption bundles (x_1, x_2) that yield the same level of satisfaction or utility, which we denote by K. In other words you've gone through the earlier section "Making your choice: The consumption bundle," but in reverse, generating an indifference curve from a utility function.

Now, you take the changes in the utility achieved when only x_1 changes. To do so, you first write that marginal utility (MU) is the change in total utility when x_1 changes. Using a formula, that makes it like this:

$$MU_1 = \frac{\Delta U}{\Delta x_1}$$

Okay, now you expand the top of the equation using the formula for a utility function. Replace U with the original expression for utility (x_1, x_2) and then the new utility when x changes becomes the following:

$$U = U(x_1 + \Delta x_1, x_2) - U(x_1, x_2)$$

This means that MU equals all the right-hand side of the equation, all over Δx_1!

Here's something interesting. The preceding section warns you not to confuse marginal rates of substitution and marginal utility, but the two concepts do have a special relationship. Recall that the marginal rate of substitution is the slope of the indifference curve and that points on the same indifference curve yield the same level of utility. Now think about a change in the consumption of both goods that leads to utility staying the same, so that both the before and after consumption bundles are on the same indifference curve. The change in the consumption bundles means that whatever utility you gained by adding more of one good, say x_1, you lost by taking away some of the other good, x_2. Overall the marginal utility gained from the change equals zero, or alternatively:

$$MU_1 \Delta x_1 + MU_2 \Delta x_2 = \Delta U = 0$$

This doesn't seem all that Earth-shattering. Now, solving for the slope of the indifference curve, which you can write as $\Delta x_1 / \Delta x_2$, we find that $\Delta x_2 / \Delta x_1 = MU_1 / MU_2$. And because MRS is the slope of the indifference curve, we can see that $MRS = MU_1 / MU_2$:

$$MRS = \frac{\Delta x_2}{\Delta x_1} = -\frac{MU_1}{MU_2}$$

So here, using a little bit of simple but clever math, you can reconstruct information about what you'd like to know (utility) from something you do know (MRS). Now *that's* microeconomics!

Ray is in conformity with the rules of choice, which makes his preferences well-behaved and therefore workable. If he isn't, inferring anything about his behavior becomes a far more challenging task. Compare Ray, for example, to Cookie Monster. As a monster, Cookie Monster "eat cookie" irrespective of how much utility he gets from cookie. Cookie Monster, therefore, doesn't behave as if he has well-behaved preferences, and you can make no inferences whatsoever about marginal substitution or utility.

Chapter 5

Considering the Art of the Possible: The Budget Constraint

In This Chapter

▶ Checking out how a budget constraint affects consumer choice

▶ Seeing how consumers want to push utility to the maximum

▶ Modeling consumer behavior in two ways

Chapter 4 discusses consumer behavior in terms of what's called *unconstrained optimization,* where the only limiting factor is the amount of utility a person achieves. Ah, such freedom!

In the real world, of course, you never quite have the time and money to accomplish all the things you want to. You could always achieve something else if it wasn't for those pesky constraints, such as buy an item if you weren't just so short of moolah. So, in reality, satisfying your wants can never be as simple as Chapter 4's model: In practice you may be unable to consume anything up to your bliss or saturation point where you no longer gain further utility.

Almost nothing in economics works in an unconstrained model. At some level, everything is constrained, if not by money then by time. When you're deciding how much of something to consume, your utility isn't the only important aspect; you also need to consider the availability of resources.

Fortunately, economists are very comfortable with the idea of scarcity. They've thought about this problem for over a hundred years and have a number of tools for describing constrained choice. In fact, at the heart of microeconomics is a model of constrained optimization, which deals with precisely this conundrum.

To make the model of Chapter 4 more fitting to the real world, this chapter adds another piece of the puzzle: the budget constraint. This chapter describes what the budget constraint does to the level of consumption that an individual consumer is able to choose. We explain what you can tell from the budget constraint and how you can manipulate it to show how people's choices are affected by changes in the prices of goods that they want to buy or the income they have for buying goods. We also use the indifference curve from Chapter 4 to show how economists model a constrained choice, and show you one important insight of the model — that the ratio between prices is the same as the marginal rate of substitution (MRS — see Chapter 4) between two goods.

Taking It to the Limit: Introducing the Budget Constraint

The key to moving from unconstrained optimization to constrained optimization is the introduction of a *budget constraint.* This is a method of conceptualizing all the ways that the choice of doing or buying something is held back by the availability of resources, whether in terms of money, time, or something else. It also provides some insights that help economists put a bit more flesh on the utility model, bringing them closer to modeling the real world.

This section presents the budget constraint, and because we expect that *your* time and effort is constrained, we do our best to keep things simple.

Introducing the budget line

Imagine, as in Chapter 4, that you have two goods x_1 and x_2 — you can think of them as coffee and tea, or season tickets to see the Yankees and vacation days in Florida. We assume you have a fixed amount of resources, which we call M for now. The two goods have prices p_1 and p_2, respectively.

The maximum amount you can spend on both goods is M, and so the budget constraint has the following formula:

$$p_1 x_1 + p_2 x_2 = M$$

This equation is known as *the budget line.*

If you remember some of your high school algebra, you may have picked up that this equation describes a straight line, and that it slopes downward. By doing some rearranging in the equation, you can express the slope of the line by the price ratio of the two goods:

$$\text{Slope} = -p_1 / p_2$$

Any bundle of the goods x_1 and x_2 up to and including the budget line is feasible; anything beyond it is unfeasible and so is ruled out. Figure 5-1 plots the shape of the set of feasible consumption choices.

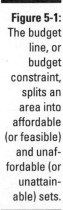

Figure 5-1: The budget line, or budget constraint, splits an area into affordable (or feasible) and unaffordable (or unattainable) sets.

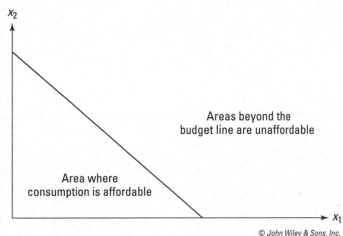

© John Wiley & Sons, Inc.

Note that points or bundles beyond the budget line — that is, those farther away from the origin than the budget line — are now ruled out. This means that when we re-introduce indifference curves, the highest possible indifference curve that you can be on is the one that is just touching or tangent in one place only to the budget constraint (assuming, that is, that the indifference curves are strictly convex, as in Chapter 2).

We demonstrate this point again in the later section "Getting the Biggest Bang for your Buck." For the moment, we show you some ways of manipulating the budget constraint and a couple of points you can glean quite simply from doing so.

Shifting the curve when you get a raise

Let's say one day your boss calls you into her office and announces that you're going to get a raise. Of course, you're delighted — but far more importantly, you've gained an opportunity to put your microeconomics to use. The way you do that is by understanding that the M (the fixed amount of resources) in the budget constraint is now bigger than it used to be, and so you can use this fact to manipulate the budget constraint to show your new purchasing possibilities.

A budget constraint maps the relative availability of two goods to a fixed amount of resources, which we call M. In the consumer choice model, this means that you take account of an increase in income by moving the budget constraint away from the origin so that the new curve is parallel to the old, as in Figure 5-2.

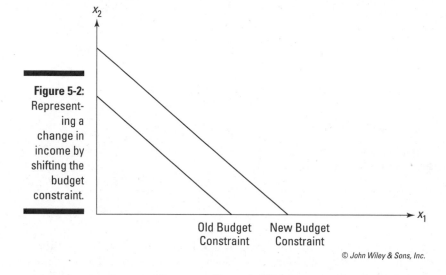

Figure 5-2:
Representing a change in income by shifting the budget constraint.

Old Budget Constraint   New Budget Constraint

© John Wiley & Sons, Inc.

You can look at this another way. If your income goes up and prices stay the same, you can afford to buy more goods. Alternatively, if your income stays the same but prices of goods all decline by the same percentage, you can afford more goods as well. Under either scenario your budget constraint shifts up parallel to the old.

A shift in the budget constraint means that some bundles that the consumer desires are now either available where they hadn't been before (if the change is positive) or ruled out (if the change is negative).

Twisting the curve when the price of one good changes

Changing income shifts your budget constraint up or down, or if all the prices of the goods you're interested in change at the same rate, your budget constraint shifts up or down in a similar fashion.

But suppose that some prices change more than others. It's more likely that some prices go up and others stay the same rather than all prices changing by the same percentage. In this case, you need to look again at the formula for the budget constraint to see how this kind of change affects your feasible consumption.

For instance, take the current consumer price index for the U.S. For urban consumers, the price index increased 0.3 percent in June 2015. The food index posted a large increase due in part to a sharp increase in the price of eggs, and the energy index rose for the second straight month as the prices of gasoline, electricity, and natural gas all increased. However, the prices for medical care, household furnishings and operations, used cars and trucks, and apparel all declined.

A price index is based on a very broad sector-based approach to measuring household consumption, and when you look further into the data, you find that the prices of some goods rose and some fell, and so the overall average picture masks these changes in *relative prices*.

Relative price changes have an important effect on consumer behavior as they cause substitution between goods. Suppose you're deciding to take a break from work for a nice hot beverage. Suppose further that coffee has become relatively more expensive. Then, under some circumstances (explained more fully in Chapter 6) you may find it worthwhile to substitute some of your consumption of coffee for tea, preserving your overall level of satisfaction.

When the price of one good, say coffee, or p_1, increases, and the price of the other good, p_2, tea, stays the same, the budget constraint changes. But instead of a shift, the constraint *rotates* so that it becomes steeper when the price of good one has risen.

Figure 5-3 shows you how we'd take account of a rise in the price of coffee.

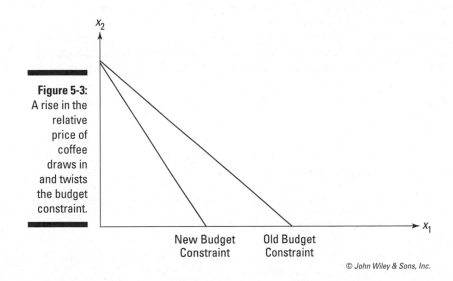

Figure 5-3: A rise in the relative price of coffee draws in and twists the budget constraint.

© John Wiley & Sons, Inc.

A rise in the price of any particular good is similar to a fall in income, because it reduces the number of opportunities to consume. However, a rise in the price of one good (relative to another or all others) restricts the choice of bundles to ones in which the more expensive good is more constrained.

Pushing the line: Utility and the budget constraint

The budget constraint divides what is feasible from what is not feasible. We can now use the model of consumer choice and take a look at what a consumer will do to optimize her utility or satisfaction when a constraint exists. To do this, we have to take a look at what happens when we put the indifference curves from Chapter 4 together with the budget constraint in this section.

As described in Chapter 4, a consumer would, up to a point of satiation (and we assume that we're some way from that point), try to consume so that she's on the highest possible indifference curve — that is, one farthest away from the origin. Figure 4-2 in Chapter 4 shows this. Each of the indifference curves has the same level of utility at all points along the curve, and the only way to be at a higher level of utility is to be on a higher indifference curve.

Figure 5-4 reintroduces the budget constraint. Okay, now, we look at three indifference curves (and associated consumption bundles on each curve):

✔ **Indifference curve I_1:** Lies entirely within the budget constraint and therefore is feasible. But would the consumer choose it? The answer is no, because higher levels of utility or satisfaction would be available by consuming right up to the budget line — all the areas above the indifference curve but within the constraint are still affordable, and all yield higher utility than any point on I_1.

✔ **Indifference curve I_2:** Also has points that are inside the constraint — although some are outside it.

Clearly the consumer would prefer points on I_2 to those on I_1, because they all confer a higher level of utility. But even though some combinations on I_2 are unfeasible, the feasible points all lie away from the budget constraint, meaning that utility is available, as long as we restrict ourselves to combinations of x_1 and x_2 that are away from the extremes.

✔ **Indifference curve I_3:** Has a multitude of unavailable points, but notice also that this has one very important available point — point D — which is exactly on the budget line (mathematically, you say that it lies on a tangent to the line). This point yields higher utility than any point on I_1 or I_2 and is feasible. Moreover, any other point on I_3 yields the same satisfaction as D, but you can't afford it with your income or M.

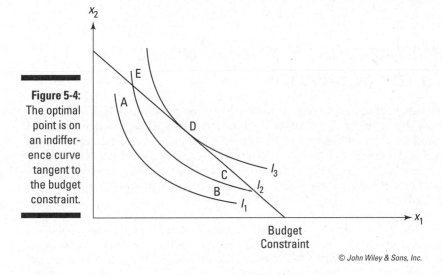

Figure 5-4: The optimal point is on an indifference curve tangent to the budget constraint.

Budget Constraint

© *John Wiley & Sons, Inc.*

When looking at utility given a budget constraint, the best available point must lie on an indifference curve tangent to the budget constraint, because that's when the consumer has spent to the last penny available and can get no more satisfaction.

Getting the Biggest Bang for Your Buck

The shape of the budget constraint itself is of great importance to micro-economists. In and of itself, the nature of the constraint provides information that's useful for looking at consumer behavior.

One of the key ways in which a tax, subsidy, or rationing affects consumers is through lowering (or, better, raising) the budget constraint. Economists manipulate the budget constraint into showing you those kinds of points in a number of ways. This section looks at two.

Economists assume that consumers want to get as much utility as possible for the least possible cost. Changes in relative prices of goods change the budget constraint and therefore the highest level of utility that a consumer can get. So, if anything affects the budget constraint, it also affects how consumers will choose which bundle of goods to consume.

Exploring relative price changes with the numeraire

Sometimes economists prefer to move away from absolute prices — for example, $4.79 for a cheeseburger — to relative prices that express prices for one good in terms of how much something else costs. For instance, the same cheeseburger costs 4.79 times the price of a bag of chips, which costs $1, so a cheeseburger on the market is worth 4.79 bags of chips. Looking at the ratios of prices rather than at the prices themselves can make choice simpler to understand.

A *numeraire* (pronounced "noomer-air") price is what you get when you fix the price of one of the goods on the budget line to 1. Doing that can be useful when you want to eliminate the effect of the absolute level of prices and just look at the effects of changes relative to the price of the numeraire good.

To get the numeraire price, start by considering that setting one price equal to 1 and allowing the other prices and income to change around it doesn't change the properties of the budget set at all. In the original budget line used earlier in this chapter (in section "Taking It to the Limit: Introducing the Budget Constraint"), the formula is as follows:

$$p_1 x_1 + p_2 x_2 = M$$

But if we fix things so that p_2 is 1, we still get exactly the same budget line, except with the intercept for x_2 (M/p_2) now just being M. The key thing is that the relative price of everything else is now expressed holding the numeraire price of x_2 at 1.

If everything in the budget set changes by the same rate, the only effect on the consumer is to shift the budget line as a whole in or out. If you multiply the budget line by a number, the optimal choice of the consumer doesn't change. So if the price of all goods and services in an economy changes by exactly the same amount in a year, inflation is *balanced* and doesn't affect consumers' purchases.

A numeraire good with a price equal to one is one way of fixing our attention on relative prices. If you're unsure about the change in price of one good relative to another, the numeraire helps you see how the ratio matters. Again, the slope of the budget constraint is the important factor, because it measures relative prices rather than absolute prices. If you use a numeraire price, you can quite simply see what's happening, because it sets one of the prices at 1, making the role of the price ratio clearer.

Using the budget line to look at taxes and subsidies

In a two-good model, the budget line is a simple straight line whose slope is the ratio of prices. But if, for instance, a tax changes the cost of a good relative to others, that is tantamount to a price change, and you can use the shape of the budget line to think about how to analyze the effect of the tax.

Before doing so, we have to be a bit more specific about the type of tax, because different taxes do different things to the shape of the budget line.

Two types of tax

We want to distinguish two types of tax (or their seemingly positive cousin, subsidies) that affect the constraint:

- ✔ **Quantity taxes:** A tax per unit of something bought. Examples are the tax that government levies on gasoline, expressed per gallon, or the "sin" taxes levied on certain goods, such alcohol and cigarettes per unit. These taxes, also called *excise* taxes, simply change the price paid for that quantity: If x_1 is the quantity of unleaded gasoline, and the quantity tax is τ per unit, the price of a gallon is $p_1 + \tau$, and you can treat the imposition of the tax as a price change.

- ✔ *Ad valorem* ("to the value of") taxes: Instead of being levied on a per unit quantity of the good, an ad valorem tax is levied as a percentage of the purchase price of the good. A common example is the sales tax.

  In the U.S., the sales tax varies according to jurisdictions within the country. For example, the sales tax in Chicago is 10.25% — consisting of 6.25% state, 1.25% city, 1.75% county, and 1% for the regional transportation authority. In Baton Rouge, Louisiana, the sales tax is 9%, consisting of 4% state and 5% local rate.

If the pre-tax price of the good is p_1, then the post-tax price is $(1 + \tau)\, p_1$ where τ is the ad valorem rate of tax. For the 10.25% sales tax that a consumer pays in Chicago, τ equals 0.1075 (convert the percentage to a decimal), and $1 + \tau$ is 1.1075. So the price of a good is 1.1075 times p.

Again, you can treat the introduction of an *ad valorem* tax as being tanta-mount to an increase in the price of the good you're considering and manipu-late the budget constraint to show it. In this case, the constraint would show the bundles of goods that can be consumed when the sale tax on good 1 is included in the post-tax price.

An interesting case to consider is what happens when a tax is only levied on consumption of a good above a certain price. In Massachusetts, the sales tax of 6.25% is not levied on clothing that costs less than $175. Any individual clothing item that is more than $175 is taxable on the amount over the basic exemption. If you buy a $200 coat, $1.56 or 6.25% of the $25 taxable amount would be added to the price. So, the microeconomics question is: How do you look at this aspect using a budget constraint?

The answer's easy: One slope of the line for purchases goes up to the thresh-old and then the line bends at that point (see Figure 5-5).

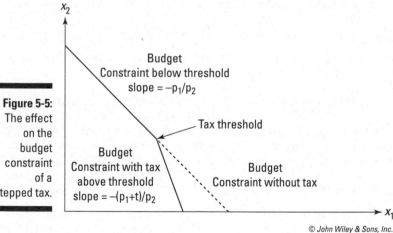

Figure 5-5: The effect on the budget constraint of a stepped tax.

To make everything easier, think about the tax being levied on a quantity rather than a value tax. Suppose, for argument's sake, that the first item of clothing does not incur a tax, but the second does. Now, while you're deciding to buy a first item, the budget constraint is the constraint for x_1 up to the point where $x_1 = 1$. Here, the slope of the budget constraint is $-p_1/p_2$ as it was earlier (see the section "Taking It to the Limit: Introducing the Budget Constraint"). However, beyond $x_1 = 1$, the slope changes to become $-(p_1 + \tau)/p_2$. As you can see in Figure 5-5, the budget line is steeper beyond the threshold.

TIP

You can do the same type of graphing with subsidies, too. A subsidy, in this case, is just a negative tax, and so instead of adding it to the price you subtract it. Therefore, if good x_1 is subsidized, the budget slope is $-(p_1 - t)/p_2$. We show this in Figure 5-6.

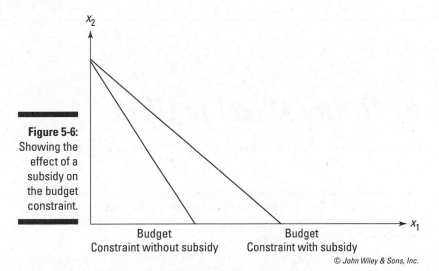

Figure 5-6:
Showing the effect of a subsidy on the budget constraint.

Budget
Constraint without subsidy

Budget
Constraint with subsidy

© John Wiley & Sons, Inc.

JARGON BUSTER

Rationing also affects the budget line. If a good is rationed, one area of the budget set becomes unavailable at any price — the set is said to be *truncated* in economics-speak.

To show this, cut a vertical line in above the maximum rationed consumption of good x_1. To the left of the line, the budget set behaves as normal. To the right, where the maximum consumption is greater than the rationed amount — call it R for the moment — the set consists of goods that the consumer could afford, but can't get. We present this example in Figure 5-7.

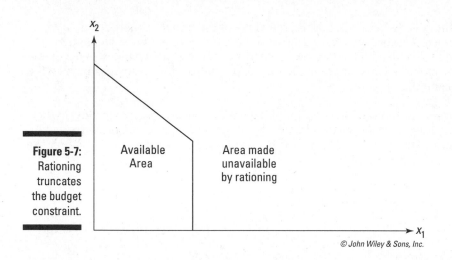

Figure 5-7:
Rationing
truncates
the budget
constraint.

© John Wiley & Sons, Inc.

Putting the Utility Model to Work

Essentially, in the standard choice model, a consumer can optimize
in two ways:

- ✔ **Utility maximization approach:** The consumer first decides on a
  budget constraint and then figures out how much utility she can get
  for that budget (discussed in the earlier section "Taking It to the Limit:
  Introducing the Budget Constraint").

- ✔ **Cost-minimization approach:** The consumer has a target level of utility
  that she wants to achieve and wants to minimize the cost that she has
  to pay to get it. As a microeconomist, you treat the amount of utility that
  she wants to get as fixed and then work out which budget constraint is
  the lowest possible constraint that allows her to afford a bundle from
  that utility function.

Ultimately, the two approaches work out to the same thing, and should
arrive at the same answer, but from two different directions. Deciding which
approach to use is a matter of *computational efficiency* — meaning you use
the version that's easiest to do in the time available — and which is more
efficient depends on how much information you have about the constraint
or the consumer's preferences, that is, indifference curves. In microeconomics, the insight that both approaches achieve the same answer is known
as *the dual*.

What's most important is the conclusion that you can derive from knowing
something about utility (see Chapter 4) and something about the budget

constraints and how the two have to be related. The relation between the two that is important in this case is that the highest level of utility possible for a constrained consumer occurs when the indifference curve is tangent to the budget constraint. Therefore the slope of the utility curve and the slope of the budget constraint are equal at that point.

The slope of the indifference curve is the marginal rate of substitution (MRS), as in Chapter 4, and the slope of the budget constraint is the relationship between the two prices ($-p_1/p_2$). Given that these have to be equal at the optimal choice for the consumer, you know that the optimizing consumer's best point occurs when

$$MRS = -p_1 / p_2$$

You need to know this equation for Chapter 6's full discussion on consumer optimization and for Chapter 9, which looks into the famous supply and demand model.

Chapter 6

Achieving the Optimum in Spite of Constraints

. . . .

In This Chapter

▶ Breaking down the effect of a change in prices into income and substitution effects

▶ How consumers' preferences are revealed

▶ Comparing income and substitution effects

. . . .

The single most important part of microeconomics is the *constrained optimization* model, which is based on the idea that people act to achieve the best they can, given some kind of constraint that limits their choice. This way of looking at people's decisions runs through most of the microeconomic syllabus, finding its way into all sorts of things from consumer choice to environmental or health economics. Yet its roots lie in the way economists look at individual decision-making.

To microeconomists, people *optimize*. When prices change, people respond to the information and react. Suppose you have $1 in your pocket to spend on a treat. You have two types of available treats, chocolate bars and cookies, and you start by getting your best mix of the two: that's two of each to begin with. Now imagine that the price of cookies goes up. What do you do? Well, if you're behaving as microeconomists suggest, you switch some of your consumption from cookies to chocolate bars so that you can keep your level of utility as high as possible.

Putting the constrained optimization model into place means dealing with the effect of prices on utility. Chapters 2 and 4 lay the foundations on consumer preferences and utility functions, and Chapter 5 deals with the budget constraint. This chapter starts from the optimum consumption bundle or point in Chapter 5, where the indifference curve is exactly tangent to the budget constraint, and shows you what happens when something changes.

We hope that, given your time constraints, this chapter helps maximize your utility.

Investigating the Equilibrium: Coping with Price and Income Changes

When investigating the effect of a price change, a good place to start is by thinking about what the change will do to the behavior of a representative consumer. Indifference curves (see Chapters 2, 4, and 5) excel in this situation!

Start at a given equilibrium to get a sense of what is happening before you make changes. In this case, the plot in Figure 6-1 is an equilibrium with well-behaved indifference curves and a standard budget constraint, and at the consumer optimum, the price ratio equals the marginal rate of substitution between goods x_1 and x_2.

Now, imagine some situation that affects your income calamitously (such as losing your job, getting a new job that doesn't pay as much, or a national economic disaster like that affecting Greece). The details don't matter; the important thing is that it reduces your income.

Starting at the equilibrium, you can draw in a new budget constraint, one that's parallel to the original one, but to the left of it. Of course, this means that the original equilibrium level of utility is now unattainable, and so you, as the representative consumer, react by reducing your consumption of goods x_1 and x_2 (see Figure 6-1). The parallel shift makes the old optimal choice unavailable, given the new constraint M_{NEW}.

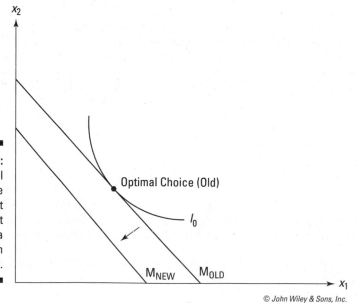

Figure 6-1:
A parallel shift in the budget constraint simulates a change in income.

Suppose instead that just one price changes (remember, you can treat x_1 and x_2 as though x_1 is the good you're interested in and x_2 represents all other goods). This is an interesting situation, because the effect on your purchasing opportunities isn't due to an overall fall in income, but to the *relative price* effect whereby x_1 is now more expensive relative to the price of all other goods available. This situation is where indifference curves fully unpack their awesome power — check out the next section.

Dealing with Price Changes for One Good

This section explores what happens when a relative price changes. In reality, this tends to happen when people talk about price rises. Only very rarely do all prices change at the same rate, but in those rare cases the budget line merely shifts in and out in parallel with the original. More often, the price of one good changes while others don't, or changes at a different rate than other goods. We take you through this scenario so that you can see its importance.

When the price of one good changes:

- The budget line, whose slope is the ratio of the two goods' prices, changes.

- The equilibrium condition requires that the marginal rate of substitution (MRS) is equal to the ratio of the two prices. So, the slope of whatever indifference curve the consumer is now on after the price change must be different from the original (the point where the ratio of prices and MRS are the same).

Don't worry if all this seems a little complicated. In this section, we break it down into simpler pieces in order to understand the behavior of the consumer.

Pivoting the budget line

In the optimization model, you take account of situations where one price changes by pivoting the budget line.

The budget line shows the maximum you can buy at the current prices. For example, you have $100, and a tennis racket costs $40, but a tennis lesson costs $20 per hour. You could buy one racket and have three lessons for the maximum, or two rackets (one for you and one for a tennis partner) and one lesson. Or you could buy five lessons and hope your old racket holds out. All these options are possible. But if the tennis lessons go up to $25, your options for substitution change. Now the maximum number of lessons you can buy while keeping your old racket falls to four.

Figure 6-2 shows the old equilibrium (with indifference curve I_0 tangent to the budget constraint, M). To this, we add the initial price change, which is illustrated by pivoting the budget line (as discussed in Chapter 5), so that the good whose price changes (x_1) becomes more expensive, drawing in the line along the x axis (representing the ability a consumer has to purchase x_1). This is the shape of the final budget line, and the slope of this line is the same as the MRS on whichever indifference curve the consumer ends up on. We label this M^{final} in Figure 6-2. In the figure, x_1 and x_2 = amounts of goods 1 and 2; M = budget constraint; U = utility at optimal bundle of goods, now unavailable; and I_0 = the indifference curve at the old optimum.

Therefore, to simulate a rise in the price of good x_1, you draw in the budget line so that maximum allocation to x_1 is reduced from x_1^{old} to x_1^{new}. The optimal point on the old constraint is no longer available.

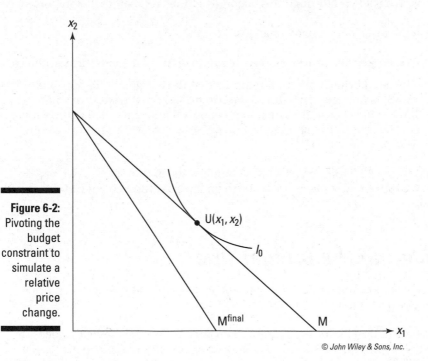

Figure 6-2:
Pivoting the budget constraint to simulate a relative price change.

© John Wiley & Sons, Inc.

But you can't get to that point yet! You have to unpack a couple new features first. Two effects occur when the price of a good changes:

- ✔ **Substitution effect** occurs when a rise in the price of a good relative to other goods leads to a substitution away from the more expensive good and towards the less expensive ones.

- ✔ **Income effect** reflects the fact that when prices rise, people have less income or less purchasing power to spend overall.

The next stage of working through the change in the price of one good is to work out the two effects in two steps so that you can see clearly how they operate, as the following two sections demonstrate.

Seeing substitution in practice

Economists are interested in how people make decisions when they want to consume up to their budget constraint, but a price hike means that their previous level of preferred consumption is no longer attainable. Consider this example: A representative consumer (call her Kirsty) likes to meet up with her friends each week to watch movies and eat noodles. Suppose she has a total budget of $60 for her entertainment activities. If a movie costs $10, and a bowl of hot noodles costs $5, we will suppose that Kirsty maximizes her utility — remember, she'll spend right up to the budget constraint if she can — when she goes to see a movie four times a week and has a bowl of noodles each time. Now suppose that — horrors! — the movie price goes up to $15: the movie becomes more expensive, relative to noodles. As a result, Kirsty can't afford her optimal bundle. Now she will want to cut back on going to the cinema and instead consume more noodles. For example, suppose Kirsty re-optimizes by going two times to the cinema and eating noodles six times a week. Economists are interested in knowing how much of the change in her consumption bundle — two fewer movies and two more bowls of noodles — was due to movies becoming more expensive relative to noodles and how much was due to the reduced purchasing power of her weekly budget?

Of course, economists would like to set up the problem so that it's as general as possible and doesn't rely on in-depth knowledge about a particular person and a particular good. Kirsty makes these choices automatically, and economists want to set things up in a way that makes consumer behavior understandable and to some degree predictable.

To show how substitution takes place, you need to know about the *slope* of the new budget line.

Start with Figure 6-2 and draw a new shadow budget line parallel to the final budget line but tangent to I_0 (though not at the original point of tangency — the slope of the new shadow budget line is different, which means that the optimal point where MRS on I_0 is equal to the slope of the new shadow budget line will be different). We do so in Figure 6-3.

The shadow budget line (M^{SHADOW}) shows how the effect of the change in the price of x_1 induces substitution, even in the absence of reduced purchasing power. In the figure, x_1 and x_2 = quantities of goods 1 and 2; M = budget constraint; I_0 = indifference curve is tangent to original budget line.

Note that we don't shift the indifference curve I_0, because the intention here is to show the substitution effect while keeping the consumer's level of welfare or happiness constant. Consumption of x_1 falls and that of x_2 rises owing to the relative price effects, but overall level of utility or satisfaction is preserved.

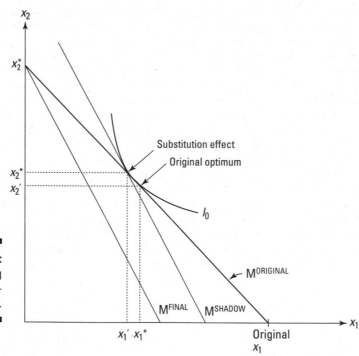

Figure 6-3:
Unpacking the substitution effect.

Adding in the income effect

When a price changes, and specifically when it increases, you feel as though you are poorer even though your income has not changed. Your reduced purchasing power will also cause you to change your consumption behavior, and this change is called the *income effect*. The change in the price of a good relative to other prices doesn't just affect the amount of the good consumed relative to the others: it also changes the amount consumed as a whole, because it generally makes your preferred amount unattainable. You feel as though you are poorer. Of course, the opposite is true if the price of a good decreases. Your purchasing power increases, and you feel richer.

Here's an example of the income effect, where someone's original best bundle becomes unaffordable and the person consumes less in total. Ian, a representative consumer, would like to spend his weekly disposable income on shoot-em-up video games and pizza. He has $50 to spend. Initially a game costs $30 and a pizza $5, so he buys one game and has pizza four times a week. But — disaster — the price of video games goes up to $35. His initial consumption bundle is no longer possible, and he now gets only three pizzas a week because he doesn't want to substitute away his game. There is no substitution effect, but still his total consumption must fall, from one game and four pizzas to one game and three pizzas. This is the income effect coming into play.

Again, economists want to generalize away from specific numbers and form a more general picture of the income effect. Follow along now as we show you the general model that economists use. The income effect occurs because the price change (and the corresponding shift in the budget constraint) means that the level of utility associated with I_0 is no longer available. Thus, the economically rational consumer optimizes by shifting down to a new indifference curve denoted by I_1 in Figure 6-4. As we discuss in the preceding section, M^{SHADOW} covers the relative price changes, and so the move from M^{SHADOW} to M^{FINAL} just deals with the fact that the purchasing power of income has gone down.

In Figure 6-4 we indicate the new optimum as U^* (the best available position for the consumer after accounting for income and substitution effects). U^* is at a different point of substitution between x_1 and x_2, and so less x_1 is consumed, and it's on a lower indifference curve, I_1. This is the "final" equilibrium point, where utility is as high as it can possibly be given the new constraint. In the figure, x_1 and x_2 = quantities of goods 1 and 2; M = budget constraint; I_0 = indifference curve at original optimum; I_1 = final indifference curve tangent to final budget constraint M^{FINAL}; U bar = consumption bundle chosen accounting for only the substitution effect, tangent to M^{SHADOW}; U^* = final best optimum after accounting for income and substitution effects.

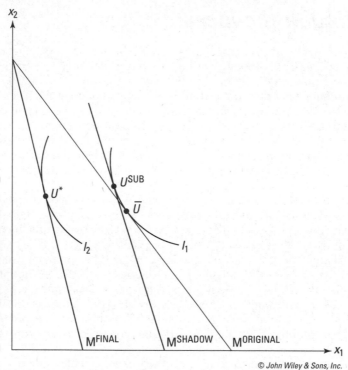

Figure 6-4:
Shifting
back the
shadow
curve to
investigate
the substitu-
tion effect
gives a new
optimum U*.

© John Wiley & Sons, Inc.

Different strokes: Different goods have different income and substitution effects

The relative size and, in some cases, direction of the income and substitution effects depend on the type of good you're examining. For instance, if (from the consumer's point of view) a good has many close substitutes, the substitution effect is likely to be large (infinitely so in the case of perfect substitutes), and the income effect negligible. But if the good has no close substitutes and the consumer continues to buy roughly the same quantity at the higher price, the income effect is likely to be much larger compared to the substitute effect.

Several factors determine the size of each effect, including the following:

✔ **Income elasticity:** Measures the responsiveness of purchasing to a change in income. Normal goods are those that have income elasticities (see Chapter 9 for details) around 1, meaning that if income rises by 10%, consumption of those goods also rises by around 10%. But some goods (such as luxuries) respond more dramatically or elastically to income changes, whereas some respond less elastically and in some cases even negatively. A good is considered inferior if consumption of it falls as you become richer. Whether a good has an income elasticity of greater or less than one or is negative depends on consumer tastes.

✓ **Existence and closeness of substitutes:** When the two goods are perfectly interchangeable from a taste perspective, the indifference curve is a straight line and so a rise in the price of one substitute results in substitution away to the cheaper option. (Given the same units of measurement, the slope of the indifference curve is 1, so unless the prices are equal, the consumer gets to the highest indifference by buying the cheaper good. When the prices are same, the indifference and the budget line coincide.)

✓ **Ability of a consumer to switch:** An implicit assumption here is that switching from one option to another is free and costless, which isn't always true — as you know if, say, you've tried to switch operating systems on your computer or your cell phone plan. Economists dealing with markets in information technology have to adapt models to add in *switching costs,* which are derived from, among other things, the cost of learning to use a technology or of giving up a network of users.

Discerning a Consumer's Revealed Preference

Given the preceding section, you can say a few more things about the relationship between preferences and the budget constraint. One is about the principle of revealed preference. Utility isn't measured, but things about utility can be found out by observing consumer choices and inferring from their choices the impact of price changes on their utility or welfare.

This somewhat back-to-front way of looking at things makes sense when you realize that economists know nothing about the consumer until he participates in a situation where inferences can be made regarding his behavior. For example, suppose the government levies a tax on a good. From the consumer's perspective, it is as though the price of the good has increased and the consumer will be made worse off and hence will not be happy about the tax. The government may try and compensate the consumer by transferring a rebate to him that's equivalent to the tax revenue collected. However, the principle of revealed preference tells us that the consumer will still be worse off under the tax and rebate scheme.

This is shown in Figure 6-5. When the consumer faces prices p_1 and p_2 and has an income M, the consumer optimizes by choosing the bundle $(x_1{}^*,x_2{}^*)$. Now the government imposes a tax on good 1 so that the price becomes $p_1{}' = p_1 + t$. At the same time, the government offers the consumer a rebate R equal to the tax revenue it collects from the consumer. With this budget constraint, the consumer chooses the bundle $(x_1{}',x_2{}')$ and we have that $(p_1 + t)\, x_1{}' + p_2\, x_2{}' = M + tx_1{}'$ where the rebate R is equal to the tax revenue $tx_1{}'$ collected. Simplifying this expression, you can see that it is equivalent to $p_1 x_1{}' + p_2\, x_2{}' = M$. In other words, the bundle $(x_1{}',x_2{}')$ lies on the original budget constraint but the consumer did *not* choose it. The consumer preferred $(x_1{}^*,x_2{}^*)$. This tells us by revealed preferences that the consumer is on a higher indifference curve or level of utility with $(x_1{}^*,x_2{}^*)$. The imposition of an income compensated tax still made the consumer worse off.

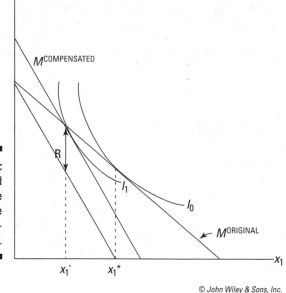

Figure 6-5:
Revealed
preference
and income
compen-
sated tax.

© John Wiley & Sons, Inc.

To put *revealed preference* as simply as possible, if a consumer chooses a bundle of goods — call it A — over another bundle — B — given that both B and A are affordable, you can say that the consumer *prefers* A to B. In other words, the act of choosing the bundle A *reveals* that the consumer preference is for bundle A over bundle B.

Until the consumer makes a choice, you don't really have a way of knowing her preferences for these bundles. Although you may be able to deduce the existence of A and B from what you know is available and affordable, you don't know a consumer's preference for sure. In the act of choosing to consume A rather than B, therefore, you gain information about a consumer's preferences that you didn't previously possess. Thus, you can infer that bundle A is preferred to B from the choice made by the consumer.

Decomposing Income and Substitution Effects

The income and substitution effects of a change in prices occur simultaneously when someone makes a choice. When introducing these two effects in the earlier section "Pivoting the budget line," however, we break them down so that the changes occur sequentially — pivoting the budget constraint indicated the substitution effect, and shifting it indicated the income effect.

Another way to gain insight into these two effects and their magnitude is to pivot the budget equation after a price change so that the consumer could afford the pre price change bundle. This approach uses a construction that is called the Slutsky equation, after the microeconomist Eugen Slutsky.

Remember that when a price changes, it causes two effects on the consumer:

- ✔ A substitution effect emerges when the budget line pivots, showing how much the change in consumption of one good changes relative to the other good.
- ✔ An income effect emerges when the budget line gets shifted to take into account a change in the total amount of money a consumer possesses.

Unpacking the effect of a price change in a model with two goods

In this walk-through, we consider a decrease in relative price that allows a representative consumer to afford more of the two goods. In Figure 6-6, the consumer substitutes towards the cheaper good: $x_{1\,OLD}$ = old level of consumption of good 1; $x_{2\,OLD}$ = old level of consumption of good 2; $x_{1\,NEW}$ = post change consumption of good 1; $x_{2\,NEW}$ = post change consumption of good 2 I_0 = original indifference curve; I_1 = new indifference curve; M_{old} = old budget constraint; M_{new} = new budget constraint.

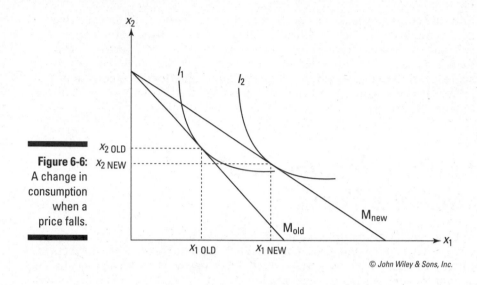

Figure 6-6:
A change in consumption when a price falls.

© John Wiley & Sons, Inc.

Here's the equation of a budget line (from Chapter 5):

$$M = p_1 x_1 + p_2 x_2$$

At this point, two things have changed regarding the original optimum point: the price of good 1 and the consumer's purchasing power have both changed. Now we consider what income M' the consumer would need, given the new price p_1' of good 1, in order to consume her original consumption bundle. The original bundle (x_1, x_2) is available and works on both M and M'.

(x_1, x_2) works on both budget lines, and so you can write two equations describing its relationship to the original budget line and the changed one:

$$M = p_1 x_1 + p_2 x_2 \qquad \text{: original equation}$$
$$M' = p_1' x_1 + p_2 x_2 \qquad \text{: pivoted budget equation}$$

For consistency, the equations show M as the original sum of money, M' as the changed sum, and p_1 as the original price of good x_1 and p_1' as the changed price.

Now subtract the first equation from the second, and here's what you get:

$$M' - M = x_1 \left(p_1' - p_1 \right)$$

Use the shorthand of Δ to indicate a change so that $M' - M = \Delta M$ and $p_1' - p_1 = \Delta p_1$, and substitute into the equation so that $\Delta M = x_1 \Delta p_1$.

Getting what you prefer

From the preceding section, you have a (slightly abstract) equation for determining what happens to income (M) and price (p_1) when a representative consumer wants to keep the quantity of x_1 he's consuming at the same level.

Here's an example to show how a consumer substitutes to keep utility at an optimum level: Carol has a bit of a coffee habit. Every week she allocates $10 of her disposable income to getting coffees at work. Each coffee — her choice is a vanilla latte — costs $2 (and she consumes up to her budget line, a maximum of $10, and has five coffees a week). Now suppose her coffee rises to $2.20, (from bad weather affecting coffee growers in Columbia) and she wants to keep her consumption at five delicious vanilla lattes a week. What must happen to her income to do so?

Given her preference, Carol realizes that if she wants to keep consuming x_1 equal to five lattes and knowing that the price of a latte has risen by $0.20, she can figure out the change in income that she must gain to keep the value of her consumption constant from the formula $\Delta M = x_1 \Delta p_1$. She does a quick piece of mental arithmetic and finds that if her income rises by $1 a week she can keep consuming five lattes a week.

Developing the substitution effect in numbers

The model in the preceding section demonstrates the changes in M that will allow Carol to keep her original consumption level the same after the change in price. But when the budget line pivots, the bundle that was optimal usually is no longer optimal, because the relative prices of the two goods have changed, making one relatively dearer than before. Thus, the consumer is most likely to optimize by substituting towards the relatively cheaper option.

Meeting the useful demand function

The demand for an amount of x_1 is generally given as a function. A *demand function* relates the quantity of the good consumed to the price of the good, the price of other goods desired by the consumer, and the amount of income a consumer possesses, supposing that all other goods are lumped together with a constant price equal to one. Not specifying exactly for the moment the relationship between income and prices, here's the demand function for good x_1 given p_1 and M:

$$x_1 = x_1(p_1, M)$$

Discerning the change in demand

The purpose of the exercise is to evaluate x_1 (the old optimum) and x_1' the new optimum when p_1 and M change. The old level of demand is in the above equation and the new one is:

$$x_1 = x_1\left(p_1', M'\right)$$

The substitution effect therefore measures the effect of the change in demand when the budget constraint pivots, allowing the consumer to achieve the original bundle, and is given by the following:

$$\Delta x_1^{\,s} = x_1\left(p_1', M'\right) - x_1\left(p_1, M\right)$$

From this equation, you can see that when you know the change in demand and the level of money required to keep x_1 the same, you can work out the substitution effect (see the next section).

Calculating the substitution effect from a demand function

Here we make an assumption about the shape of a particular demand function and take a look at the substitution effect. Adam needs to use his car for transport and buys gasoline in gallons from the local garage. His demand is described by the following function:

$$x_1 = 20 + M/(10p_1)$$

His allocatable income, M, is \$240, and we assume that gas costs \$3 a gallon. Prices for benchmark crude oil have plummeted and — somewhat implausibly — all that is being passed on to consumers, meaning Adam now pays \$2 a gallon. As his microeconomist friend, you're fascinated by this change in his fortunes, and you want to calculate how large the substitution effect is as Adam changes consumption in response to price (as his demand function tells you he will).

You know from his choices which of two feasible bundles Adam would prefer, because that was revealed when he chose. But to make a calculation, or prediction, you need an idea of the general relationship between the price of gasoline and the quantity demanded, derived by knowing how much gets bought at any particular price.

You're in a quandary: You really want to show how much of the change in quantity consumed depends on substitution and how much on change in income, but you can't know that until you know the relationship between price and total change in demand. As described in the earlier section

"Discerning a Consumer's Revealed Preference," microeconomists never know what preferences exist until they're revealed by a consumer making a choice. You can't know until you've worked out that general relationship, but underlying that relationship are the substitution and income effects. As a result, you have to start by gaining intuition about how Adam may behave and then building up a consistent picture of the relationship between price and quantity.

Therefore, learning consumer theory is a little circular and requires you to work backwards in order to move forward. In this example, Adam's demand function (see the preceding equation) relates quantity consumed (x_1) to the price of good $1(p_1)$ and the amount of income he had M ($240). So you can start performing your clever calculations given this simple relationship to work with.

To evaluate the size of Adam's substitution effect, you go through a four-stage process:

1. **Take Adam's demand function and evaluate x_1 for M and p_1.**

   You know Adam's original demand, and so you calculate x_1 for the demand function. Plugging in 240 for M and 3 for p_1 you get 28 gallons of fuel bought per week.

2. **Find the value of M' that keeps x_1 the same when p_1 changes.**

   You apply the formula $\Delta M = x_1 \Delta p_1$. You know that x_1 equals 28 and that $\Delta p_1 = (2 - 3) = -1$, and so M must change by $-$28. That means the new value of M' must be 240 – 28, which equals (ta-da!) $212.

3. **Plug M' and p_1' back into the demand function to evaluate new demand.**

   Going back to the original equation for Adam's demand for gas, you put in the new numbers for M ($212) and p_1 and now calculate: $X_1 = 20 + 212 / (10\text{x} 2) = 30.6$ gallons.

4. **Apply the formula for the substitution effect.**

   You use the equation

   $$\Delta x_1^s = x_1(p_1', M') - x_1(p_1, M)$$

   and plug in 30.6 for x_1 (p_1', M') — the new compensated demand from step 3 — and 28 for x_1 (p_1, M) – the original demand. Therefore, the substitution effect is responsible for 2.6 gallons of extra fuel being purchased per week.

If you simply plug in a value for p_1' in the original demand function, you get an answer for the total change in demand (which you can verify by plugging in the numbers and see that it comes to 4 gallons). But this way, you identify that of the 4-gallon increase in demand, the substitution effect is responsible for 2.6 gallons, or 65% of the total change in demand.

You calculate the substitution effect by stripping out the effect of income (in other words, step 2): finding the level of income that compensates for the change in price is key. If you don't find the compensated demand, you're looking at total change in demand and not the size of the substitution effect.

Adding up the income effect

The other effect of a change in price is to change the purchasing power of the consumer. If the price of a good changes, it's tantamount to arguing that a consumer's income has also changed, because the new budget line either restricts the level of demand (when the price of a good goes up) or allows consumption of goods that were previously unavailable (when the price of a good goes down).

In the preceding section, you model the change in purchasing power by shifting the budget line out. But you can also use some clever adaptations to that process to make a calculation of the income effect on Adam's demand — and of course adapt them to other demand situations.

To do so, define the income effect as the change in demand for a good when purchasing power or income changes from M to M' and price is held constant at p_1'. This definition keeps the mathematical treatment in line with the graphic example in Figure 6-4, where the budget line first pivoted and then shifted.

To express the income effect mathematically, write the following:

$$\Delta x_1{}^i = x_1\left(p_1',\text{M}\right) - x_1\left(p_1',\text{M}'\right)$$

Here p_1', the new price post-change, is held constant and you evaluate the demand for x_1 given that M changes to a new value M'.

Now plug in Adam's numbers from the preceding section. For the expression $x_1\left(p_1',M\right)$ calculate his demand using the changed price of 2, but the uncompensated level of income, 240. You get this:

$$x_1 = 20 + 240 / \left(10 \times 2\right) = 32$$

Evaluate demand given the compensated income from step 2 in the preceding section:

$$x_1 = 20 + 212 / \left(10 \times 2\right) = 30.6 \text{ litres}$$

Apply the formula for the income effect, taking the second answer from the first, to get an answer of 1.4 gallons of gas.

The sum of the two effects comes to the total change in demand, and so although his demand changes by 4 gallons overall, the income effect is responsible for 1.4 gallons and the substitution effect for 2.6 gallons.

Putting the two effects together using the Slutsky equation

Put simply, the Slutsky equation says that the total change in demand is composed of an income and a substitution effect and that the two effects together must equal the total change in demand:

$$\Delta x_1 = \Delta x_1^s + \Delta x_1^i$$

This equation is useful for describing how changes in demand are indicative of different types of good. Indifference curves are always downward sloping, and so the substitution effect must always turn out to be negative. But the income effect may not be, depending on how consumption of a good changes with income. A normal good has a negative income effect, and so if the price goes down and hence purchasing power or income goes up, then demand goes up. The reverse holds when price goes up and purchasing power or income falls, because then so does demand.

But not all goods are "normal." Some are inferior in an economic sense. We don't mean that they're of poor quality but that they have a negative income profile — as income goes up, a person consumes less of them. Instant noodles, for instance, aren't generally held to be a product that people consume unless they're constrained in terms of money; as you get richer, you consume less of them. In this case, the substitution effect is negative, but the income effect is also negative. For the opposite situation, see the nearby sidebar "Giffen goods."

Giffen goods

Although unusual, there are some cases where extreme trading down occurs so that as income goes down, the income effect is positive and the total change in demand turns out to be positive. These goods are known as *Giffen goods,* after the economist who first investigated their existence during the Irish famine. As the price of potatoes went up, so did their consumption. Giffen goods are often thought of as curiosities, but they do exist, albeit as a small subset of the total set of inferior goods.

Part III
Uncovering the Alchemy of Firms' Inputs and Outputs

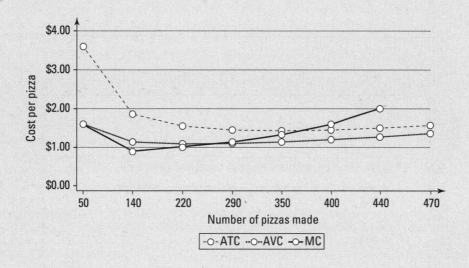

In this part . . .

- ✔ Distinguish the different types of costs that firms face.
- ✔ Discover how firms choose between using capital and labor.
- ✔ See how firms and individuals come together to make markets.

Chapter 7

Working with Different Costs and Cost Curves

- -

In This Chapter

▶ Learning two different views of costs

▶ Distinguishing average, total, and marginal costs

▶ Connecting costs to staying in business

- -

Much of the production in an economy comes from firms. In a market-based economy, these firms make their decisions based on an indicator, *profit,* which expresses the difference between the revenues the firm takes in and the costs it expends in obtaining those revenues. To understand how a firm makes such decisions, as well as how economists look at them, you need to examine more closely the relationship between the different types of cost a firm faces — what economists call its *cost structure.*

In a market economy, and certainly in an economically liberal society, a firm can't simply march people to its showrooms, lock the doors, and force them to buy its product, much as they might like to. So, although a firm may know a lot about how to organize production or how to produce, it doesn't necessarily know how much a consumer will want to buy at a given price — at least until it starts to get data from transactions. And it certainly can't control how much people will buy at that price (though it may have a good basis for guessing). Therefore, economists look at the aspects of a firm's operations that it *does* control, which means looking seriously and carefully at its costs.

This chapter examines a firm through its *cost curves,* which provide a relationship between a given cost incurred to produce and how much a firm will produce for that cost. We define and then investigate a firm's total, marginal, and average costs, see how they interact within a firm, and discuss their importance in firms surviving and continuing to trade or going under.

Understanding Why Accountants and Economists View Costs Differently

Economists look at costs in a particular way, which may not be what you expect. Every firm in every industry in every country incurs costs of one kind or another, and accounting systems provide a way of measuring and recording them. But economists are interested in more than the record of what was done in the past. They also want to know what opportunities the firm did not pursue or what the firm could have done had it not made the decision it did. Therefore, economists tend to look at costs in a different way.

In a set of company accounts, you find many items that describe costs, from costs of goods sold to overheads to general expenditures (these are *accounting costs*). Company accounts are produced to a set of standards that reflect the accounting profession's view of how best to describe the costs of a company, given that those costs are incurred in different ways and at different stages of production. As a result, companies report many different cost measures, and accountants know how to interpret these measures as needed.

Economists treat costs in a slightly different way, called, unsurprisingly, *economic costs*. Whereas an accountant needs to know what costs *have accrued* over the past year, an economist wants to examine costs as they relate to the firm's decision-making. This involves some key subtleties, the most important of which is that economic costs account for the opportunities the firm had to give up in order to do what it's doing. Economists call these *opportunity costs*. In principle, a firm has to account for them before going on to make any decisions about production or investment so that it knows it's making the decision on a rational basis.

If you're scratching your head a little, here's an example to relieve that itch.

Suppose you gave up a decently paying job to start a business and at the end of your financial year your accountant sends you a statement saying that your revenue was in excess of your costs by $25,000. You're happy with this, considering that an accounting profit of $25,000 is a decent return on your business. But then your economist friend points out that the job you gave up was paying a net salary of $35,000, which means that you gave up an opportunity to make $10,000 more than you received from your new business.

In fact, your *accounting profit* of $25,000 was an *economic loss* of $10,000 when you factor in the opportunity cost of giving up your old job to start your business. (Economics is called *the dismal science* for a reason.)

The upshot is that when looking at the individual types of cost a firm incurs, you can assume that economists (and this book) are talking about *economic costs* that include *opportunity costs*.

Looking at a Firm's Cost Structure

When considering a firm, economists place emphasis on its cost structure, which means looking at the different ways to break down or measure costs, depending on the parts of the picture they're looking at.

Typically microeconomists use three different ways to express the costs of a firm:

- ✔ **Total cost** looks at total cost for a given level of production.

- ✔ **Average cost** looks at how much producing a given level of output will cost *per unit* of output.

- ✔ **Marginal cost** looks at how much costs increase to produce an additional unit of output.

Economists also tend to break down costs according to the planning horizon or period of the firm and use these relationships to discover something about the structure of a firm or the technology of production it engages in:

- ✔ **Fixed costs** do not vary for the planning horizon considered. These costs are fixed and do not depend on the size of output.

- ✔ **Variable costs** vary for the planning horizon considered and depend on the size of output.

Taking in the big picture: Total costs

When talking about the types of cost a firm faces, economists start with the biggest and least detailed view of costs and then break them down in ways that make sense for economic decision-making.

The most global view of a company is in terms of its total costs (TC), which economists use quite simply to arrive at a number for total profits (you don't need to worry about gross or net terms here). *Total costs* are simply the overall cost of making a product and serving it to a market after all those relevant cost elements are accounted for.

If you start with a number for total revenue received (TR) and then subtract all those costs, you arrive at a figure for profit. We write that as an equation here:

$$\Pi = TR - TC$$

The Greek symbol Π in the equation stands for profit, so that economists don't get confused with price (generally denoted with a P).

When you take the view of firm owner, you may want to start looking at aspects of the total cost a little more closely. The simplest way to break down total costs is into two categories:

- ✔ **Costs that depend on the amount you've produced:** These include all things that are ongoing in the sense that the more you produce — or for a service, the more activity you undergo — the more you pay, which means things such as costs of each input used or the cost of utilities. These are called *variable costs,* and economists usually denote them VC when talking about variable costs as a component of total costs.

- ✔ **Costs that don't depend on the amount you've produced:** These include all the elements that your firm would have to pay regardless of how many items it produces. These may be the cost of premises, such as rents, or licenses if needed, or even the cost of advertising that the firm has to buy to let people know about its business. Economists call these *fixed costs* and usually abbreviate them FC.

Together, the two types of cost must sum to the total cost at which the firm operates, so we can say:

$$TC = FC + VC$$

Here's an example: A bicycle manufacturer makes bikes using labor, materials, and utilities costing $10 a bike. Assuming that she makes 100 bikes in a production period, the variable costs (VC) she faces will be 100 bikes times $10 a bike, which equals $1,000. However, in order to do this she needs a factory with the capacity to make the bikes: That factory costs $10,000 to rent per period. So her total costs are fixed costs (FC) of $10,000 plus the VC of $1,000, which equals $11,000 total costs.

Here are two important points to bear in mind:

- ✔ You have to pay fixed costs even if you produce absolutely no output whatsoever. If, for instance, you take out a rental contract for an office, you have to pay the rent irrespective of whether you produce anything at all.

✔ Variable costs depend on the amount of output you produce. If you have a pizza restaurant and you make no pizzas, you don't need any flour, tomatoes, or even power for a pizza oven. But the more pizzas you make, the more you spend on these inputs.

Measuring by unit: Average costs

By itself, total cost doesn't say much about the firm and still less about how it makes its decisions. Economists want to discover a little more about how the firm operates, so they look at the relationship between total cost and the number of units produced. To do so, they divide the cost of production by the number of units produced to derive the *average costs*.

Making use of average costs

Average costs or the cost per unit, measured at a level of production, are useful things to know in and of themselves, but they also have some important properties that economists use to find out about the efficiency of production. To compute average total cost (ATC), you divide total costs (TC) by the quantity produced (Q):

$$ATC = TC / Q$$

Now, here's an interesting thing. As already mentioned, total costs break down into fixed costs (FC) and variable costs (VC). Therefore you can divide each of these components by quantity of output produced to get average fixed costs (AFC) and average variable costs (AVC), which are the amount of fixed cost per unit and the amount of variable cost per unit, respectively. Or to put it another way:

$$ATC = TC / Q = (FC + VC) / Q = AFC + AVC$$

To discover an interesting feature of a firm's costs of production, take a look at average fixed costs. Fixed costs don't change whatever the level of production, but as you go on producing more and more, the AFC per unit falls as you divide by a higher level of output each time.

Here's a very simple example: A baker needs to incur a cost of $100 to set up his premises and can then make cakes for $2 per cake. The total cost is the sum of fixed and variable costs. Let Q denote the number of cakes produced. This allows us to write the following formula for his total costs:

$$TC = 100 + 2Q$$

Now divide through by quantity of cakes produced to get average total cost:

$$ATC = 100 / Q + 2$$

We now plot some numbers for the average total cost (ATC), or more simply (AC). Table 7-1 computes total and average costs according to this formula.

Table 7-1	Relationship between Total, Average, Fixed, and Variable Costs					
Quantity Produced	_1_	_2_	_3_	_4_	_5_	_6_
Fixed cost	100	100	100	100	100	100
Variable cost	2	4	6	8	10	12
Total cost	102	104	106	108	110	112
Average total cost	102	52	35.333	27	22	18.667
Average fixed cost	100	50	33.333	25	20	16.667
Average variable cost	2	2	2	2	2	2

Take a look at the average total cost row. If you notice that it falls as we add more units, that's good. Now look at the next two lines, the costs broken down into fixed and variable components. Note that the average fixed costs are particularly falling. Why? Well, a fixed cost doesn't depend on how much a firm produces — it still has to pay the same cost. In this case, though, because it's making more units, the fixed cost is being _divided_ by more units each time, which means that as the firm makes more, the average fixed cost gets smaller.

This fact is a key principle behind the concept of _economies of scale_. As the baker produces more cakes, he does so for a lower cost per cake.

Visualizing economies of scale by plotting average costs

One way to see how this works is to plot the average cost over a range of production. Generally the average cost curve is U-shaped. Over the range of output, as more gets made, the fixed costs get spread out over more output and average costs fall. Average costs stop falling when the increase in average variable costs in expanding production outweighs the decrease in average fixed costs. This does not happen in Table 7-1's example because average variable costs are constant and do not go up as production increases.

Average costs typically fall up to a point, beyond which the increase in average variable costs from adding an extra unit is greater than the decrease in average fixed costs by adding an extra unit. At this point, economists say that the firm has fully exploited economies of scale and is experiencing *diseconomies of scale*.

Figure 7-1 shows that average fixed cost is always falling, because the same number is divided by a bigger number each time, but that average variable costs start to rise beyond a certain point. That point, where the average cost of production rises again, is the *minimum efficient scale* of production and is important for considering the efficiency of a firm. Just note it for the moment: we say more about what efficiency means in this context in Chapter 8.

Figure 7-1: Average costs, average variable costs, and average fixed costs for a typical firm.

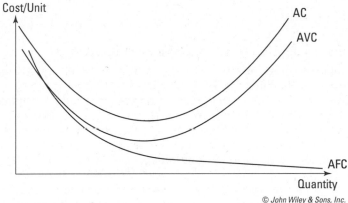

© John Wiley & Sons, Inc.

Adding only the cost of the last unit: Marginal cost

The breakdowns used in the preceding sections show costs for a particular level of production. But economists also use another important measure to consider when considering a firm's costs: *marginal cost*.

Meeting marginal cost

Put simply, *marginal cost* (MC) is the cost of adding one extra unit of output to your current output level. (A unit of output could be a ton of steel, a cake, a bushel of wheat, an hour of dental cleaning services, all depending on the output and the units of measurement.) Imagine that you produce 10 beach balls for $10 in total cost. If you add an extra beach ball to your production and make the total cost $11, the marginal cost of the 11th beach ball is $1, because that's how much producing an extra beach ball adds to your total costs.

Economists express marginal costs in terms of the *change in total costs,* which means that they measure a change in total cost for a change in quantity. Thus marginal costs are a measure not of how much something costs but how much those costs are changing as you do something to production.

"Marginal *anything*" in economics is important, because it is often the case that decision-making occurs at the margin. If you are already doing something, say making 100 units, and have already made that decision, then you must decide whether to make the 101st unit. That's the marginal decision you face.

You can calculate MC fairly simply, even across a number of units by remembering that it's the change in cost for a small change in quantity (Q). So, quite simply taking the change in total cost (TC) and dividing by the change in quantity gives you an answer:

$$MC = (Change\ in\ TC) / (Change\ in\ Q)$$

Tracking where MC crosses the AVC and ATC curves

Marginal cost curves always cross the average variable and average total cost curves at the minimum of those curves — that is, at the bottom of the U-shapes that make up both curves. (Average fixed costs are different: they can fall over the whole of the production range and therefore not have a bottom of the U). This intersection has to happen because marginal costs capture the change in costs that determines whether or not average variable or average total costs are rising or falling.

To see why, let's move away from costs and think about worms for a while. Suppose a biologist is working out the average length of wiggly worms in a sample. Suppose she's measured 10 of them and come up with an average length of 5 inches. Now imagine that she's given an 11th sample. If the 11th worm is longer than 5 inches, the *average* length of the worms in her sample goes up. If it's less than 5 inches, of course, the average in the sample goes down. But if the *marginal worm* is exactly 5 inches long, the average stays at exactly 5 inches.

Back to costs. Suppose the average cost of producing ten units is $1. If the cost of adding an extra unit is greater than $1, the total cost of producing all the units is more than $11, and the average cost of production is more than $1. But suppose that the marginal cost of an extra unit is 90 cents. Then the total cost is $10.90 and average cost is 99 cents — average cost has fallen. On the other hand, if the marginal cost is exactly $1, average cost is also exactly $1.

So we have three cases:

✔ *Average cost falls* when the marginal cost of producing an extra unit is less than the average cost of producing all previous units.

✔ *Average cost rises* when the marginal cost of the extra unit is greater than the average cost of producing all preceding units.

✔ *Average cost stays the same* when the marginal cost of producing an extra unit is exactly the same as the average cost of producing the previous units.

You can see this effect illustrated graphically in Figure 7-2. These "typical" average curves are split at their minimum points (bottom of the U) by a marginal cost curve.

Figure 7-2:
Relationship
between
average
(AC) and
marginal
cost (MC).
AVC =
average
variable
costs.

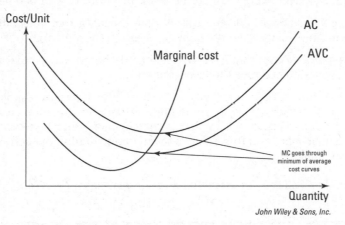

John Wiley & Sons, Inc.

Here's a key implication. To minimize costs, you want to be at the minimum of the average total cost curve (i.e. the minimum of AC in Figure 7-2). You're at that point when the marginal cost of adding an extra unit of production is exactly the same as the average costs of all the preceding units. So, to produce for the lowest possible cost, you know not to produce when the marginal cost is greater than average cost, and that if your marginal cost curve is below average cost, you're better off in terms of average cost when you expand your production up to the point where they're equal.

Putting it together: Cost structure of a simple firm

This section considers a simple firm example to show how microeconomics looks at the cost structure of firms in general.

Zio Enzo's Pizza makes authentic Italian-style pizzas and is considering how to minimize its costs. Enzo asks his daughter, Maura, to use her first-year microeconomics training to look at the firm's cost structure. She deduces the following:

- ✔ Fixed costs will be $100 per week, no matter how many pizzas are produced.

- ✔ A pizza-maker is paid $10 per hour for an 8-hour day, or $80 per day.

- ✔ Enzo's has no variable costs other than the labor that goes into making them (implausibly, out of all the pizzerias in the world!).

- ✔ The variable cost that's relevant is the number of pizza-makers employed to produce the firm's output.

- ✔ The output initially improves as the firm hires more pizza-makers, because two can produce more output than one. But soon enough a bench full of pizza-makers start getting in each other's way as they fling dough around, and this reduces the net contribution of each successive pizza-maker.

Maura collects all the data together and summarizes it (see Table 7-2).

Table 7-2				Cost Structure of Zio Enzo's					
L	Q	Q/L	FC	AFC	VC	AVC	TC	ATC	MC
0	0	-	100	-	0	-	100	-	-
1	50	50	100	2	80	1.6	180	3.6	1.6
2	140	70	100	.71	160	1.14	260	1.86	.89
3	220	73.3	100	.45	240	1.09	340	1.55	1.00
4	290	72.5	100	.34	320	1.10	420	1.45	1.14
5	350	70	100	.29	400	1.14	500	1.43	1.33
6	400	66.7	100	.25	480	1.20	580	1.45	1.6
7	440	62.9	100	.23	560	1.27	660	1.50	2
8	470	58.8	100	.21	640	1.36	740	1.57	2.7

L = Labor (number of workers), Q = Quantity (output), Q/L = Output per worker, FC = Fixed cost, AFC = Average fixed cost, VC = Variable cost, AVC = Average variable cost, TC = Total cost, ATC = Average total cost, MC = Marginal cost

Here's what Maura can tell about the business from this breakdown of the cost structure. From the output per worker column she notices an interesting, but entirely normal phenomenon: more gain in output comes from adding the first incremental worker than from adding the eighth. As she suspected, the firm gains *increasing returns* from the first additional pizza-maker joining the team. But after adding the third, they start to get in each other's way, making their additional contribution to output decrease. The more workers she adds, the smaller their contribution to output becomes.

Economists call this a case of *diminishing returns* which occurs when adding additional increments of labor to a production premise or plant of fixed size.

Now let's plot the data points for average and marginal costs in Figure 7-3.

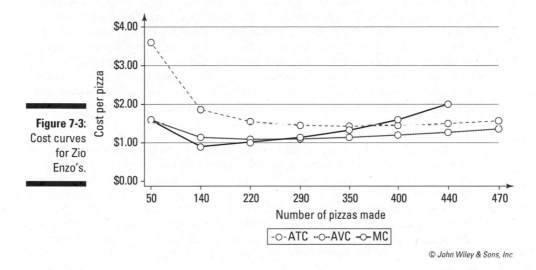

Figure 7-3:
Cost curves for Zio Enzo's.

© John Wiley & Sons, Inc.

Although both average cost curves are shallow (because of the low numbers of workers relative to the number of pizzas produced), they are, more or less, the U-shaped curves mentioned in the earlier section "Tracking where MC crosses the AVC and ATC curves." Also note that the marginal cost curve goes through both of those minimum points.

Applying microeconomic thinking to the cost-minimizing level of production, Maura can tell her father that he makes himself best off at the point where he's employing three pizza-makers to do the work. (Clue: The lowest average variable cost of making pizzas is, as you can see from Table 7-2, at three workers. When you increase the number of pizza-makers by one, the marginal cost added is greater than the average variable cost, and so you can see that you've passed the sweet spot and costs are now increasing again.)

Relating Cost Structure to Profits

The motivation for a firm staying in business is that its revenues exceed its costs (including opportunity costs — see the earlier section "Understanding Why Accountants and Economists View Costs Differently" for a definition). When revenues exceed costs, the firm is making profits. Therefore, we need to consider a firm's revenue side. This section introduces the ideas of profit maximization and shutdown conditions.

Looking at firm revenue

How much a firm produces — or whether it produces at all — also depends on how much revenue a firm takes in. The firm can control its costs better than it can control its revenue, but it still needs to be taking in money in some way, or it is unlikely to remain a business for very long. Because profits are the difference between revenues generated and costs expended, you have to know something about how the firm's revenue relates to its costs to know something about profits. So, in this section, we show you how to manipulate revenue equations to see how much profit a firm might make, and when not making anything and shutting down is the wisest option.

We begin by extending the example of Zio Enzo's Pizza from the preceding section. We make a simple and probably ridiculous assumption that Enzo's is a price taker (check out Chapter 10 for more on price takers and their opposite, price makers). Being a *price taker* means, quite simply, that Enzo's has no influence on the price that the market is willing to pay for the delicious, imaginary pizzas that Enzo makes. Instead we assume that the market is willing, in general, to pay $2 a pizza (it must be in a student area), and that no relationship exists between Enzo and any competitors.

Remember the formula to work out profits:

$$\Pi = TR - TC$$

Now we take the term for total revenue and expand it. Total revenue (TR) received for selling Q units of a product at price P is:

$$TR = P \times Q$$

So how can the firm discover whether total revenue is greater than total costs, and if so by how much? Here's a trick: Average total cost (ATC) is TC divided by Q, and so ATC multiplied by Q will give you TC. Therefore:

$$\Pi = (P \times Q) - (ATC \times Q)$$

The two terms for revenue and costs contain Q, and so we divide both sides by Q to drop it out.

Let's focus on the two terms on the right-hand side of the equation. If P (the price a firm receives for its output) is greater than average total cost, the firm supplying that good makes economic profits greater than zero. If the price is less than average total cost, the firm is taking losses. When the two are equal, revenues are equal to economic costs, and the firm makes economic profits of zero.

The optimal condition for how much output a firm should be willing to supply (the best that it can possibly do given its costs and revenues) is satisfied when the marginal cost (MC) of producing an extra unit is equal to the marginal revenue (MR) received from selling it.

Hitting the sweet spot: When MC = MR

When the marginal revenue gained from an extra sale is equal to the marginal cost incurred in making the good, the firm is maximizing its profits. Put another way, if supplying an extra unit costs more than the firm receives by selling it, the firm is better off not doing it. If supplying an extra unit costs less than the firm receives from selling it, the firm is better off producing it.

When making a decision, the firm is interested only in the last incremental unit of the product, whether you're talking about revenues or costs. All previous production is irrelevant: The firm just needs to focus on whether to make the last unit and, given that, whether producing the unit yields a profit.

Figure 7-4 adds a new line (compared to Figure 7-3) for the marginal revenue gained from selling an extra pizza. The assumption made in the preceding section — Enzo's is a price taker — means that in this case, marginal revenue is a horizontal line at a price of $2.

Notice that the marginal cost line crosses this line when MC = MR, which is exactly at 440 pizzas. So, Enzo's will be making the optimal production decision where it produces 440 pizzas — where exactly as much is yielded from selling one more pizza as it costs to make.

This concept is so important that we now think about it in another way. Look back at Table 7-2 and notice that the marginal cost of all the pizzas before the 440th is less than $2. Now look at the 400th pizza, which Enzo can make for a marginal cost of $1.60. If he were to make 400 pizzas, the marginal pizza would yield revenue of $2 but have a cost of only $1.60, which, you'd suppose, would make for one happy Enzo.

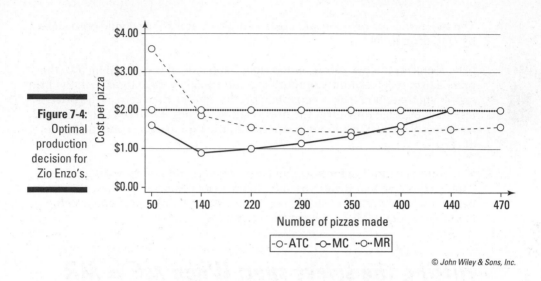

Figure 7-4:
Optimal
production
decision for
Zio Enzo's.

But Enzo could even be made happier by selling pizzas numbers 401 to 440. He would be better off in terms of making more money by expanding his production to the level where the cost of producing the last pizza and the benefit or revenue from selling it are equal. On the other hand, if he were paying more than $2 to make a pizza that only yields $2, he'd be better off reducing his output until the two were equal.

The very best production decision a firm can make is when MC = MR.

Viewing profits and losses

Here are two observations concerning profits and losses for a firm under the condition of producing optimally:

- Finding Q* where MC = MR allows the firm to make the optimal output.

- At Q* (the optimal amount of production), the firm isn't guaranteed a positive profit, but this is the point at which it maximizes profit (and if it must take losses, this output minimizes losses).

We now walk you through understanding whether a firm will or won't make a profit in a very simple way. Figure 7-5 shows the costs and output for a generic company (we're not using the specific numbers as we did for Zio Enzo's). The optimal output (where MC = MR) is indicated with Q*. Now at Q*, price is greater than average total costs.

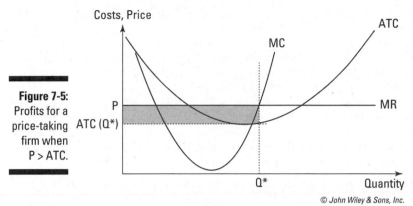

ATC = Average total cost, MC = Marginal cost, MR = Marginal revenue,
Q* = Optimal amount of production, P = price

Figure 7-5: Profits for a price-taking firm when P > ATC.

At this point you can use a little sleight of hand to show profits: Remember that revenue is simply price times quantity. On our mapping of price and quantity that's also the area of a rectangle bounded by the axes, the MR line, and Q*. Then move on to the total cost, which is going to be ATC times Q* — that is, the average total cost of making each unit times the number of units. That also gives you a rectangle, but one bounded by ATC, the axes, and Q*. Take the cost rectangle from the revenue rectangle, and you're left with the shaded area in Figure 7-5, which is the total level of profits for this firm.

Peer deeper into the cost and revenue equations and you'll see that the only difference between the sizes of the rectangles is the difference between P and ATC. Taking P – ATC gives you the height of the box, and multiplying by Q* provides its width. And there you have it — profits and another nice new formula for it:

$$\Pi = (P - ATC) \times Q$$

If, of course, the price received by the firm is less than average total cost of producing the good, the firm isn't making profits but taking losses. We use this important condition for the firm in the next section, where we talk briefly about why a firm may want to stop producing and under what circumstances.

Staying in business and shutting down

The simple fact is that if a firm doesn't make profits, it doesn't tend to stay a firm for very long. Even companies that are well run, well capitalized, and innovative — or have other advantages — can find themselves in this position, which is one reason why a firm's decision to exit a market is as important a consideration to an economist as the decision of whether to enter one or not.

Chapter 10 describes a specific model that helps understand the exit and entry decision in *perfectly competitive* market structures, but here we look briefly at this issue in a much simpler way.

Economists are interested in two cases:

- ✔ What would induce a firm to exit a market in the short run (*short run* meaning a planning period in which *some* of its costs are fixed)?

- ✔ What would induce a firm to exit in the long run (*long run* meaning a planning period in which *all* of its costs are variable)?

Not making a contribution? Shut down in the short run

In the short run, the assumption is that a firm can operate, for a limited amount of time, without fully covering all costs of operation, as long as it's covering the variable cost of operating. In other words, the price received for a sale covers the average variable cost of producing the item. If you're doing this, you can at least get forbearance from people for the fixed costs of production in the hope that times improve and you'll be able to pay them back.

Thus the short-run shutdown condition is that if P < AVC, then continuing to produce does not make sense. If you do continue producing at this level, everything you receive from an extra unit is less than the variable or avoidable costs of producing it, and therefore every unit you sell makes a loss that you could have avoided. At this point, the best thing you can do is *not* produce, because the more you produce, the more you lose.

Factory gets the blues

You rarely find a business operating when the price is less than average variable cost (P < AVC). One cherished example, however, comes from the celebrated British record label Factory, which agreed to produce a single, "Blue Monday" by New Order, in an extremely expensive laser-cut sleeve. The packaging was so expensive that the first pressing lost money on every copy sold (eventually the firm realized this and came up with cheaper packaging for future releases).

A lot of copies were sold, and Factory lost a large amount overall, taking greater losses the more it sold. The single is often regarded as a classic, both in music and design, but Factory is never cited as a positive example in business textbooks.

Not covering all costs: Shut down in the long run

In the long run, a firm needs to cover all its costs of operation, even those for which it can get short-term forbearance. For instance, if you borrow money for a business loan, when times are hard, you may be able to get your bank to agree to you deferring some of the payment or making reduced payments.

Suppose that the fixed costs of operation were $1,000 and that the firm is producing, optimally, Q*. Suppose further that the variable costs at Q* are $500, and the revenues coming in are $800. In this case, the firm is covering its variable costs of $500 and so doesn't have to shut down in the short run. It can make a bargain with its creditors to pay only $300 of the fixed costs back, for a while, and depending on their grace they may agree to that bargain. The result to the firm is an overall loss of $700 rather than a loss of $1,000 if it produces nothing, and so producing is better than not producing.

These payments can't be put off forever, however, only deferred temporarily. As a result, the long-run shutdown condition is one in which the firm would still be better off not accruing losses. Instead, the firm operates for a while on the grounds that it's better off producing than not producing, but eventually accrues losses that it can't restructure away and it will have to shut down.

Chapter 8

Squeezing Out Every Last Drop of Profit

In This Chapter

▶ Examining whether a firm is a profit maximizer

▶ Looking at how a firm maximizes profits in the short and long run

▶ Understanding how firms minimize costs

*E*conomists tend to begin their analysis of firms with the assumption that the firm is a *profit maximizer* — that is, the firm's ultimate aim is making the most profit it can. Although microeconomics doesn't stop there (and has produced a number of more in-depth analyses of managerial motivation and results that don't rely on this assumption), the profit-maximizing firm is the basic building block of microeconomic analysis.

In this chapter we justify the idea that a firm is in practice a profit maximizer. We also look at profit maximization more closely, showing how it rests at the heart of economists' conception of efficiency and how profit-maximizing firms choose the optimum amount of stuff to produce. In addition, we also discuss the opposite approach to achieving the same end: minimizing costs while maintaining the desired output.

Take a moment to catch your breath. You have quite a ride ahead!

Asking Whether Firms Really Maximize Profits

In most cases, economists assume that firms want to maximize their profits and that, as a result, they make their decisions on this basis.

Here's a possible objection to this assumption: Economists are thinking about a firm as a very simple decision-making unit, quite unlike the complex entities that firms are in reality. All the following conditions characterize the standard approach to the firm in economics:

- ✔ Managers act in the interest of shareholders whose goal is profit maximization.
- ✔ Management has unified interests.
- ✔ There are no internal issues between or inside internal divisions of the firm.
- ✔ People turn up on time and do the job for which they're employed.
- ✔ There are no hidden incentives not to make profit in the tax system.

Suppose you know nothing about a company and you don't know that all those things are the stuff of working life. How would you then make a representation of a firm? What goals, behaviors, or practices would you guess that this representative firm would engage in?

In this scenario, profit maximization is a reasonable assumption to make. Of course, if you know about particular reasons why a given entrepreneur has made a decision, you can guess at a lot more information about the firm. But if you know next to nothing about the individual case, the only assumption that makes sense is that the firm intends to maximize its profits.

None of this, of course, means that profit maximization is always the goal of the organization. As a simple example, think of a company whose shareholders want to receive the highest possible level of returns, whereas the management of the company wants to hold on to their jobs or take as many of the potential returns for themselves. If the managers have sufficient bargaining power over the shareholders, they can affect the decisions of the firm in their own interests.

Talking about efficiency, in the long and short run

When a firm maximizes its profits effectively, it's acting efficiently. Economists like efficiency and deplore waste. Whatever you do in business, they prefer that you make efficient use of your capital and other resources. If you take the lowest point of the average cost curve — where the marginal cost curve crosses the average cost curve — you've found the most efficient level of production. In addition, profit maximization occurs at the point where marginal revenue equals marginal cost (that is, MR = MC). See Chapter 7 for much more on this. Let's take a moment now to explore — ahem, efficiently — why these two efficiency conditions are so important.

When economists discuss efficiency, they're most likely talking about the following two conditions:

- **Productive efficiency:** Exists when output is being produced at a level that minimizes the average total cost of production.

- **Allocative efficiency:** Exists when making one party better off is impossible without making another party worse off (also called *Pareto efficiency* after celebrated Italian economist Vilfredo Pareto).

These two definitions are distinct, meaning that satisfying allocative efficiency without satisfying productive efficiency is possible. To see why, we look at the two concepts in a bit more detail.

Productive efficiency: Producing for the lowest possible cost

Productive efficiency is satisfied when a firm can't possibly produce another unit of output without increasing proportionally more the quantity of inputs needed to produce that unit of output. It's met when the firm is producing at the minimum of the average cost curve, where marginal cost (MC) equals average total cost (ATC). (Sometimes you will see ATC as just AC, or average cost. They mean the same thing.)

Why is that? At the minimum of the average total cost curve, economies of scale are exhausted, and production at this level yields the lowest per unit cost. The firm is producing an output level at the lowest possible cost. If a firm expands production beyond that point, it incurs a marginal cost higher than the average cost, and the per-unit cost of output increases. Recall the profit-maximizing conditions discussed in Chapters 3 and 7. A firm maximizes profits by producing where marginal revenue equals marginal cost, or MR = MC. If this occurs at the same output level where MC = ATC, then profit maximization leads to productive efficiency.

In Chapter 13, you can use the concept of productive efficiency to tell you a lot about how a market is operating. One application we mention here is in considering how society should treat *natural monopolies* — those companies that yield sufficient economies of scale relative to the size of the total market that they're unlikely to ever face a direct competitor. One thing economists notice is that these companies tend to operate inefficiently; that is, that they don't tend to operate at the lowest possible cost (and that consumers are consequently hurt by this, as inefficiencies get pushed on to the consumer in the form of lower quality or quantity and/or higher prices).

Figure 8-1 summarizes productive efficiency: The two shaded areas reveal how the firm can become better off by making itself more productive.

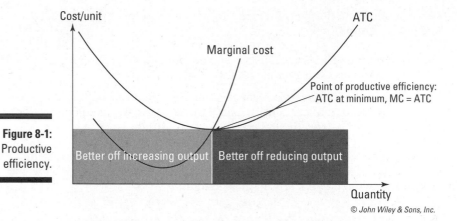

Figure 8-1:
Productive
efficiency.

© John Wiley & Sons, Inc.

Allocative efficiency: Can you make one party better off without making another worse off?

Allocative efficiency is related to the concept of Pareto efficiency that economists use to look at social welfare (see Chapter 12 for more on that), but it has important aspects that are driven by efficiency in production. Essentially, if something is allocatively efficient, one party can't possibly be made better off without making another party worse off. Here's a simple example to illustrate the point: Suppose Alice and Bob are allocated money from a central pot of $100, and you record the allocations twice:

✔ In the first round you allocate the whole $100, and Alice and Bob each get half, $50. Now within this framework, you can't give either Alice or Bob more without making the other worse off, and so the distribution is allocatively efficient.

✔ But if you hold back $1 and distribute $99 to Alice and Bob, any distribution between the two isn't allocatively efficient, because you can simply release the $1 and make either party better off, *without making the other worse off!*

In the context of production, when a firm is operating at lowest possible cost, it's also allocating efficiently its budget for inputs between capital and labor. This occurs — you guessed it! — when the average cost of the firm is at a minimum.

Chapter 12 uses this concept of efficiency when it talks about welfare in general. For the moment, we just want to introduce the idea that when all firms operate at their minimum cost, welfare in society is maximized.

Checking the long and the short run

Economists distinguish between the long- and short-run positions of a firm. They do so because a firm can find itself, in the short run, in a number of positions where it is constrained. It can't fully react to change immediately and therefore makes slightly different decisions than it would if there were no constraints — in other words, different than it would in the long run if it were fully capable of reacting to whatever change (pricing, technological, demand, and so on) was taking place.

Economists want to be more precise about what the terms *long run* and *short run* mean, without specifying a particular time interval (for example, a month) that will be different for firms in different industries. For example, finding an exploitable oil deposit may take longer than writing a couple lines of code. The definition economists use is conceptually simple: In the long run, the firm is able to change its use of all factors of production — labor, capital, and land. In the short run, the firm is not able to do that; it's limited to imperfect adjustment, usually of only one factor, often labor.

As an example, imagine that a firm employs ten people to do a job working on ten machines. And suppose the wage it pays its workers has become more expensive, so that the firm would be better off employing only eight machines and eight people. But the lease for the machines is not up until the end of the year, whereas it can lay off workers at any time:

- ✔ **In the short run:** The firm adjusts its use of labor without adjusting its use of capital or machinery — having nine people operate the ten machines. Over this short-run period, the firm isn't operating at its most effective use of resources.

- ✔ **In the long run:** After the firm negotiates a new lease, it can operate even more cheaply. Assuming profit maximization is its aim, it moves towards doing so.

Microeconomists express this situation by looking at costs in the short and long run. To an economist, any short-run average total cost (SRATC) curve must be by definition less *elastic* — that is, less responsive to price — than a long-run average total cost (LRATC) curve. Therefore, in a diagram, a SRATC curve is steeper, reflecting the lower ability to adjust in the short run (as costs go up, output doesn't change as much as in the long run). The LRATC is always less than or equal to the SRATC at any given output level, reflecting the fact that the firm can use its inputs more efficiently in the long run than in the short run.

Figure 8-2 illustrates this condition. Remember that a short-run marginal cost curve goes through the minimum of each of the SRATC curves, and the long-run marginal cost (LRMC) is more elastic — price and cost responsive — than in the short run.

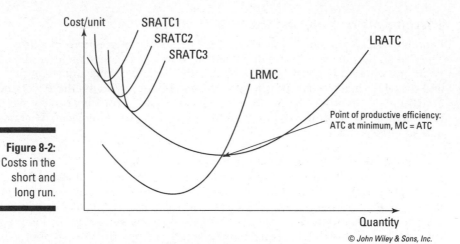

Figure 8-2:
Costs in the
short and
long run.

© John Wiley & Sons, Inc.

Going Large! The Goal of Profit Maximization

Now it's time to find out a little more about the profit-maximizing process. To do so, we need to make a few little extensions to the model of the firm used in Chapter 7 to take account of how the firm changes its decisions when the costs of inputs change. And to do that, we're going to express output in terms of two inputs — capital and labor — and their respective prices, the cost of capital and the wage rate.

Firms can use two methods to work out how to use their inputs to make outputs: the profit-maximizing approach of this section and the cost-minimizing approach (see the later section "Slimming Down: Minimizing Costs"). Although eventually they lead to the same place — assuming you do the relevant calculations right! — they arrive via slightly different journeys. Wherever you're going, though, you need a place to start, and we begin with a production function.

Understanding a production function

A _production function_ is a mathematical description of how a firm makes its output. For a simple firm with only one input, a production function may be expressed by the following:

$$f(x_1)$$

Here, *f* is the firm's production function, and x_1 is the amount of an input —
for example, labor. If you know the amount of the input x_1 and the shape of
the function *f,* then you know how much output the firm will produce. We
now add the second input — holding it constant because we're going to look
at the short run first — and then use a little math to figure out the relationship between output and costs.

We call the production function *f,* the two inputs x_1 and x_2, and their respective costs w_1 and w_2. We begin by spelling out the production function:

$$f\left(x_1, x_2\right)$$

That shows a relationship between inputs and outputs but not profit: The
f part of the expression explains that there is a relationship between the
amount of output produced and the level of inputs engaged in production,
the x_1 and the x_2. For the moment, we're not spelling out exactly what that
relationship is mathematically. To know about the firm's profits, we need
to know about the revenue gained from selling the output and the cost of
obtaining the inputs. The revenue side is very simple if the firm sells its
output all at the same price *p*. Then if you know the output level, multiply it
by price (*p*) and you have total revenue (TR):

$$TR = p\, f\left(x_1, x_2\right)$$

And for total costs (TC):

$$TC = \left(w_1 x_1 + w_2 x_2\right)$$

Because we're holding the second input constant in the short run, we call it
$\bar{x}_2$. It won't be changing, and so we can treat it as a constant.

From the original production function, we can combine the two preceding
equations to make a profit function that we want to maximize:

$$\max\, pf\left(x_1, x_2\right) - w_1 x_1 - w_2 x_2 \text{ with respect to } x_1$$

Meeting the isoprofit curve

We now substitute output, *y,* for the production function for a moment and
use that to draw a picture. Again, we'll use the Greek letter π for profit. The
equation is now like this:

$$\pi = py - w_1 x_1 - w_2 x_2$$

We want to use this equation to derive an *isoprofit* curve, which is a curve
on which all points yield the same level of profit. In the preceding equation,
profits could change if *p, y,* or one of the *w*s or one of the *x*s changes. On an
isoprofit curve, we hold π, profits, constant for any point on the same curve,

and we plot the relationship between inputs and outputs for a given level of profit. We rearrange the equation so that y is on the left-hand side:

$$y = \frac{\pi}{p} + \frac{w_2}{p}x_2 + \frac{w_1}{p}x_1$$

This equation shows that the terms on the right-hand side and specifically all those terms that don't include an x_1, are constant. The intercept is where the curve intercepts the y axis. The expression on the right, referring to x_1, gives the slope of the line, $\frac{w_1}{p}$.

Looking at profit maximization using isoprofit curves

Now we turn to the concept of the *marginal* — the incremental change (see Chapter 7). In this case, the incremental change we're interested in is the change in production at the margin. The slope of the production function is the measure of how production changes as x_1 changes. In general, the marginal change in output is called *marginal product,* but here the relationship only exists between x_1 and output, because we kept x_2 constant.

Figure 8-3 illustrates maximization using the short-run production function $f(x_1,x_2)$ with x_2 held fixed, and three isoprofit curves. Only isoprofit 2 is possible and optimal. Why?

Figure 8-3:
Profit maximization for one factor using three isoprofit curves.

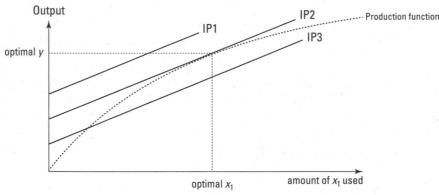

© John Wiley & Sons, Inc.

IP1 = isoprofit 1, IP2 = isoprofit 2, IP3 = isoprofit 3

At isoprofit 2, the marginal product (MP, slope of the production function) is equal to the cost of the input used divided by the price received at market for your output. Or to put it more succinctly:

$$MP_1 = w_1 / p \text{ or } pMP_1 = w_1$$

To discover what this means, we ask Jeph the Joiner, proprietor of Jeph's Joinery. He has a job at the moment making chair legs for an interior designer. He wants to know, given that all his equipment is fixed in the short run, how many people to employ at a given wage in order to make as much profit as possible. His cousin Emma the Economist takes a look at his figures and says that he should employ up to the point where the contribution of the marginal worker is such that multiplying the output produced by the marginal worker by price equals the wage that Jeph will pay.

Jeph knows his hardwoods but not his margins and asks for the answer with less jargon. Emma says: "Suppose you're making your chair legs and you know that the next one — the marginal one — is going to yield $10 in revenue. Now suppose you have to hire someone for a cost of $11 to make the leg. If the cost is greater than the marginal revenue, you make yourself better off by *not* producing that unit ($11 is greater than $10 and you'd lose $1 on the output). If the cost of hiring is only $9, though, you'd make a surplus of $1. You can make yourself better off still, assuming that you can sell the product, by hiring up until the cost of hiring equals the value of the marginal product — that is, the marginal revenue — you yield from selling the output."

Microeconomics lays great stress on the concept of the margin for exactly this reason. The best that a firm can possibly do is when the marginal benefit it gets is equal to the marginal cost of achieving it.

Maximizing profit in the long run

Here's a quick question for you: What's the difference between the short and the long run to an economist? If you say that in the long run all factors are variable, you're correct! If not, take a look at the earlier section "Talking about efficiency, in the long and short run" before reading on. When you're clear on this issue, you can go on to the next section, safe in the knowledge that extending the model to two inputs isn't so difficult.

I wonder if, after reading the preceding section, you want to say, "Hang on a minute; that situation's unrealistic — only one factor changes!" You're right, because in the example Jeph's Joinery is considering only the short run. What happens in the long run?

An output level that minimizes average costs in the short run could lie on the long-run average cost curve (refer back to Figure 8-2) and be the best possible option in the long run too. We use that fact to point out that the only thing that has changed when moving to the long-run equilibrium is that now the last equation in the preceding section must apply *to each input* and not just one. Thus for two inputs x_1 and x_2 you get a pair of conditions:

$$p \, MP_1\left(x *_1, x *_2\right) = w_1$$

$$p \, MP_2\left(x *_1, x *_2\right) = w_2$$

Here, * denotes that these are the optimal levels of inputs given the cost of inputs.

Profit-maximization problems tend to follow these forms, though they can get more complicated than this simple presentation. Sometimes economists are interested in a different (though related) type of question, such as what to do if the price of one input changes but not the other, or what happens when firm technology changes. The next section discusses an adaptation of the model for that — the cost-minimization model.

Slimming Down: Minimizing Costs

The preceding section discusses a firm maximizing its profit by choosing a level of inputs that allows it to produce a given level of profit. Now we rearrange the problem slightly and assume that the firm wants to reduce its costs to the minimum level while producing a desired level of output. To do so, the firm chooses how much to use of two inputs, called x_1 and x_2, as defined in the earlier section "Understanding a production function." But unlike in that section, we want to choose a way of minimizing the cost.

Economists write this problem in a new way, using two equations to represent it:

$$\text{Min } w_1 x_1 + w_2 x_2$$
$$x_1, x_2$$
$$\text{Such that } f\left(x_1, x_2\right) = y$$

The min means choose values of x_1 and x_2 that make everything in the equation $(w_1x_1 + w_2x_2)$ as small as possible. The values we're choosing for the inputs are optimal values, and we call those x^*_1 and x^*_2, with the * meaning an optimal value.

The second equation, which uses the production function, shows all the feasible combinations of inputs that produce a desired level of output. This is called an *isoquant* — meaning that all points or input combinations on an *isoquant* yield the same level of output, in this case y.

Now we alter the first equation to see another facet of the equation: We look *for a given level of cost,* which we denote C. We do so by rearranging a little:

$$w_1x_1 + w_2x_2 = C$$

Rearrange this so that you can put the input x_2 on the vertical axis in the graphs (see Figure 8-4), and you get this:

$$x_2 = \frac{C}{w_2} - \frac{w_1}{w_2}x_1$$

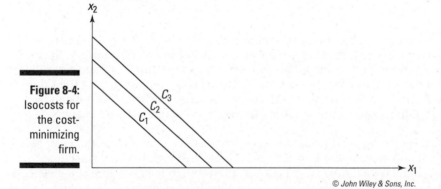

Figure 8-4:
Isocosts for
the cost-
minimizing
firm.

© John Wiley & Sons, Inc.

In this rearrangement of the equation, the quantity of x_2 used is a function of constant level of cost and the relative price of x_1. Given that the price of x_1 is w_1, the *relative* price of x_1 is w_1/w_2. Now, when plotted on a graph, it becomes a straight line with a slope of $-w_1/w_2$ and an intercept on the vertical axis of C/w_2.

We allow C to change to create a set of lines, each of which has the same total cost, and has the same slope of $-w_1/w_2$. Called *isocosts* (see Figure 8-4), these are all downward-sloping parallel lines. Every point on an isocost has the same cost and higher isocost lines have higher costs.

The final step is to put the isoquant and isocost together. We restate the problem as finding a point on an isoquant line with the lowest possible isocost associated with it. This happens at a point of tangency between the isoquant and isocost, which is a more mathematical way of saying that at the optimal point or input combination, the slopes of the isocost and the isoquant are equal (see Figure 8-5).

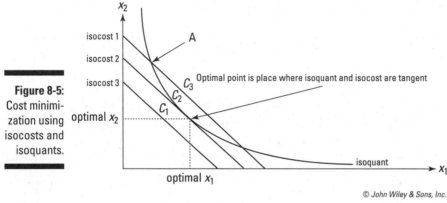

Figure 8-5:
Cost minimization using isocosts and isoquants.

© John Wiley & Sons, Inc.

The only input combination that can be optimal to use is the point where the two curves are tangent. Taking a look at the isoquant, you can see that an infinite number of combinations of inputs can make up that fixed desired level of output. However, point A for example is on a higher isocost than the optimal and therefore wouldn't be chosen, because the same output can be produced for a lower cost, and the firm wants to minimize those costs.

You can derive a cool further condition from knowing about the slopes of the isoquant and isocost and how they must match. Remember that the slope of something is generally an indication of how much it's changing at a given point. Economists are interested in what the changes along the isoquant reveal about the marginal product (MP) of the two inputs x_1 and x_2, and what the ratio of the marginal products says about the technology a firm is using.

The slope of the isocost must match the slope of the isoquant. You already know the slope of the isocost: $-w_1/w_2$. You also know that the slope of the isoquant matches the ratio between the prices of the inputs. Now the slope of the isoquant is the ratio of the marginal product of each of the inputs, and so at the optimum point:

$$MP_1 / MP_2 = -w_1 / w_2$$

The bit on the left side is the ratio between the marginal products of the two inputs at the optimum. It's also known as the *technical rate of substitution,* because it describes the rate at which a firm gives up one input in order to add increasing units of another input while keeping output constant. Because economists generally assume diminishing productivity when substituting, the isoquant must slope continuously downwards when production technologies are what economists call *well behaved* — this captures diminishing returns to substituting one unit of one input for one unit of another.

Chapter 9

Supplying the Demanded Information on Supply and Demand

. . . .

In This Chapter

▶ Looking at the supply curve

▶ Demanding to see the market demand curve

▶ Seeing how a market equalizes supply and demand

. . . .

*I*f anything exemplifies microeconomics, it's the well-known model of supply and demand in a marketplace. Aspects such as constrained optimization (Chapter 6) or firm production decisions (Chapters 7 and 8) are of course important, but microeconomics really comes into its own with the supply and demand model. In many ways, it's the most powerful tool in the microeconomist's toolkit.

The supply and demand model is a centerpiece of economics because it adds to the understanding of the consumer and producer by letting them interact through the medium of exchange. This exchange is voluntary and, as such, benefits both parties, though not necessarily to the same extent. The supply and demand model is also the bedrock of the discussions of different types of markets covered in Chapters 10–12.

So if you — ahem — *demand* an explanation on supply and demand, and how the market seeks equilibrium between the two, we're happy to — ahem, ahem! — supply one.

Producing Stuff to Sell: The Supply Curve

As you probably know by now, producers in a market are generally organizations called firms. Firms set their levels of production to be optimal in terms of costs, seeking to produce (that is, *supply*) up to the point where marginal revenue equals marginal cost and attempting to get their long-run average costs down to as low a level as they can. The marginal (and indeed average) costs of production are related to the technology a firm chooses to get the best level of output for the combination of inputs chosen.

These features of production characterize the individual *rational* firm, which seeks to maximize its profits or minimize its costs – given the conditions in the marketplace.

But economists also want to analyze what a *collection* of firms does — that is, an *industry* — as well as the actions of just one firm. They want to aggregate the decisions of individual firms so that they can clearly see how this simple behavior at the firm level influences the prices and quantities of things made and exchanged in a market. The supply curve is a way of going from an individual firm to an entire industry provided that no one firm is able to influence the price at which the good sells in the market. Firms in this case are called *perfect competitors,* and the industry is perfectly competitive.

Moving from marginal costs to firm supply

You can go easily from an individual firm's supply to industry supply by adding up, horizontally, the marginal cost curves of the individual firms in the relevant industry. This section describes how this process works.

Marginal costs

The *marginal cost* (abbreviated MC — see Chapter 7) of producing anything is the cost of producing only the last unit of that good; it tells you what happens to cost when adding one extra unit to production. At the margin, the firm produces up to where MC of producing a new unit equals marginal revenue (MR), the revenue gained from selling one extra unit. Thus, the rational profit-maximizing firm chooses its production so that MC = MR.

If the market in which the firm operates is perfectly competitive — the firm is a *price taker* that accepts the market price without being able to influence it — the MR received is just the same as the market price, p, and so price, p, equals MC.

Another way of telling how competitive a market is in reality is by seeing whether the price at which producers can sell their product is at or close to MC. If it is, the market is very likely to be competitively supplied. If not, the market is likely to be dominated by one firm or have some other anti-competitive features. The firm in the competitive market uses this relation between MC and MR = p to solve the profit-maximization problem, so that it can set its best, or optimal, level of output given the price it can get in the market. That means maximizing the difference between total revenue and total costs.

A perfectly competitive market has an important feature: The price received by the firm isn't related to its strategic decisions. Whatever the firm decides with respect to its output, price doesn't change — which is another way of saying that a firm is a price taker.

We start by making the total costs of the firm a function of its output, meaning that as output changes, total cost changes. We write that function as $c(q)$.

In other words, total costs (c) are dependent on the output produced (q). This is called the *total cost function* for the firm.

Revenue side

For the revenue side, total revenue (TR) is given by the quantity produced, which is — again — q times the price of the good, p: TR = pq.

Profit equal the difference between cost and revenue, and so the firm wants to maximize: $pq - c(q)$. Plus, it wants to do so by choosing the best level of q.

If you look at the marginal terms as described here and in Chapter 7, you can see that marginal revenue is the rate of change of revenue when output changes. If a firm increases its output by a change in q (write as Δq) then the change in revenue, ΔR, is ΔR = $p\Delta q$.

But because the firm's supply does not affect market price, price does not change as q changes, and marginal revenue is quite simply given as ΔR/Δq = p.

The expression for MR tells you that you are evaluating the change in revenue as output changes, which is exactly, by definition, what marginal revenue expresses! And because price in this competitive market does not change in response to a firm's decision, price equals MR.

Cost side

We write marginal cost (MC) in this case as $\Delta c/\Delta q$, which tells you to look at the change in costs as q changes. Doing so, you can rewrite it as MC(q).

Firm supply curve

Okay. Now that you have an expression for MR and MC, notice that if price isn't dependent on a given firm's output, the firm profit maximizes by producing up to the point where p = MC(q).

This relation is the foundation of the supply curve for a firm. It relates the price of a good to the marginal cost of supplying one extra unit of this good. Therefore, it expresses the firm's decision in terms of price and quantity, which is the relationship shown in a supply curve!

In Figure 9-1 we plot the marginal cost curve for a price-taking firm as a relationship between the cost or price of a good and the quantity that the firm will make of the good: this is the *firm supply curve*.

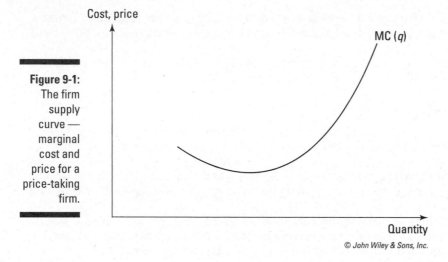

Figure 9-1:
The firm supply curve — marginal cost and price for a price-taking firm.

© *John Wiley & Sons, Inc.*

Adding up the numbers from firm to industry

Given the information in the preceding section, you now need to aggregate the decisions of all the firms in the industry.

The firm supply curve is really just its marginal cost curve given an assumption of price taking (meaning no one firm in the market can individually influence the price of a product). Therefore, if you add up all the marginal cost curves of all the firms in the relevant industry, you arrive at the industry supply curve.

You need to add up the firm supply curves *horizontally*. You have to add the quantity made by each firm at a given price in order to see the relationship between price and quantity supplied.

The firms are price takers acting optimally, so marginal cost and price are the same.

Figure 9-2 summarizes this situation. It shows two marginal cost curves added up for an industry of two firms. Figure 9-3 sets this out arithmetically for four prices.

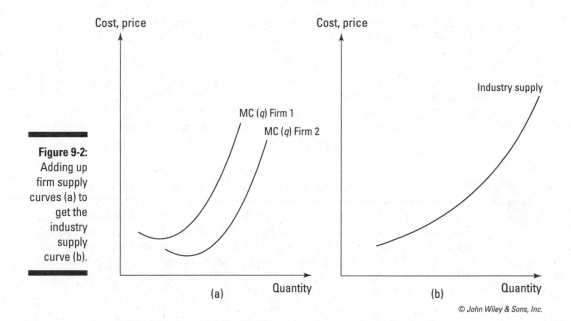

Figure 9-2: Adding up firm supply curves (a) to get the industry supply curve (b).

© John Wiley & Sons, Inc.

Figure 9-3: Adding marginal cost curves horizontally to make the supply curve.

Price	Firm 1 supply at price P		Firm 2 supply at price P		Industry supply
1	10	+	15	=	25
2	15	+	25	=	40
3	20	+	35	=	55
4	25	+	45	=	70

© John Wiley & Sons, Inc.

Giving the People What They Want: The Demand Curve

Supply decisions are important in and of themselves, especially in understanding how a firm chooses optimal production (see the earlier section "Producing Stuff to Sell: The Supply Curve"). But it takes two to tango (as all *Dancing with the Stars* fans know), and two sides to make a market. Markets can't exist without customers because, of course, buyers need to exchange with someone.

The buyers in a market comprise the demand side of the market. Whereas looking at the supply side lets you see how producers produce more or less given the price that they receive for their goods, the *demand side* plots the relationship between the price of a good and the quantity that buyers purchase at that price. The *demand curve* summarizes this relationship.

When deriving a demand curve, bear in mind that the demand curve plots the relationship between price and quantity, *holding other factors constant.* In other words, any individual demand curve holds income, the price of other goods, and preferences constant in order to focus simply on the one relationship that matters in this model — the relationship between price and quantity. This condition also means that in contrast to the preference and choice model from Chapter 6, any given demand curve describes the relationship between price and quantity demanded of one good and not relative changes in consumption of one good with respect to another good.

Going from preferences to demand

In Chapters 2 and 4–6, all the examples involve substitution with two goods. A consumer allocates a set budget between consuming a quantity of good 1 and good 2 to achieve the best possible utility. A budget constraint sets a maximum level of consumption and the consumer chooses the consumption bundle that makes her best off in utility terms. Figure 9-4 summarizes the optimal choice given the budget constraint.

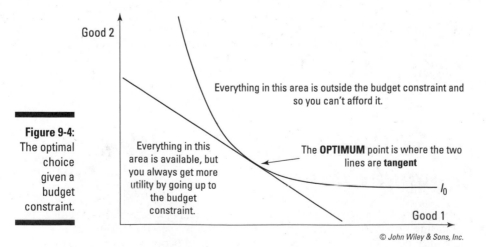

Figure 9-4: The optimal choice given a budget constraint.

Good 2

Everything in this area is outside the budget constraint and so you can't afford it.

Everything in this area is available, but you always get more utility by going up to the budget constraint.

The **OPTIMUM** point is where the two lines are **tangent**

I_0

Good 1

© *John Wiley & Sons, Inc.*

The demand curve answers a slightly different question. Given that consumers behave as they do in the preceding paragraph, what's the relationship between the price of a chosen good and the quantity of the good demanded — not usually by one consumer, but by all consumers participating in that particular market? To answer this question, you have to understand how the choices presented in Chapter 6 add up to make a demand curve. The simplest way is to consider a situation where the only thing allowed to change is the price of one good, whereas income and the price of all other goods are held constant.

Here's an example using simple numbers: Carol has $10 and wants to allocate it to slices of pizza. We assume only one good (slices of pizza) and one sum of money allocable to buying pizza (a disposable income of $10). With no other goods, you can take anything referring to the price or quantity of anything other than the slice of pizza to be zero.

If a slice of pizza costs $1, Carol can afford ten slices (assuming non-satiation — though to some other person that much pizza may not be experienced as utility but discomfort). Table 9-1 shows this and five other per-slice prices.

Table 9-1	Pizza Slices Carol Can Buy with $10
Price per Slice	*Number of Slices Affordable*
$1	10
$2	5
$3	3
$4	2
$5	2
$6	1

Figure 9-5 plots Carol's quantity demanded against price. You can see a nice, clear, though in this case not quite straight, line describing the relationship between price and quantity. As the price of a pizza slice rises, the quantity demanded falls. This relationship is Carol's *demand curve*.

Now we take Carol's demand and add it to the demand of the only other patron of the pizza place, Doug. When you add up all the decisions of all the consumers in the market, holding constant their income and the price and availability of any other substitutes, you arrive at the market demand for pizza slices and you've derived the market demand curve (see Figure 9-6). For this, we've assumed that Doug has similarly well-behaved preferences, although we haven't gone through the exercise of quantifying them in the same way as with Carol. The key point is that whatever they are, you derive market demand by adding them up.

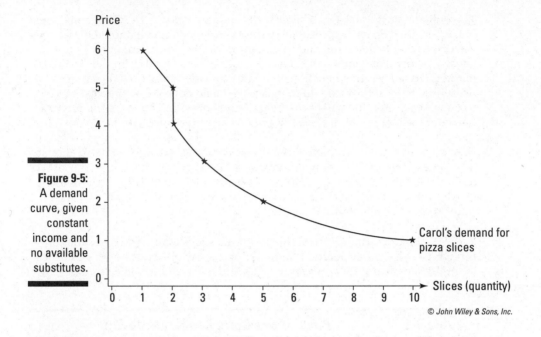

Figure 9-5:
A demand
curve, given
constant
income and
no available
substitutes.

© John Wiley & Sons, Inc.

Figure 9-6:
(a) shows
Doug and
Carol's indi-
vidual
demands for
pizza slices.
(b) shows
market
demand is
the sum of
individual
demands.

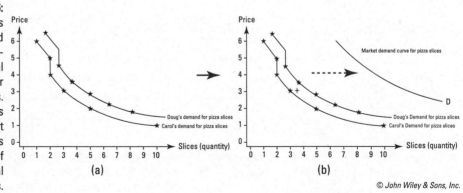

© John Wiley & Sons, Inc.

Economists are sometimes lazy about making the distinction clear, but strictly speaking at any point on a demand curve, you're talking about the *quantity demanded* at a given price, whereas the term *demand for* is talking about the more general relationship between price and quantity for a given good. So, this section's example discusses *the demand* for pizza by looking at the *quantity demanded* by Carol and Doug at different prices.

Seeing what a demand curve looks like

The demand curve in the last section maps only two variables, price and quantity demanded, holding all other things, such as income and tastes and prices of other goods, as constants. Thus, the demand curve tells you that any point along the curve is a relationship between price and quantity: When price goes up, the quantity demanded of a given good goes down.

You can read price and quantity off the axes of the curve, but for some types of applications using a function to describe demand is more useful. In this approach, you use numbers to describe the price-quantity relationship.

Quite simply, a *demand function* is any mathematical formula that describes a demand curve. Here's a very simple formula for a demand function: $x_1 = 100 - p$. This expression relates the quantity consumed of a good (x_1) to a price of the good and a constant (which you can interpret as income that may be allocated to the good). The key point is that the only variable that's allowed to change is the price of the good.

Despite some reasonably rare exceptions (see the nearby sidebar "Exceptions to downwards demand curves"), *demand curves slope downwards*, indicating that any given point on a demand curve will have a lower quantity demanded where the price is higher. Two main interpretations follow:

✔ When looking at an individual consumer, a higher price means that holding income constant, an individual consumer will substitute away from the good whose price has risen and therefore consume less of it.

✔ When taking all the consumers in the market together, at a higher price fewer consumers are willing to pay up to that price to receive the good.

The curve shifts when anything other than price changes

When looking at demand curves, you hold absolutely everything except price constant for any given curve, meaning that price changes are movements along a demand curve. If something other than price changes, you have to analyze the change by comparing different curves. To simulate such changes, you shift the demand curve horizontally to show a change in one of the factors that was held constant. (See Figure 9-7).

Let's continue the preceding section's pizza slice example. If, say, Carol now has $20 to allocate to pizza (rather than $10), her demand at $1 a slice is 20 slices and at $2 a slice, her demand is 10 slices. We illustrate that by shifting her demand curve to the right to show that she can now afford twice as many pizzas as before. Similarly, if a noodle bar opens up on her campus, we shift the curve horizontally to the left to show that her demand for pizza falls as a new rival opens.

Exceptions to downwards demand curves

Sometimes a demand curve may not apparently behave as you expect. These exceptions tend to occur at the extreme ends of the income spectrum (or quality spectrum).

At the bottom end of the quality spectrum are *Giffen goods,* which are so inferior that as your income is constrained your consumption rises through an extreme trading-down effect. Because you can think of a rise in price as a relative fall in income, you can see Giffen goods as being so inferior that their demand curve at least partially slopes upwards.

At the top-quality end are *Veblen goods,* whose consumption also depends on the value of other people knowing that you're capable of affording those goods (rare artworks, couture fashion, supercars). Here a rise in price can lead to an increase in demand precisely because a higher price increases your ability to boast about your

consumption. This phenomenon, identified by sociologist Thorsten Veblen, is called conspicuous consumption and relates the utility gained from consuming a good to the fact that other people see you as "well off" if you can.

Economists debate hotly the rarity or not of these phenomena. Giffen goods were often treated as a theoretical curiosity, but extreme trading-down does occur, such as among food prices in exceptionally constrained situations (in fact, the example was developed after looking at one such crisis situation, the Irish famine 1845–52). Veblen goods have received more attention recently as economists seek to explain consumption behavior in developed societies where at least some percentage of the population is rich enough to base its consumption decisions on being seen to consume.

Figure 9-7:
(a) For changes in price, read off the same demand curve. (b) When something other than price changes, shift the demand curve.

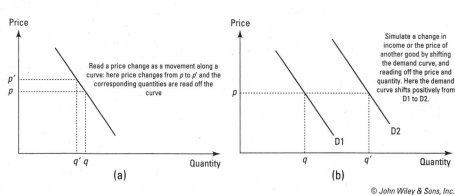

Don't confuse the two operations of *moving along* a curve and *shifting a* curve. If, for instance, you observe a rise in prices and at the same time an increase in demand, most likely that happened because something shifted demand, such as income or tastes, as opposed to an individual demand curve sloping upwards. When you get the hang of distinguishing between movements along the demand curve and shifts in the demand curve, you can start to see how they work in the real world.

In the 1990s, the brewer of a somewhat generic lager repositioned itself in a more premium segment of the market: First it raised the price and second it advertised the lager as a premium brand. A microeconomist can look at the price movement along the curve and read off that quantity demanded was likely to be lower. But the second stage of the brewer's strategy created a taste effect that raised, in some way, the utility gained from consuming the lager so that at any given price, the quantity demanded would be greater. Thus the demand curve *shifted outwards,* leading to a greater level of consumption for any given price (see Figure 9-8).

Read the situation in two stages, bearing in mind that a demand curve holds everything except price constant. That means, if you're looking at something else — a rise in income or a change in tastes, for example — you need to shift the demand curve to model the change.

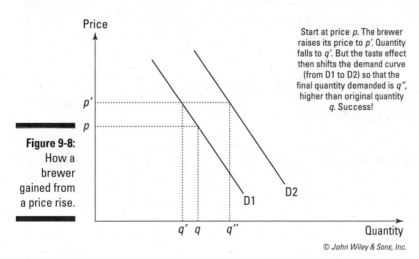

Start at price p. The brewer raises its price to p'. Quantity falls to q'. But the taste effect then shifts the demand curve (from D1 to D2) so that the final quantity demanded is q'', higher than original quantity q. Success!

Figure 9-8:
How a brewer gained from a price rise.

© *John Wiley & Sons, Inc.*

What you can glean from supply and demand

When you know the shape of the supply and demand curves, you can use them to investigate changes in price and quantity using a method called *comparative statics,* where you compare two states of the market at two different periods as if they're simple camera snapshots. Then you can investigate how price and quantity have been affected after a change has been enacted.

Be aware, however, that comparative statics leaves out some detail of the adjustment process between the two states of your relevant market.

This omission isn't usually a problem in and of itself: You can discover a large amount about how a market behaves by comparing two snapshots in time. But sometimes *dynamics* — that is, adjustments and changes over periods of time, like in a moving picture — are important and have to be considered. A change where a market adjusts suddenly and sharply to a change in price is very different from a change where a smooth path of adjustment occurs. At this level of economics, pretty much all models you're likely to pick up are examples of comparative statics, but at more advanced levels, you can add extra tools to your toolbox to compare dynamic adjustments.

Identifying Where Supply and Demand Meet

Plotting supply and demand curves on the same diagram gives an upward-sloping supply curve and a downward-sloping demand curve, and — except in rare circumstances — a point where the two cross. At that point, price and quantity have values that keep producers and consumers happy so that exactly as much is produced at that price as customers want to buy. That point is called *equilibrium*.

Returning to where you started: Equilibrium

In the supply and demand model, markets are *equilibrium-seeking,* meaning that after an adjustment, everything ends up back at a point where prices and quantities are equal (no unsold goods and no running down of inventories). Typically, using supply and demand analysis, you start and end at an equilibrium, even if not at the same equilibrium point as before.

Equilibrium and equilibrium-seeking are extremely important concepts to microeconomists. At the equilibrium, markets *clear:* Exactly as much is produced as consumers need, and producers have no *stock building* (no *excess supply*) or running down of stocks and shortages (as would be caused by *excess demand*). In this model, equilibrium comes about because the price can adjust to ensure that quantities demanded and supplied are equalized.

To see this process in action, suppose (as in Figure 9-9) that a situation occurs where price is temporarily higher than the equilibrium. This case sees excess supply, because the quantity supplied at that price is greater than the quantity demanded. With excess supply the price adjusts, falling so that, first, more potential buyers are tempted back into the market and, second, the marginal producers decide that producing that much is no longer worthwhile and cut their production. These two effects lead to the equilibrium-seeking market returning to its equilibrium where the market clears.

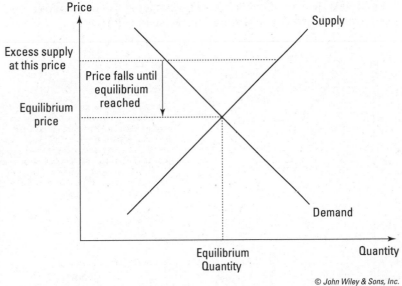

Figure 9-9: Price falls in response to excess supply.

© John Wiley & Sons, Inc.

This equilibrium-seeking tendency is one reason why economists require good evidence before recommending action to control a market. In the view of the majority of economists, unless proven otherwise, the price mechanism is sufficient to adjust markets until they clear. Examples of interferences in markets that have merely made things worse are many — often it comes about because any one policy maker knowing as much about a market as the people participating in it is difficult.

Not all economists prefer no intervention in all cases. We just mean that the profession wants to ensure that intervention doesn't make things worse.

When affordable housing is in short supply, there is often public pressure for rent control. Rent control policies have been implemented in many U.S. cities, first during World War II and then later in the 1960s and 1970s. Today, relatively few places have rent control, and it is prohibited in many states. Rent control allows landlords a maximum rent and problems occur when the maximum is below the equilibrium. Setting the rent ceiling at that level led to an excess demand for rentals from potential tenants, while marginal landlords were unable to get as much in rent as they felt compensated them fairly for the value of their properties. As a result, many landlords left the market at exactly the same time, because more people wanted to rent from them and the rent controls prevented prices from adjusting to create an equilibrium that may have kept landlords and tenants happy.

The result can be a collapse in the private rental market, and the additional effects included lower labor mobility (because private rents are often the most flexible way of being housed when a person moves from one town to another). We walk you through this case in Figure 9-10.

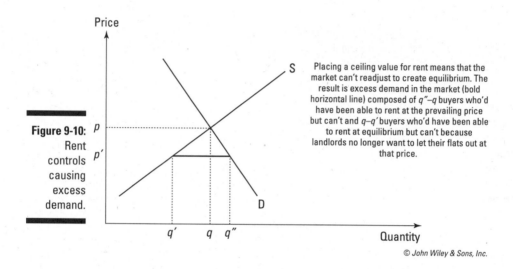

Figure 9-10: Rent controls causing excess demand.

Placing a ceiling value for rent means that the market can't readjust to create equilibrium. The result is excess demand in the market (bold horizontal line) composed of q''–q buyers who'd have been able to rent at the prevailing price but can't and q–q' buyers who'd have been able to rent at equilibrium but can't because landlords no longer want to let their flats out at that price.

© John Wiley & Sons, Inc.

Reading off revenue from under the demand curve

At the equilibrium, you can see on the supply and demand curves a unique price and quantity at the point where they intersect. The interesting thing is that, if you multiply price by quantity at a given point on a demand curve, the result is the revenue yielded from selling q units of a good at price p.

Total revenue always equals price times quantity and also corresponds to the area of a rectangle under the demand curve. When testing the responsiveness of demand using *elasticity* (a measure of how demand changes for a given change in price — discussed in the later section "Testing the responsiveness of demand using elasticities"), one result shows whether a producer's revenue will be higher after a price change. You can find that by comparing the size of the rectangles before and after a price change. Later in the "Testing the responsiveness of demand using elasticities" section, we show you the simple formula for how that happens. But for the moment, take a look (in Figure 9-11) at the rectangles under the demand curve for an old price of p and an old quantity of q and for a new price (after a change) of p' and a new quantity of q'. The change in revenue from p to p' and q to q' is as follows:

$$(p \times q) - (p' \times q')$$

In Figure 9-11a, original revenue before the change is given by Price times Quantity. In 9-11b, after a price change, the area under the demand curve changes — the revenue gained at the new price and quantity is shown by the shaded area; the dotted lines indicate the old amount of revenue for comparison.

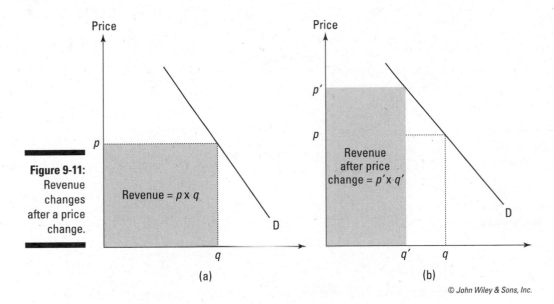

Figure 9-11: Revenue changes after a price change.

(a)   (b)

© John Wiley & Sons, Inc.

Summing the gains to consumer and producer: Welfare

The equilibrium price at which a market clears provides another useful thing to ponder when analyzing a market: gains made simply by trading, which economists call the *gains to trade*. The idea is that for any given equilibrium in price and quantity, some consumers would be happy to buy at above the market price, and some producers would be happy to supply at less than the market price. Both parties have made a trade that makes them better off, because they'd have been willing to buy (sell) at a higher (lower) price and don't have to; so each party captures some value from the trade.

The consumers' gain is called *consumer surplus* (see Figure 9-12), which comprises the gain for those willing to have bought at a price above the equilibrium price but don't have to. It's given by the area formed by

- The equilibrium price and quantity in the market.

- The highest price that consumers are willing to pay on the demand curve ($p^{\max}$ in Figure 9-12).

- The point where a horizontal line from the equilibrium point crosses the vertical axis (the intersection with the line is p, equilibrium price).

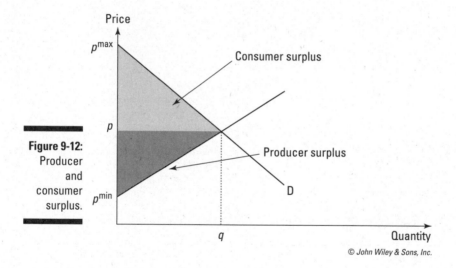

Figure 9-12: Producer and consumer surplus.

© John Wiley & Sons, Inc.

The length of the line between the first and third points in the list is q, and so the size of the area under the demand curve is the area of the triangle, given by:

$$\text{Consumer surplus} = \tfrac{1}{2}q\left(p^{\max} - p\right)$$

A similar reasoning applies to the area above the supply curve and below the market equilibrium price, which comprises producers willing to supply the good for a price lower than the equilibrium price, but who don't have to because the market clears at that equilibrium. Here, the only substitution is to use p^{min} for the price at which the cheapest producer is willing to provide the good (see Figure 9-12):

$$\text{Producer surplus} = \frac{1}{2}q\left(p - p^{min}\right)$$

Welfare, the term used, is the sum of the gains to trade between the two parties, and so is given by the sum of producer and consumer surpluses (summarized in Figure 9-12). Check out Chapter 12 for more on welfare.

Welfare has several meanings in economics, but when you're using the supply and demand model, it means the sum of consumer and producer surplus. The same also applies to the model of oligopoly in Chapter 11 and monopoly in Chapter 13. You will see that in the long run perfect competition model in Chapter 10, all the welfare goes to the consumer (nice!).

Testing the responsiveness of demand using elasticities

The most direct calculation you can make from the supply and demand model relates to responsiveness to a change in price, or to a change in something else that has been held constant in the particular market you're considering. The way we measure responsiveness is called an *elasticity*.

In this section, we discuss the three most important cases:

- ✓ **Own price elasticity of demand** measures the percentage change in quantity demanded in response to a percentage change in the price of the good. This measure corresponds to movement along the demand curve.

- ✓ **Cross-price elasticity of demand** measures the percentage change in quantity demanded in response to a percentage change in the price of another good. This measure corresponds to shifts in the demand curve.

- ✓ **Income elasticity of demand** measures the percentage change in quantity demanded in response to a percentage change in income. Again, this measure corresponds to shifts in the demand curve.

Effect of an own price change

The own price elasticity of demand measures the effect of the change in the price of a good on quantity demanded of the good. Hence, it can tell us whether the revenue that producers get increases or decreases as the price changes.

You can arrive at the revenue change by reading off prices and quantities and comparing the size of the rectangles under the demand curve (see the earlier section "Reading off revenue from under the demand curve"). But you can measure the size of the effect more simply by using the own price elasticity of demand formula. A change in price from p to p' is $p' - p$. Using the mathematical shorthand Δ to indicate a change, we write this as Δp.

Now we do the same for quantity, again reading off the change in quantity for the two points p and p' (whose associated quantities are given by q and q'), which gives Δq. To find the percentage change in quantity demanded we divide Δq by q and to find percentage change in price we divide Δp by p. Own price elasticity is the ratio of the $\Delta q/q$ to $\Delta p/p$ and measures the responsiveness of demand.

Economic variables come in different types of measurement units, from different currencies to different sizes of supply (diamonds, for example, aren't generally supplied by the ton, and steel isn't generally supplied in ounces). A great advantage of the elasticity measure is that it doesn't depend on units of measurement. By using percentages, elasticity measures are not affected by whether we measure gold in kilograms or ounces.

The own price elasticity of demand (P.E.D) can be expressed as follows:

$$P.E.D. = (\Delta q / q) / (\Delta p / p)$$

Or the other way is to start by using percentage changes so that

$$P.E.D. = \%\Delta q / \%\Delta p$$

Both ways are valid and give the same number. Sometimes, percentage changes are given to you by the data you receive, and sometimes you have to calculate them. But for both methods, the inferences you can make are the same.

The own price elasticity of demand is almost always a negative number. This reflects the fact that an inverse relationship lies along a demand curve between price and quantity, and so it follows that as price rises quantity falls. This is also a backhanded way of saying that a demand curve slopes downwards.

Three cases exist for the own price elasticity of demand:

- ✔ **Elasticity of demand is more negative than –1 (or its absolute value is greater than 1):** A percentage increase in prices leads to a greater percentage decrease in quantity demanded and hence to a fall in revenue. The reverse is true for a percentage decrease in price. In this case, revenue rises.

✔ **Elasticity of demand is less negative than –1 (or its absolute value is between 0 and 1):** A percentage increase in prices leads to a smaller percentage decrease in quantity demanded and hence to an increase in revenue. The reverse is true for a percentage decrease in price. In this case, revenue falls.

✔ **Elasticity of demand is exactly 1:** A percentage increase in prices leads to the same percentage decrease in quantity demanded and hence revenue stays the same. The same is true for a percentage decrease in price. In this case, revenue also stays the same.

Economists don't always put the minus sign before an own price elasticity of demand, because in the overwhelming majority of cases they assume it to be negative. In these cases we're considering the mathematical operator absolute value and so we strip off the minus sign. Unless there's a very important reason why the own price elasticity may be positive — for instance, in a Veblen good — the general practice is to assume that own price elasticity of demand has a negative sign as the downward-sloping demand curve indicates.

The price elasticity of demand divides into cases where the elasticity is more negative than –1 (that is, the absolute value is greater than 1 as, for instance, in the elasticity of –1.2) and those where it's less negative than –1 (for instance, an own price elasticity of –0.8). If it's more negative than –1 you've found a case of elastic demand:

✔ **Demand is elastic:** A decrease in price results in greater revenue, but a rise in price results in lower revenue.

✔ **Demand is inelastic:** A rise in price results in greater revenue, but a decrease in price results in lower revenue.

At some point on a linear demand curve, demand is *unit elastic*. At this point any rise in revenue caused by raising prices is exactly counterbalanced by the fall in revenue from selling fewer units of the product. In numerical terms, this is the same thing as saying that the own price elasticity of demand is exactly –1 at that point. Examples of demand functions do exist that yield elasticities of –1 at all points along the demand curve: These aren't straight lines.

Effect of a cross-price change

The cross-price elasticity of demand measures the effect of a change in the price of another good. Typically, you calculate it by knowing the prices and quantities before and after the change for two goods, i and j. So the effect of a change in the price of good j on the quantity demanded of good i is like this:

$$\%\Delta q_i \, / \, \%\Delta p_j$$

The cross-price elasticity of demand measures the effect of a shift in the demand curve, not a movement along it (it's changing something other than the price of the good in which you're interested). Three basic cases exist here:

- ✔ **Cross-price elasticity of demand is positive:** A rise in the price of good *j* has a positive effect on the sales of good *i* and so the two goods are substitutes. The greater the value of a positive cross-price elasticity of demand, the more substitutable the two goods are. So an estimate of the cross-price elasticity of demand that finds a high and positive sign allows the inference that the two goods, such as Coke and Pepsi, are in the same market.

- ✔ **Cross-price elasticity of demand is negative:** A rise in the price of good *j* has a negative effect on the sales of good *i* and thus you can infer that the two goods complement each other in consumption. They are complements. An example is that when the price of gas goes up, sales of big gas-guzzling cars fall because the two are complementary goods.

- ✔ **Cross-price elasticity is zero or very near:** The two goods have very little quantifiable effect on each other.

Effect of a change in income

The income elasticity of demand measures what happens to consumption of a good when income changes. Income is of course held constant along the demand curve, and so the income elasticity measures the effect of a shift in the demand curve caused when income moves from *M* to *M'*. (Check the earlier Figure 9-7b for an example of a demand curve shifting.)

Typically, economists use ΔM or Δy for a change in income — more usually *y*. They then evaluate a percentage change in quantity caused by the percentage change in income. Unlike the effect of an own price change, however, the income elasticity doesn't simply rely on the slope of the demand curve being negative, and so the income elasticity may be positive or negative. Here we evaluate the formula for the income elasticity of demand:

$$\%\Delta q \, / \, \%\Delta y$$

Here are the four general cases:

- ✔ **Quantity demanded rises as income rises:** Makes the income elasticity of demand positive (economists call these types of goods *normal goods*).

- ✔ **Quantity demanded rises by far more than income rises:** For example, when a 10% rise in income yields a 20% rise in quantity (so that the income elasticity of demand is 2). This behavior is associated with a *superior good* (often associated with consumption of luxury products).

✔ **Quantity falls as income rises:** The income elasticity of demand is negative. This is associated with *inferior goods,* where demand falls as income rises.

✔ **Income elasticity is zero:** Consumption of the good is unaffected by income. Necessities generally have income elasticities between zero and +1, and you'd expect their consumption to rise as income rises, but not by as much as the rise in income.

Chapter 10

Dreaming of the Consumer's Delight: Perfect Competition

In This Chapter

▶ Introducing perfect competition

▶ Understanding the requirements for a perfectly competitive market

▶ Explaining why perfect competition is a benchmark

*I*s perfection attainable? Although from time to time you may use the term casually ("I've made the perfect cappuccino," "Reality TV shows are a perfect nuisance," and of course, "This is the perfect book on microeconomics!"), most people understand that achieving perfection in the real world is impossible. But that doesn't mean that they can't imagine the perfect situation.

Perfect competition is the name economists give to a market with many interchangeable firms, none of which can independently influence the market outcome. This scenario isn't all that likely in the real world, because it depends on a set of conditions that are unlikely to hold. But some markets do get quite close to approximating perfect competition; of course, many others do not come close. When they do get close, they bring a number of benefits, which are most likely to go to consumers.

In this chapter, we look at the equilibrium of output and price in perfect competition — an ideal situation that economists use as a benchmark. We go through some of the conditions that determine which markets are oh so perfect and which fall below the standard. We also discuss the important factors of firm entry and exit, which lie behind the model of the perfectly competitive market. Do we have your attention? Perfect!

Viewing the "Perfect" in Perfect Competition

The word *perfect* means something very specific to economists. This section outlines what exactly that is and discusses some of the necessary conditions for perfect competition.

Defining perfect competition

Perfect in the sense of perfect competition means that it fully satisfies a set of conditions that economists have placed on the model.

By way of an analogy, economists mean *perfect competition* in the same way as mathematicians describe a perfect circle as exactly satisfying a set of mathematical conditions regarding curvature.

The term certainly doesn't mean that in a perfectly competitive market everyone's always happier. In fact, for producers, a perfectly competitive market may be a difficult one in which to operate, because the forces of competition constrain their behavior.

Identifying the conditions of perfect competition

A number of factors are required for a given market to be in perfect competition:

- Each firm is small relative to the market and has no influence on price.
- Firms and products are substitutable.
- Each consumer is small relative to the market and has no influence on price.
- Perfect information about prices and quantities is available.
- There is easy entry into and exit from the market.

We go through them all in a little more detail in this section.

If you fail to find any of these conditions holding in a given market, the market is not perfectly competitive.

Each firm is small relative to the market

In a perfectly competitive market, no firm is individually able to influence the price or quantity sold of a given good. For this to be the case, each firm has to be a small producer relative to the quantity demanded. Typically, this means there are many firms to supply the market, none of which has a significant share of the market. This is obviously not always the case in many markets, because many markets are *dominated* by one firm or a small group of firms.

The *small firm* condition leads to economists describing firms in the market as *price takers* (the opposite being *price makers* or *price setters*). None of them can influence market price or demand, and so firms have no option but to take whatever price is determined by the market *as a whole*.

Firms and products are substitutable

Products in a perfectly competitive market are said to be *homogenous*, that is, indistinguishable from one another. If, for example, you're shopping at a fruit and veg market with many sellers (so that none can influence the price paid for apples), the apples that each sells must be the same: no better or worse apples and no stalls that are the only ones selling Macintosh or the only ones selling Granny Smith. Instead, all must be selling the same, indistinguishable product.

Similarly, the firms must have the same production technology. If they don't, long-run differences between firms are possible, which leads to differences between the firms in the market. This would open up the possibility of one firm being different enough from the other firms to be considered as being in a different market altogether and to be able to influence that market.

Again, these conditions may not reflect real-world conditions. Although some goods are entirely homogenous, they aren't necessarily always produced by firms with the same production technologies. Take commodities, which are defined by their homogeneity: Gold is either gold or something else. An atom of the metal is either a gold atom or an atom of a different metal, not a different kind of gold atom. But this isn't to say that firms mining gold produce it to the same level of efficiency everywhere in the world.

Each consumer is small relative to the market

A similar issue is the degree to which consumers are small relative to the market. This means that there is not a consumer whose purchasing behavior is able to influence the price. For many markets, this is a pretty plausible condition. A regular at Starbucks does not influence the price of a latte. However, a large pharmacy chain such as CVS is likely to be able to influence the price it pays for the prescribed medications it sells to consumers.

Perfect information about products and prices

A perfectly competitive market contains no hidden surprises. Consumers are perfectly informed about what products are available, the qualities of the products, where they are sold, and at what prices. Thus they're immediately able to assess whether they want to purchase from one firm or another.

This information does not come at a cost. If consumers have to work to find out prices, the competition may not be perfect.

Easy entry and exit

Easy entry into and exit from the market is an extremely important condition. If an entrepreneur sees profits being made in a perfectly competitive market, he's able to enter that market immediately and begin competing profits away from the firms in the market. Similarly, if he's in a market and not making profits, he's able to pack up and leave without his leaving incurring any costs that can't be recovered.

This condition doesn't mean that starting up involves no costs — just that it doesn't involve any costs above and beyond those of producing whatever he's producing in that market: no fees for entering and no costs of closing.

Putting the Conditions Together for the Perfectly Competitive Marketplace

In a long-run equilibrium in a perfectly competitive market, firms make *economic profits* (those assessed after all costs have been reckoned) equal to zero and produce output at the minimum possible cost. Zero economic profit does not mean that the shareholders of the firm are losing — rather, it means that the rate of return they are earning is comparable to what they could earn elsewhere in the economy. To see why economic profits are zero and productive efficiency holds in the long-run equilibrium of a perfectly competitive market, this section investigates the equilibrium conditions for perfect competition. (To read more about supply, demand, and equilibrium, check out Chapter 9.)

Seeing the supply side

Firms in perfectly competitive markets are price takers. To understand the competitive position among the firms in a competitive market, it is helpful to look at the supply decisions an individual firm will make. This means that if you want to see what's happening in the market, you have to return to look-ing at the firm's cost curves (see Chapter 7 for a full explanation).

To go from a firm's decision about how much to produce to an industry supply, as Chapter 9 does, you need to add up the marginal cost curves of all the firms in the industry and read off the output that's produced in aggregate at each possible price. That gets you the industry supply curve that you use to find equilibrium output.

The thing is, in perfect competition the assumption that market entry and exit for firms is costless means that supply in a perfectly competitive market looks a little different. What we're going to do first is show you how horizon-tal addition works to get the figure for industry supply in the short run.

We use the example of the paper clip industry. Table 10-1 shows the output of three firms in the paper clip industry for three different values of marginal costs. At a marginal cost of 1, for instance, firm A makes 10 paper clips, B makes 11, and C makes 12. To get the industry supply in the short run, you add up the output of A, B, and C at each of the three marginal costs — so when all competitors produce at a marginal cost of 1, industry supply is 10 + 11 + 12, which equals 33.

Table 10-1	Marginal Cost and Industry Output in the Paper Clip Industry		
Firm Marginal Cost	*1*	*2*	*3*
Output per firm			
A	10	11	13
B	11	12	15
C	12	14	17
Total	33	37	45

The supply curve for the industry gives the relationship between output and cost for the industry. Adding up the marginal costs for each of the firms pro-vides the short-run supply curve for the industry.

We're adding horizontally so that we have to add up the output for all the firms.

Now, because firms are price takers, profit maximization means that marginal revenue is equal to price is equal to marginal cost or MR = p = MC. Table 10-2 shows industry output for three different prices. (You may notice that industry output is the same as in the bottom row of Table 10-1. The difference is that we're using the marginal cost equals price relationship to make the inference that makes up the supply curve.)

Table 10-2	Supply Curve for the Paper Clip Industry		
Price	*1*	*2*	*3*
Industry output	33	37	45

When you plot the output for the three firms, you get the typical upward-sloping supply curve (see Figure 10-1). Using the relationship between marginal cost and marginal revenue equal to price, you can express the profit-maximizing supply with price on the vertical axis and quantity on the horizontal axis, and lo and behold, you can say that if the market price of a box of paper clips is 3, then the industry would produce 45 boxes. In other words, the sum of the marginal costs of the firms in the industry leads to an output equal to 45 when marginal cost is equal to 3.

Figure 10-1:
Adding marginal costs horizontally to make industry supply.

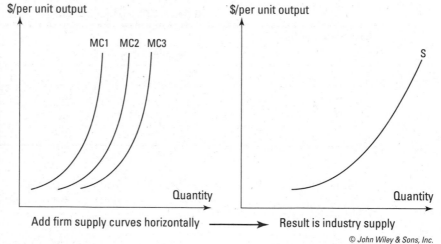

© John Wiley & Sons, Inc.

This situation is fine for looking at most cases of industry supply and market demand, but the costless entry and exit condition in the long run (check out the earlier section "Identifying the conditions of perfect competition") adds something new to how we work out supply in the long run.

Costless market entry and exit means that in the short run, if any firm is making economic profits, then that situation will attract in the longer run a new firm to enter the market. That entry would compete away the profits made by firms in the industry. What matters in the long run, therefore, is what a firm would do when considering whether to enter the industry. Economists ponder that by considering something called the marginal firm.

Marginal, as usual in economics, means at the margin. At the margin, only one firm is deciding whether to enter the industry, stay in it, or leave it. At equilibrium, the marginal firm will have no preference between those decisions. How can that possibly be the case? Well, given the profit-maximizing rule for firms — that production is set where marginal revenue equals marginal cost (see Chapter 3) — you know that this can happen only when a firm receives exactly as much for its last unit of output as the incremental amount it cost to produce it. At equilibrium in perfect competition, therefore, economists look at the marginal revenue received by the last firm and find that it must equal the marginal cost of producing that output. The marginal condition holds in the short run where capital (for example, production facilities) or the number of firms is fixed and in the long run when the condition refers to the last firm to enter the industry.

Digging into the demand side

The preceding section's discussion on supply is a start, but you also need to look at the other side of the market — demand — to get the market equilibrium.

The demand curve that faces any individual firm in a perfectly competitive market is infinitely elastic. Each firm can sell as much as it wants at the going price — otherwise, it could influence price by its production decision, which by assumption of perfect competition is not possible. Alternatively, any attempt to sell at a price above the market price would drive every potential customer running to your competitors. The upshot is that the demand curve facing a perfectly competitive firm must be a flat horizontal line at the current market price.

Here's another way of understanding what it means to not be able to influence market price. Imagine that you're in the middle of an aisle of many vegetable sellers in an outdoor market. They all sell identical yams and tell you their prices by clearly barking them out so that getting that information involves no cost to you. They're all very near to each other too, so you incur no cost going from one to another to find a yam for your dinner (sounds yummy!).

For argument's sake, assume that yams are on sale at the market cost of $1 per pound. But then imagine that one seller has the ability to get hold of yams for less and can therefore bring them to the market for 90 cents. You hear his price, and immediately realize (as a rational consumer) that his price being lower means that you can buy more and (following the model of the consumer in Chapters 4–6) make yourself better off by doing so. You're economically rational, so it's a no-brainer. You buy from the cheaper seller.

But you aren't alone in this market — you're only one of many rational consumers. All the other consumers in the market have also heard his price, and they all want to have more utility rather than less. So they all follow, leaving all the other sellers barking their prices to precisely no one.

When you get to the cheaper seller, you find him looking absolutely exhausted. The entire market has come to him, and he can't possibly keep up. His stock is going to run out, leaving him scratching around trying to find more yams to sell. What does he do? He has no choice. He's going to have to put his price back up to the market price — as stated in the earlier section "Identifying the conditions of perfect competition," he's a price taker — and return to market equilibrium.

Returning to equilibrium in perfect competition

This section aims to put supply and demand together to get equilibrium (where, of course, supply equals demand). In the earlier section "Seeing the supply side," we state why we consider the marginal firm. We now combine what we know about the marginal firm with what we deduced about demand to consider what happens when the marginal firm meets the rational consumer in perfect competition.

Economists are only interested in the marginal firm out of all the firms, and we can understand the output in the industry by just using the cost curves for that one firm. (To revise cost curves, pop over to Chapters 7 and 8. Don't worry, we'll still be here.) Figure 10-2 puts the equilibrium conditions into a picture.

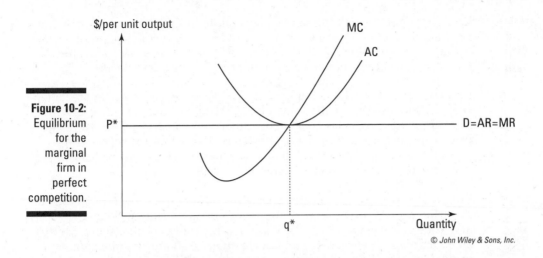

$/per unit output

Figure 10-2:
Equilibrium
for the
marginal
firm in
perfect
competition.

MC

AC

P*

D=AR=MR

q*

Quantity

© John Wiley & Sons, Inc.

The demand curve facing a firm describes not only price or average revenue, but because it's horizontal and perfectly elastic, it describes the marginal revenue gained from selling an additional unit to a customer. Putting them together, as in Figure 10-2, the marginal firm sets output, assuming it is a rational profit maximizer, so that MC = MR, thus producing where the marginal cost curve crosses its demand curve.

Now here's an interesting thing from Chapter 3:

$$\Pi = TR - TC$$

Π is profit. You can get TR (total revenue) and TC (total cost) from the demand or average revenue function and from the average cost function. If you multiply AC by quantity (q), you get TC. Similarly, if you multiply average revenue (AR) by q, you get TR. Thus you can divide through by taking the quantity out of the cost and revenue terms:

$$\Pi = (AR - AC) \times q$$

In a long-run equilibrium, the marginal firm is just indifferent between entering and not entering the market, and this means that it must earn zero profit. Average revenue equals average cost, or that (AR – AC) has to equal zero so that if you multiply zero by quantity, you get zero. Moreover, in the long run, the marginal firm must be producing at the minimum possible average cost (AC) — otherwise, there is potential profit to be earned by changing output and lowering average cost. So there you have it: Profits for the marginal firm in perfect competition have to equal zero, and the firm is producing at minimum average cost.

Economic profits aren't the same as accounting profits. There are many ways to assess accounting profits, but there's only one for economic profits, which is that they're assessed after *all costs have been reckoned.* This includes all wages, capital used, and the opportunity cost of any alternatives.

Now let's go back to the example of the vegetable sellers from the preceding section. Suppose the equilibrium price of a delicious package of veggies is $10 per package, which is equal to the unit cost of a package, and the seller prices the package at $9. What happens next? Well, first the seller is now pricing in a way that TR < TC. If that's the case, the seller will make losses and have to decide whether to go on selling in this market.

But the lesson from the demand side is that, at that price, customers rush to the seller's stall. In fact, because the seller's demand curve is infinitely elastic at a price of $10 per package, the entire market rushes to that seller. Serving an entire market below cost isn't a sustainable position, and the marginal vegetable seller has to put prices back to the equilibrium in order to stay in business — if he decides not to shut down, that is.

Now what if the price is above average cost? Well, in this case you can work out from the equation that the seller now makes economic profits above zero. But then other entrepreneurs see the marginal veggie seller making economic profits and so are attracted to enter. They then compete away those profits until the point where the marginal firm is *indifferent* between staying in the industry and leaving it. In other words, after they enter, the marginal seller or firm, again, makes economic profits of precisely zero.

Thus in the long run — which economists define as that length of time it takes for all production decisions to be changeable — the marginal firm in a perfectly competitive industry makes economic profits of zero.

Examining Efficiency and Perfect Competition

Economists derive two conditions for efficiency (check out Chapter 8 for more on profit maximization):

- **Allocative efficiency:** The market price for a product equals the marginal cost of producing it.

- **Productive efficiency:** The firm produces for the lowest possible average cost.

Both these conditions are satisfied in perfect competition, which means that from the overall viewpoint of cost, equilibrium in perfect competition is allocatively and productively efficient. Thus, on the grounds of cost, perfect competition produces the most desired products for the lowest possible cost.

This sounds wonderful, but it is important to remember that the key requirement for a perfectly competitive market is that each firm is *small* relative to the market and cannot influence market price. We live in a world where firms such as Apple, Toyota, Walmart, Anheuser-Busch InBev, and Comcast are large relative to the market and can influence market price. If Toyota stopped producing cars or Walmart shut down all its stores, there would be an impact on market prices. These firms do not face perfectly elastic demand curves — they have market influence or market power.

Understanding that perfect competition is a boundary case

The best way to see perfect competition is as a maximum possible efficiency case and not necessarily a depiction of the real world.

We draw an analogy with an engineer's concept of perfect efficiency, where 100 percent of the energy put into a machine gets transformed into useful work. In reality, that's not true. But investigating the case where it does apply, as a model, the engineer is able to understand the degree to which her machine falls short of ideal and explore the reasons for it.

Economists use the idea of perfect competition in a similar way. Few markets in the world, if any, satisfy all the conditions of a perfectly competitive market, but that's not why economists are interested in its features. The real reason is to enable some comparison of the efficiency of a given market with that of the perfectly competitive market, and to assess the degree to which it falls short.

Also, although the zero profit condition and selling at a price equal to minimum average cost may sound nice in theory, in practice profits don't just get stacked in a bank vault. They can also be retained for investment — for instance, in research and development (R&D) of new products. R&D is often an intensive and expensive process, and most economists point out that firms that don't make long-run profits have less capital to spend on R&D and less incentive to make that investment. Thus high levels of competition may have a drag effect on levels of R&D investment and not be conducive to forming research-intensive companies and developing new technologies.

Considering perfect competition in the (imperfect) real world

Often students ask whether the model of perfect competition is realistic or whether it's just a textbook case. Our answer is that it may *almost* happen in some situations, and although they're interesting, the primary interest in perfect competition is more as a benchmark for understanding the effects of competition. Examples in this chapter include a commodity market (because commodities are homogeneous products) with many buyers and sellers, such as a fruit and vegetable market. Perhaps the closest example is something like Uber offering taxi services in a town where there are many potential drivers and users. In this case, you could expect to get quite close to the perfectly competitive situation. Confronted with a market like this, each driver would be making close to zero economic profits as a whole. They may be making a salary's worth of money, but remember that the salary is the opportunity cost of their time and car use.

Part IV

Delving into Markets, Market Failure, and Welfare Economics

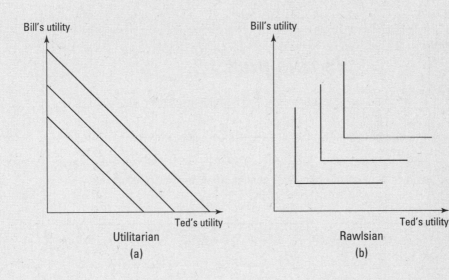

Bill's utility

Ted's utility

Utilitarian

(a)

Bill's utility

Ted's utility

Rawlsian

(b)

In this part . . .

- ✔ Find out why consumers love perfect competition but firms may not.

- ✔ Get to grips with what welfare means in economics.

- ✔ Discover why monopolies produce less for a higher price.

- ✔ Understand how things change when one side of a market knows more than the other.

Chapter 11

Stepping into the Real World: Oligopoly and Imperfect Competition

*O*ligopoly is the name economists give to a type of market with only a few firms (it comes from the Greek word *oligos* meaning few). The classic example of an oligopoly is the airline industry, where a few airlines compete among themselves for customers, and the bulk of the domestic market is locked up among the four largest competitors: American, Delta, United Airlines, and Northwest. But oligopoly is visible everywhere, in industries as different as cable television services, computer and software industries, cellular phone services, and automobiles.

One of the ways in which economists analyze oligopoly is by comparing it with other market structures. Compared to perfect competition, described in Chapter 10, consumers don't get as good a deal. But compared to monopoly (which has no competition, see Chapter 13), they do better under oligopoly.

Economists use the term *imperfect competition* to describe market structures with a few competitors, as in oligopoly, or two competitors *(duopoly)*.

In this chapter, we discuss the basic attributes of an oligopolistic market, three ways of describing how firms operate in such a market, and how firms are able to differentiate themselves from their rivals and gain market power.

Outlining the Features of an Oligopoly

The important difference between the model of an oligopoly and the model of a perfectly competitive market is that firms in oligopoly can influence market outcomes. As a result, firms behave strategically and try to anticipate the *strategic interactions* among each other. This means that they form beliefs about what their rivals might do in response to their acts. This behavior makes oligopoly a useful jumping-off point for looking at even more complex markets, and for understanding how the concepts of game theory are relevant to microeconomics. (Part IV covers game theory.)

The first thing you have to do when looking at oligopoly is describe the key characteristics that make a given market an oligopoly. Besides having only a few firms in the market, here are some other features to note:

- ✓ **Firms have market power and can affect market prices:** The demand curve facing a firm in this case is downward-sloping rather than a flat line (as for perfect competition — check out Chapter 10).

- ✓ **Firms, as ever, are rational profit maximizers:** They set prices or quantities where marginal revenue equal marginal cost (see Chapter 3).

- ✓ **Firms interact by anticipating how their rivals will react to their decisions:** These guesses about their rivals' behaviors affect the price that a firm will charge or the quantity it will supply.

- ✓ **Entry into the market typically incurs sunk costs:** Sunk costs are costs, such as advertising or product development, that have no recoverable value after the cost has been expended. These make entry costly and exit not costless.

- ✓ **Consumers are rational utility maximizers:** Therefore, demand works in the same way as in Chapter 9.

One of the most important of these conditions is that entry and exit is no longer costless. Oligopoly often comes about as a result of the existence of *barriers to entry*. In a perfectly competitive market, entry and exit are assumed to be costless (see Chapter 10). Changing this condition makes a large difference, because rivals can base their behavior on each other's actions without worrying about potential competitors who aren't currently in the industry. Thus firms in an oligopoly can make economic profits in the long run, whereas perfectly competitive firms cannot.

Barriers to entry are anything that imposes a non-recoverable cost on entering a market, and they come in many kinds:

> ✔ **Innocent:** Large capital investments that have no resale value. For example, setting up a manufacturer of aircraft costs a lot of money for specific plants and equipment.

> ✔ **Strategic:** Incumbent firms may engage in costly behavior strategically designed to keep entrants out, including preemptive moves.

> ✔ **Prohibitive regulations:** Such as the result of government allowing only a few licenses to trade in that industry. For example, in 1927 the U.S. government nationalized the airwaves and since then licenses their use. Wireless broadband providers like Verizon and AT&T must bid for the spectrum licenses they use. Television broadcasters, on the other hand, are issued licenses by the Federal Communications Commission.

Discussing Three Different Approaches to Oligopoly

A helpful way to start understanding oligopoly is to consider the special case of a *duopoly,* where only two firms are operating in the market. After you get the hang of thinking about how two firms interact with each other, you can adapt your modeling to think about the harder cases involving three or more firms.

Investigating how firms interact in a duopoly

The first thing to consider is how firms interact in the market place to influence price. Some firms, such as those in service industries, produce to order and set their prices. For example, a restaurant sets a menu price, and customers decide how much to order at that price. In this case, we say that the restaurant *produces to order*. These kinds of firms are price setters. On the other hand, firms in manufacturing industries, such as those making automobiles, textiles, and leather goods, produce to stock or inventory and price adjusts to clear the market. These firms compete in quantities. The two different approaches to how firms influence price and are associated with the following models:

> ✔ **Cournot model:** Where quantity is the strategic variable.

> ✔ **Bertrand model:** Where price is the strategic variable or the thing that firms control.

In both models, we assume that firms either choose quantity (Cournot) or price (Bertrand), simultaneously.

Choosing quantity as a strategic variable has very different results from choosing price.

Instead of having the two firms make their choices simultaneously, an alternative approach is to let one firm choose first and the other second, or move sequentially. When choices are made sequentially, we are interested in whether there is a *first mover advantage*.

The Stackelberg model allows one firm to have a potential leadership advantage over the other firm by moving first. We discuss a version where the firm has an advantage over choosing how much to produce, called *quantity leadership*.

Next you want to work out the equilibrium in each case so that you can compare them — the results are interesting even in a simple model.

Competing by setting quantity: The Cournot model

In the Cournot model of a duopoly, the two firms in the industry — which both make an identical or highly substitutable product — simultaneously decide what quantity to produce for the market, given each one's beliefs about how the rival will react to its decision. You want to know how much each firm will produce in order to have the best chance of making maximum profits.

Imagine the simple scenario of two Canadian lumber companies, Fort William and Port Nelson. Lumber is a useful example because it's reasonably indistinguishable as a product.

You solve the model by first considering just one company's decisions and calculating its *reaction function* or *best response function*. This is an expression that gives the firm's profit-maximizing or best response to its conjecture about what the rival firm will do. In Cournot oligopoly, the firm's conjecture on its rival and its best response or reaction to it is expressed in terms of quantity.

Spelling out customer demand

Begin by looking at customer demand, Q, as a function of market price P. This is something neither company can change. In a quantity-setting model, the firms choose quantities to produce, and price adjusts to clear the market.

In a price-setting model, firms set their prices, and consumers decide how much to buy at those prices. For a simple example, suppose a linear demand function:

$$P = 30 - Q$$

Fort William and Port Nelson produce Q_{FW} and Q_N, respectively. The total market size depends on both firms' production, and so:

$$Q = Q_{FW} + Q_N$$

To make things simple, though a little unrealistic, set the model up with a marginal cost (MC) for both firms of zero (this keeps things a little simpler than reality, but as you progress with the model, you can change this assumption and see what happens):

$$MC_{FW} = MC_N = 0$$

The last thing is to find an expression for the total revenue of one of the firms. We choose Fort William and use the identity that total revenue equals price times quantity. Knowing the demand function, you can write:

$$TR_{FW} = P \times Q_{FW} = (30 - Q)Q_{FW}$$

This gives the total revenue for Fort William as an expression of the total amount of lumber produced by the two firms — allowing you to move on to calculating the profit-maximizing level of production.

Finding the optimum production for Firm 1

The optimum is at MC = MR, so finding the optimum level means setting MR equal to zero (as MC was assumed to be in the preceding section). MR is the change in total revenue when quantity increases by one. In order to find it, take the slope of the expression for total revenue for Fort William.

Beginning with the expression for TR_{FW}, multiply it out to see what all the parts of the expression are:

$$\begin{aligned} TR_{FW} &= (30 - Q)Q_{FW} \\ &= 30Q_{FW} - (Q_{FW} + Q_N)Q_{FW} \\ &= 30Q_{FW} - Q_{FW}^2 - Q_N Q_{FW} \end{aligned}$$

Finding the slope of this equation with respect to a change in Q_{FW}, you get an expression for marginal revenue (MR). You can do so by plotting total revenue for Fort William against its output and taking the slope of the line (but if you trust us, you can go straight there by using calculus):

$$MR_{FW} = 30 - 2Q_{FW} - Q_N$$

Now you know that MC = MR (because the firm is a profit maximizer) and MC is zero in this model, so you know that if you set MR equal to zero and solve for Q_{FW} you get:

$$Q_{FW} = 15 - \tfrac{1}{2}Q_N$$

This result is the reaction function for Fort William that tells you what profit-maximizing quantity Fort William will produce in response to what it believes Port Nelson is producing.

Plotting reaction curves for the two firms

You can go through the same reasoning as in the preceding section to get Port Nelson's reaction function — or you can trust us that it works out as being:

$$Q_N = 15 - \tfrac{1}{2}Q_{FW}$$

The next stage is to plot the two reaction functions against each other. Each axis measures the quantity produced of one of the companies. The two reaction curves give the amount of lumber each will produce given the production of the other.

The two lines cross at one unique point (because they've been set up as straight lines — so this may not be true if revenue and cost functions were more complex).

Figure 11-1 shows that point, called the *Cournot equilibrium.* To find it, you first recognize that both firms want to be on their profit-maximizing best response functions, and this happens only at that intersection point. To solve for that point, you substitute the reaction function for Q_N, which is in terms of Q_{FW}, into the reaction function for Q_{FW} and solve for Q_{FW}. Then use that solution to solve for Q_N. Because the two reaction functions are identical to each other, you get $Q_N = Q_{FW} = 10$. Therefore, industry total production is 20.

Seeing why the equilibrium isn't as good as a competitive market

If you feed back the total output of both firms into the demand curve, you can get an expression for the price each will receive. Market demand is given by $P = 30 - Q$ and total production is equal to 20, and so the price that the market is prepared to pay is 10.

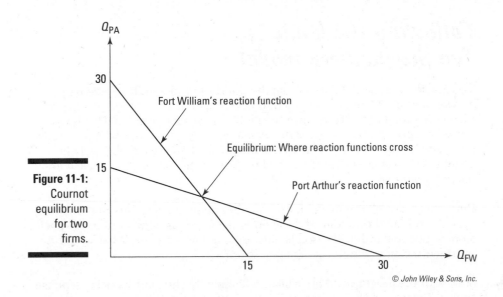

Figure 11-1:
Cournot
equilibrium
for two
firms.

© John Wiley & Sons, Inc.

When each firm produces 10, the price received from selling the last unit is greater than the assumed marginal cost, which was zero. So, an oligopoly in Cournot equilibrium produces at a higher price than a competitive market, and firms in the industry make *economic profits* — that is, profits greater than zero. Solving for a price of zero (so that price equals marginal cost, as in a competitive market), industry output is 30. So, a competitive market produces a higher output than an oligopoly in Cournot equilibrium.

Seeing why the equilibrium isn't as bad as a monopoly

Suppose the two firms coordinate their decisions so that you can treat them as a monopoly — a single firm that supplies the whole of the market. Then the firms together maximize their revenue based on combined demand.

Going through the scenario in the preceding section, marginal revenue in this monopoly case is MR = 30 − 2Q, because now only one firm is in the game. Setting MR = MC, which is zero in this example, the output that maximizes profits is 15. This amount is less than the Cournot equilibrium, and so an oligopoly in Cournot competition produces less than a competitive market, but more than a monopoly.

Collusion among firms in an oligopoly to coordinate on the monopoly outcome is not surprisingly bad for consumers. When firms collude successfully, the result is a *cartel* and is highly illegal, precisely because it results in a lower quantity produced (and therefore higher prices). Check out Chapter 16 for more on cartels.

Following the leader: The Stackelberg model

The Stackelberg model differs from the Cournot model of the preceding section in that one firm is assumed to have the ability to set its quantity as market leader and the other firm then follows with its decision. One firm has what economists call a *first mover advantage* and it exists whenever one company has an ability to lead in a market. If, as happens in oligopoly in general, entry occurs over time, the first firm in the market may have a first mover advantage.

Deriving a Stackelberg model for the lumber companies means that one firm sets its optimal production and the other firm reacts to the first firm's deci-sion. Suppose that Port Nelson is able to be the first mover. What would it produce and how would Fort William react?

Start with the insight that Fort William will react by choosing its best response to Port Nelson's decision. In the Cournot model, Fort William makes a guess about Port Nelson's decision, whereas in the Stackelberg model, Fort William knows exactly what Port Nelson has chosen. Port Nelson can work out how Fort William will react and input Fort William's decision into its reaction function.

Suppose — as before — that the demand curve is given by this:

$$P = 30 - Q$$

Now Port Nelson makes its decision based on what it can predict the follower, Fort William, will do. It predicts Fort William's behavior by knowing that Fort William will be on its best response or reaction function. Port Nelson can substitute Fort William's reaction into its own total revenue function:

$$TR_N = 30 - Q_N^2 - Q_{FW}Q_N$$

$$Q_{FW} = 15 - \tfrac{1}{2}Q_N$$

This gives Port Nelson's revenue function given Fort William's reaction:

$$TR_N = 30\,Q_N - Q_N^2 - \left(15 - \tfrac{1}{2}Q_N\right)Q_N$$

That looks unwieldy, and so we gather like terms to simplify:

$$TR_N = 15\,Q_N - \tfrac{1}{2}Q_N^2$$

Find the slope of this line to get marginal revenue for Port Nelson:

$$MR_N = 15 - Q_N$$

You can now set MR = MC = 0, which gives production for Port Nelson as 15. Now, using Fort William's reaction function, you can plug Port Nelson's production back in and get 7.5.

Comparing to the Cournot results where both firms made 10 units (from the preceding section), you instantly see that Port Nelson makes 15 units of lumber and Fort William only 7.5! Also, summing the total output of the two firms, you get 22.5 units rather than the 20 under Cournot conditions. So, if one firm gets to lead and move first, output for the industry as a whole is higher. Plug that into the demand function and you see that this is tantamount to price being lower.

The first mover advantage allows the leader to produce more output and to squeeze or limit the rival's share of the market. The equilibrium that emerges favors the leader, in terms of market share, and the result is better for the consumer, lower price, than when there was no first mover advantage and both firms had equal market shares.

Competing over prices: The Bertrand model

In the Cournot and Stackelberg models, the two firms compete in quantities and price adjusts to clear the market. The firms choose quantities, which influences market price. However, in many markets firms set prices and often try to undercut rival's price in order to steal the rival's customers. The Cournot and Stackelberg model do not capture that cut-throat kind of competition. For that, we turn to the Bertrand model of price competition.

The *Bertrand model* of oligopoly looks at what happens when firms compete by setting prices. It can explain what happens during a price war and why cut-throat price competition tends to be undesirable for firms. You can illustrate this situation easily by considering what happens when our two lumber companies compete in price instead of quantities.

Let's start at the Cournot outcome (refer to the earlier section "Competing by setting quantity: The Cournot model" and Figure 11-1), in which each firm is selling 10 units at a price equal to 10. Now suppose that the two firms compete in price instead of quantity, each firm sets its price of lumber, and consumers place their orders. Will one of our lumber companies have an incentive to deviate and set a price different from 10?

From the consumer's perspective, the goods are identical, so if Fort William cuts price to 9, all customers will order from it, the lower-price supplier, and this move is profitable. However, Port Nelson will react and cut price a small amount below Fort William's. Then *it* takes the entire market. Neither company wants to be the one quoting higher prices in this scenario.

Under price competition, each producer has an incentive to cut prices below its rivals and so each continues cutting prices until it reaches the limit. What's that limit? Well, it's when price equals marginal cost, which is — ta-da! — exactly the competitive price.

This finding bears out the important observation that price competition isn't in the interests of producers in this type of market. If each firm gets the competitive price, profits made are zero and neither producer gets to benefit from the lack of entry.

Comparing the output levels and price for the three types of oligopoly

We now take a look at what happens to price, output, and profit under the three types of competition covered in the three preceding sections:

- ✔ **Cournot competition:** The lowest industry output and highest price appears when firms are Cournot competitors, reacting to their conjecture at what each other's output will be. The price here isn't quite as high as under a cartel or a monopoly, but it's higher than in other types of oligopoly.

- ✔ **Stackelberg competition:** The outcome leads to not quite as high a price and not quite as low an output as Cournot, but it isn't quite as good as under a competitive market.

- ✔ **Bertrand competition:** The outcome leads to the same price as under a perfect competitively supplied market (and therefore the highest quantity).

In reality, competition among firms is often not as cut-and-dried as these models make out. An offer of a lower price isn't always a signal that the industry is about to enter into a frenzy of Bertrand competition. Take, for instance, "lowest price guarantees," which are frequently advertised at big retailers such as Best Buy and Walmart. Far from being a signal that a company is willing to beat the best price in the market, the strategy can be used as a price-cutting deterrence strategy. If you offer to beat anyone else's price, it actually removes the incentive for anyone else to try and undercut you.

In the Stackelberg and Cournot models, equilibrium price exceeds marginal cost, which means that firms make economic profits. In the case of Bertrand competition with undifferentiated products, price hits marginal cost, and therefore firms make zero profits in equilibrium.

Making Your Firm Distinctive from the Competition

In the hard-nosed world of competitive business, firms have a strong incentive to differentiate their products to separate themselves from rivals. Car manufacturers, for instance, produce many different brands of car rather than a single generic item called a car. Even when the goods are relatively homogenous, such as matches or sticky tape, firms still want to identify their product as different from others in consumers' minds. These strategies can soften competition.

This practice raises a question: At which point are products different enough that thinking about them as being in the same market stops making sense? Economists examine this issue by looking at the cross-price elasticity of demand between two products (for details, check out Chapter 9): The more positive the cross-price elasticity, the more likely the two products are indeed in the same market. Looking at it from the perspective of a firm that wants to make as much profit as possible, branding and making its product different to competitors' products reduces the cross-price elasticity of demand.

Economists look at these behaviors in two ways:

- ✔ They adapt oligopoly models to allow the products to be differentiated.

- ✔ They use a model called *monopolistic competition,* which allows for profitable product differentiation to work in the short run, but not in the long run (because if you hit on a winning formula, someone is bound to copy it).

Reducing the effects of direct competition

Companies reduce the effect of direct competition in many ways. These strategies all seek to reduce the degree of direct competition faced by firms making similar or substitutable products. They include the following:

- ✔ **Integrating their supply chains:** For instance, selling through preferred partners or through retail networks that they themselves own allows a company to differentiate its product through the retail services it provides. Antitrust laws may prevent firms with dominant market positions from doing this, because of fears of excluding rivals. But otherwise it is fine. A Honda dealership that only sells Honda cars and vans is an example of a producer owning a retailer — what economists call *forward vertical integration in the supply chain.*

- ✔ **Branding products:** Branding strategies center on advertising and packaging so that consumers identify the products as being different. Sometimes branding is a way to highlight that a product is in fact different — think of detergents, where brands and formulas are interlinked. But sometimes branding exists where products are minimally different — gas, for instance.

- ✔ **Competing on some other dimension that consumers care about:** Location is one such example; returns and payment options are another.

The supermarket industry in the United States is an oligopoly that is undergoing a major transformation. At one end are the big box retail stores such as Walmart that offer grocery service as well. (Walmart's market share in groceries has grown in the past decade to nearly 30%.) At the other end are natural grocers and specialty stores such as Whole Foods and Trader Joe's. The traditional chain grocery stores like Safeway must adapt to the changes.

Economists build upon the basic oligopoly models talked about in the earlier section "Discussing Three Different Approaches to Oligopoly" in order to capture the importance of product differentiation and sunk costs. Here are two basic ways:

- ✔ **Adapt the oligopoly models to include product differentiation with significant barriers to entry.** If firms differentiate their products and at the same time incur sunk marketing and advertising costs to communicate these differences to consumers, then price cutting a la Bertrand competition (described in the earlier section "Competing over prices: The Bertrand model") is muted. Customers will develop loyalty and not switch to lower-priced rivals. Moreover, entry is difficult because of the marketing and distribution costs incurred to reach consumers. Both factors mean firms can make economic profits in a long-run equilibrium.

- ✔ **For markets where product differentiation is important but barriers to entry are relatively low, economists use a model called monopolistic competition in which entry can occur in the long run.** This adaption looks at competition with differentiated products from the perspective of a firm that can make economic profits in the short run, but not in the long run (check out the next two sections for more).

A consequence of barriers to entry is that it enables firms to make long-run economic profits, which is one reason economists tend to dislike them. The thing is, in reality, many industries show a turnover in membership. Although some industries are nice examples of oligopoly with little entry — think of the soft drink industry — others show significant amounts of entry and exit. The car manufacturing industry, for example, has lost names such as the DeLorean, the Nash, and the Oldsmobile, over the years, but gained a Lexus, a Tesla, and a Kia along the way.

Economists call the possibility of entering an imperfectly competitive market *contestability*. When markets are contestable, potential rivals can enter the market relatively easily because there are relatively small sunk costs. As a result, they exert competitive pressure on the incumbent firms in the market to keep prices low. The displacing of incumbent firms by new firms is a process called *creative destruction*. New entrants see the behavior of incumbent firms and work out new ways of making the product better or doing it cheaper. If successful, they enter the market and gain advantage over the already-present firms, growing bigger while their rivals decline. That leads to a constant turnover of firms in the market and continual improvement in quality and novelty.

The average lifespan of a company listed in the S&P 500 index of leading U.S. companies has fallen from 67 years in the 1920s to just 15 years today, according to Professor Richard Foster from Yale University. Over that period, the economy became more complex, and innovation happened at a greater pace, leading to more competition and more entry and exit.

Competing on brand: Monopolistic competition

When a market is contestable and firms in that market face likely entry but are able to differentiate their products, economists turn to the *monopolistic competition* model. As its name suggests, it assumes firms are in a competitive market, but unlike in perfect competition, the firms sell differentiated products that are not perfect substitutes for each other. Firms in this case can influence the market outcome or, in other words, face downward-sloping demand curves. Hence the monopolistic part of the name of this model is that each firm is trying to be the sole supplier of its "flavor" of product.

This situation applies to many industries, from cereals — a relatively generic product with some degree of differentiation on brand — to broadcast television. These industries have in common the fact that the firms have to invest continually in their product or their brand — or both — or risk losing their profits to an entrant.

Seeing how brands compete

In monopolistic competition, the demand curve that each firm faces is downward sloping. (Recall that in perfect competition, the firm faces a perfectly elastic demand curve, whereas in monopoly the firm's demand curve is the market demand curve.) The market demand curve is always downward sloping — except of course for Giffen goods, and the demand faced by an individual firm in monopolistic competition is, however, more elastic in the long run than in the short run, because entry is possible only in the long run and consumers can in the event of a price increase switch to a rival more easily. The demand curve is downward sloping, reflecting the fact that the firm competes by making its product or brand different from its rivals' products.

Firms, as usual, operate where marginal revenue equals marginal cost. They use that to set quantity and receive the price consumers are willing to pay (from the demand curve).

Because firm demand is downward sloping, price or average revenue is greater than marginal revenue, so the firm makes profits in the short run (see the shaded area in Figure 11-2a, with markup being the difference between price and average cost). However, in the long run, in Figure 11-2b, entry has shifted the firm demand curve downwards, and as a result the new equilibrium, though still having the firm producing where MC = MR, results in the firm making no economic profits.

Figure 11-2:
Monopolistic
competition —
firm
equilibrium.

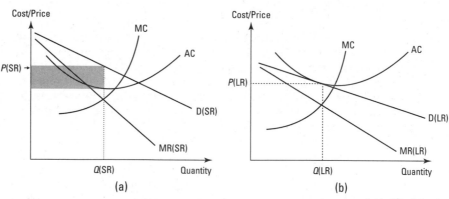

(a)   (b)

© John Wiley & Sons, Inc.

MC = Marginal cost; AC = Average cost. (a) In the short run: P(SR) = Price in the short run; Q(SR) = Quantity in the short run; MR(SR) = Marginal revenue in the short run; D(SR) = Demand in the short run. (b) In the long run: P(LR) = Price in the long run; Q(LR) = Quantity in the long run; MR(LR) = Marginal revenue in the long run; D(LR) = Demand in the long run.

The firm in monopolistic competition therefore has to deal with the continual threat to its profitability from entry. It can try to respond to this threat by investing continually in the value of its brand, perhaps by advertising — and by investing in the quality of its product.

Trading efficiency for diversity: Monopolistic competition for consumers

Compared to a perfectly competitive market, some welfare loss (described in Chapter 13) occurs under monopolistic competition. The monopolistically competitive industry produces less total output than under a competitive market, which means a deadweight loss — a loss of consumer surplus in particular. Figure 11-3 depicts this as a shaded triangle (the area under the demand curve but above marginal cost for units of output not produced).

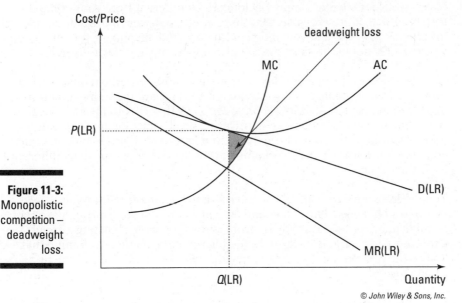

Figure 11-3: Monopolistic competition — deadweight loss.

© John Wiley & Sons, Inc.

P(LR) = Price in the long run; Q(LR) = Quantity in the long run; MR(LR) = Marginal revenue in the long run; D(LR) = Demand in the long run.

Although consumers may lose out through lower quantities and higher prices compared to a competitive market, they also gain something else: diversity of products. Each firm in monopolistic competition wants to be the monopolist of its own particular segment of the market, so no two firms market identical products.

Certain biases can exist in monopolistic competition. Not every desirable good, from the point of view of consumers, is necessarily produced. In particular, monopolistically competitive industries have a bias against products with a very high elasticity of demand because this makes maintaining the price premium of the brand difficult.

The price premium that a firm gets when it competes in this way is, in itself, part of the measure of the value of its brand. If you take the difference between the price of a branded good and a generic product, and multiply by quantity sold, you have a simple method for evaluating the value of a given brand.

Understanding differentiation: The median voter

Many people think that simply deciding to be different from your competitors is sufficient . . . wrong! In fact, there are boundaries to the amount of difference: too little and you end up with no brand advantage; too much and you're really not in the same market as competitors and the consumers.

In 1929, the great economist Harold Hotelling came up with an observation, now known as Hotelling's law — though it's less a law and more something observed in many markets. *Hotelling's law* says that eventually markets that have differentiated products tend toward a position with minimum differentiation. Products that are a little different adapt to each other and eventually converge on a space in the marketplace where neither is especially different from the other.

To see Hotelling's reasoning, consider a simple example. Fifth Avenue in Manhattan between 49th Street and 60th Street is a major thoroughfare that attracts many potential shoppers from across the globe: locating a retail shop there is desirable because of the big potential market. Assuming that you're the first person to think of this idea, where would you put the first retail store?

Well, if you assume that the throughput of people going up and down this stretch is roughly the same in both directions, the best place to put the first retail store is right in the center, between 55th and 54th. Exactly halfway (given a little geographical latitude for planning constraints) maximizes the share of the people walking from one end to the other.

But where would a rival firm position a competing retailer, the second in this road? The answer is directly opposite you. To see why, consider if the rival built it somewhere else, such as halfway between 60th and 55th. It would capture customers towards the one end, but you'd be getting 75 percent of customers because yours is closer to more of the strolling shoppers. Therefore, a rival will situate its offering as near to yours as possible — and successive openings will continue to open as near to this cluster until the center is "mined out." Then, and only then, will entrants open between the middle and end.

Also informally called the *median voter theorem,* this result is used to identify why political parties tend to cluster their offerings around the center of the political spectrum. The reasoning is much the same as with retailers. If the voter that matters is the swing voter, parties tend to cluster around those voters found in the center of the political spectrum.

Chapter 12

Appreciating the Fundamental Theorems of Welfare Economics

Some things just seem wrong, don't they? Hooters serving champagne, Adam Sandler starring in a serious film, Vladimir Putin singing "Blueberry Hill" . . . . Well, microeconomics has its own "just doesn't feel right" moment, too.

When studying any particular market, you want to identify where supply and demand are equal for that particular good. This is called a *partial equilibrium*. But what happens when you ask the question about *all* markets rather than just one? Can economists find a general result that holds so that all markets are in equilibrium together? Although it seems to jar with everyday experience and often just doesn't seem right, surprisingly such a result does exist — given special circumstances. Economists call it a *general equilibrium* and it's one of the most startling and least understood parts of microeconomics.

 A general equilibrium is needed so that many of the models that macroeconomists and policy makers use to describe an economy make sense. It can also, if used carefully, inform policy decisions about the best way to shape an economy.

Along the way to building a general equilibrium model, you arrive at two other results, which are quite startling and profound. These are called the *fundamental theorems of welfare economics*. Now, *welfare economics* is the part of microeconomics that looks at how people can be made better off and it is ultimately tied to the idea of productive efficiency or making things for the lowest possible cost. But how much of a good should be produced and who should get it? We also need a way of understanding how much of the various goods that people want should be produced and how to distribute these goods in a way to make people better off.

Economists in general believe that people in a society as a whole gain more utility and are therefore better off when some people gain utility and none lose, what economists call a *Pareto improvement*. Economists say that welfare is increased when a Pareto improvement happens. (The following section explains welfare and its multiple meanings.)

The two fundamental theorems developed in this chapter are important stages in learning about welfare. Without them, most modern economic modeling would be impossible. The mysteries are how to get to those results and how to interpret them. If you enjoy mysteries, join us as we show you what's really going on!

Getting the Welfare Back into Welfare Economics

Welfare is a difficult thing to define in general. Often people ask about other people's welfare, talk about a "welfare state," or discuss different types of "welfare benefit." This vagueness is unfortunate because welfare needs to be tied down a little more closely in order for us to put it to use in economics.

Economics is concerned with things that you can ultimately measure, so the meaning of welfare has to be related to measurable entities such as prices and quantities. These, in turn, are things that economists hope capture the concept of well-being or utility (see Chapters 2 and 4–6 for a fuller discussion of utility). When economists talk about *maximizing welfare,* they're relating the concept of utility to groups of economic decision-makers — whether producers, consumers, or society as a whole.

Economics uses more than one type of definition of welfare — depending on whether we're talking about a partial or a general equilibrium model:

> ✔ **Partial equilibrium model:** In this context, *welfare* is the sum of the areas bounded by the supply and demand curves in the market for that particular good — the consumer surplus and the producer surplus.

✔ **General equilibrium model:** In this context, *welfare* means social welfare, the aggregate level of utility across all individuals in the economy. Therefore, seeking the highest level of welfare means making the aggregate level of utility as high as possible.

Meeting two social welfare functions

Economists consider the issue of equity through the lens of a *social welfare function*. This function is often described by a curve drawn in a way to reflect different valuations among individuals in the society for different degrees of equity in distributing goods and services. These different degrees in turn tend to be drawn from the standpoints of ethical philosophies. Many views exist with interesting implications for how the social welfare function is drawn.

Figure 12-1 shows two different types of indifference curves corresponding to two different social welfare functions:

✔ **Utilitarian function:** Sums the level of utility for each individual, so for two individuals, Ted and Bill, it's entirely indifferent between Bill having 100 percent of the utility and Ted having 100 percent.

✔ **Rawlsian function:** Seeks to maximize the welfare of the least well-off individual, so it has only one unique sweet spot, at the corner of the L shape.

Figure 12-1:
Two social welfare functions.

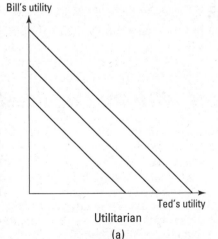

Utilitarian
(a)

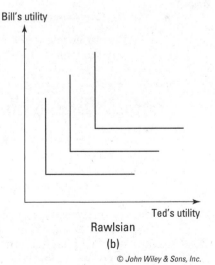

Rawlsian
(b)

Understanding Why Partial Equilibrium Isn't Enough

The equilibrium in any given market — for instance, for shoes or for fish — is a partial equilibrium, because it applies only to that one market. But economies are complex things, and if something affects one market, it affects many others as well through income or substitution effects. For example, a rise in the price of fish affects the amount of money that consumers spend on fish, which affects the equilibrium in related markets — perhaps consumers substitute other foods for fish. More generally, because everything competes at some level for a consumer's consumption spending, the rise of a price in one market affects the equilibrium in all other markets.

To describe an economy in all its complexity, you need to have a way of describing a general equilibrium where the interrelationships among all the markets are considered. The problem, of course, is that doing this for a complex economy could be a nightmare task. Imagine the effort necessary to describe every partial equilibrium and extend that analysis to every market in an economy.

Instead, economists use a framework to simplify the process of getting to a general equilibrium. The framework outlined in this chapter is about as simple a version as anyone can use — but don't worry, you can extend it later as you get more confident in using your knowledge of microeconomics.

You need two things for the framework:

- ✔ **An Edgeworth box:** A tool for depicting exchange between individuals
- ✔ **Pareto efficiency:** A concept for categorizing which equilibrium results are efficient

Modeling exchange with an Edgeworth box

In the constrained optimization model (see Chapter 6), we depict levels of utility based on the preferences of one person for two goods. But now our task is to look at exchange, so we need two people making choices (including whether to exchange with each other) based on their preferences.

Microeconomics sets up this scenario by using the *Edgeworth box* (see Figure 12-2 for a generally applicable example), which allows us to depict the utility of two people on the same diagram. This generalized Edgeworth box has two origin points, each associated with an allocation in which one person gets zero utility and the other person gets his highest possible utility. At the bottom left corner is the origin for the first person (here Wesley) and at the top right the origin for the second (Buttercup). For this example, we imagine that the two goods are fish and shoes.

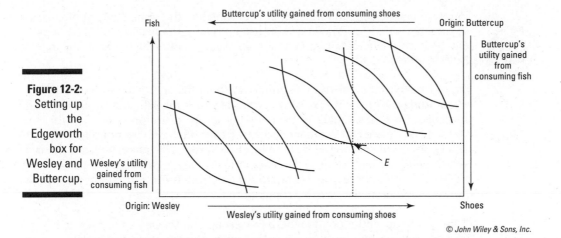

Figure 12-2:
Setting up the Edgeworth box for Wesley and Buttercup.

© *John Wiley & Sons, Inc.*

Each participant has well-behaved preferences, so you can depict their preferences with indifference curves (as described in Chapters 4–6). You get a series of indifference curves going away from the origin in both directions. Point *E* in Figure 12-2 is special: It specifies an initial endowment of fish and shoes for both Wesley and Buttercup so that:

- ✔ E_W^F is Wesley's endowment of fish.
- ✔ E_B^F is Buttercup's endowment of fish.
- ✔ E_W^S is Wesley's endowment of shoes.
- ✔ E_B^S is Buttercup's endowment of shoes.

Investigating Pareto efficiency

Having set up the initial endowment in the preceding section, you now want to know whether everyone is happy with it, which means using the concept of Pareto efficiency.

Pareto efficiency is a specialized version of efficiency for discussing distributions of things — income, resources, goods, or wealth — between people. A distribution is Pareto efficient if the following aspects apply:

- ✔ You can't make all people better off.
- ✔ You can only make one person better off if you make at least one other person worse off.
- ✔ No potential gains can be made from trading.

Pareto efficiency doesn't mean that everyone has the same amount of goods or income. A distribution where Buttercup has all the fish and all the shoes can be Pareto efficient, if you can't make Wesley better off without making Buttercup worse off.

So, to return to the question, is point *E* Pareto efficient? The answer is a resounding no. At point *E* Wesley can trade shoes for fish, and Buttercup can trade fish for shoes, and both be made better off. Therefore, points in the "lens" above *E* are all Pareto superior to *E* (although they're not all Pareto efficient — some of the points are closer to Pareto efficiency, without themselves being efficient points). For the points to be Pareto efficient, they must be points where there are no potential gains from trading. This occurs where the two indifference curves are tangent to each other.

Connecting up all the points where Buttercup and Wesley's indifference curves are tangent gives you a line that goes through every Pareto optimal point in the box. This is called a *contract curve* (see Figure 12-3). You know by looking at the contract curve whether an allocation of the goods between the two individuals is efficient. If the point is not on the curve, you could make both parties better off by moving to an allocation on the curve.

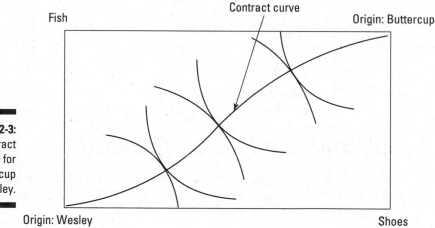

Figure 12-3:
Contract curve for Buttercup and Wesley.

Fish

Contract curve

Origin: Buttercup

Origin: Wesley

Shoes

© *John Wiley & Sons, Inc.*

Trading Your Way to Efficiency with Two Fundamental Theorems

Given the setup in the preceding section, we now need to investigate how you go from a Pareto inferior allocation of endowments to a final efficient distribution. At the moment you have an initial endowment, *E*, which isn't on the contract curve, so the potential exists to get to a better — Pareto optimal — distribution on the contract curve. This section describes how.

Bidding for the general equilibrium

The 19th century French economist Léon Walras examined this situation with a thought experiment, in which an auctioneer is calling out prices for every possible good in an economy. Walras wants two things to happen: prices are quoted in each market, and there is no excess supply or excess demand in any market. The trades that take place at the prices that satisfy that condition will get you to an allocation on the contract curve for that economy.

The auctioneer can, in theory, keep calling out prices until these two conditions are met. Seeing how this works isn't always obvious. Let's look at an example.

You need two earlier results:

- ✔ At any point on a contract curve, Wesley and Buttercup's indifference curves are tangent. That means that the marginal rate of substitution (MRS — check out Chapter 2 for details) of fishes for shoes must be the same for both.

- ✔ At any optimum position for any one consumer, the MRS must equal the price ratio between the two goods (check out Chapter 6 for details).

Calling out successive prices for fish and shoes, a process economists call *tâttonement* (after all, Walras was French — it means "groping" or "trial and error"), the auctioneer eventually finds an equilibrium that satisfies Wesley and Buttercup. At this price, they trade some of their endowments of fish for shoes, or vice versa, until they arrive at the point where their MRS for fish and shoes are equal to the price ratio. This point is the *general equilibrium* for this — very simple — economy.

A general equilibrium model implies one simple result: All markets can't be in excess demand or excess supply simultaneously. If an excess supply of fish exists in this model, you must also see excess demand for shoes — otherwise both markets would clear. Even more startlingly, if one of the markets in this two-good model is in equilibrium, then the second must also be — if the market for fish clears, then the market for shoes must also clear. This result is known in economics as *Walras's law,* illustrated in Figure 12-4. Here, *E* represents an initial, nonoptimal endowment. In this scenario, the process of tâtonnement will lead to an optimal point where Wesley and Buttercup's indifference curves are tangent to each other and to the line measuring the final price ratio of the two goods.

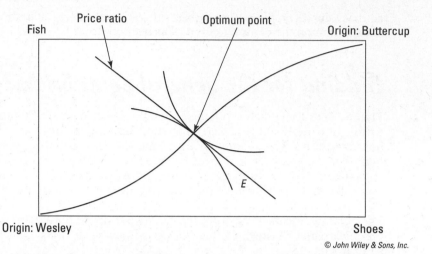

Figure 12-4:
The optimum arrived at by the Walrasian auction.

Grasping for efficiency: How markets set prices through tattonment

The auctioneer is a nice imaginary device, but he doesn't exist in reality, so Walras went further with his analysis.

Markets have a tendency to lead to prices consistent with people's preferences all by themselves. Walras named this process *tâttonement* to indicate that markets are consistently equilibrium-seeking — for instance, when there is excess demand, prices rise until enough buyers drop out of the market and the market clears. This happens through participants' actions without any form of coordination at all, simply by economic agents continually responding to excess demand or supply in any of the individual markets within the whole economy.

Nobody "knows" what that equilibrium might be, but markets find it by continually adjusting. That's tâttonement, folks.

The first fundamental theorem: A free market is efficient

Walras's logic leads to the *first fundamental theorem of welfare economics:* A free market left to itself ultimately gives you a Pareto efficient outcome. (Flip to the earlier section "Getting the Welfare Back into Welfare Economics" for more on welfare economics.) Another way of saying this is that eventually, through tattonment, the free market arrives at a condition where no more gains to trade are available. In this case, all consumers have exchanged goods with each other to arrive at a position where no one wants to move any further or exchange any more.

However, and this is a huge *however,* the market only does so if four fundamental assumptions are met:

- ✔ **No externalities:** No costs fall on parties other than those engaged in exchanging. This is probably not true in reality where many trades involve an external cost falling on another party. For example, when paper mills produce and trade paper, there are pollution costs, which are borne by those who live near the mill.

- ✔ **Perfect competition in each market:** Very few markets meet this condition in reality. For perfect competition to hold, each producer must be small in terms of its market share and not able through its trading decisions to influence price. Consumers must be perfectly informed about all products and their prices.

- ✔ **No transactions costs:** There are often costs associated with market transactions, such as the time it takes to find a seller or buyer to trade with. Transactions costs can be significant enough to spur the development of whole industries — for instance, comparison search engines on the Internet can reduce the transactions costs associated with buying insurance or finding a hotel room.

- ✔ **Full information:** Consumers must be perfectly informed about all products — their qualities and their prices. Firms must be able to know and observe the productivity of their workers. Chapter 15 is devoted to dealing with cases where people don't have full information, so you can probably guess that assuming that they do is not a defensible assumption about reality.

Although this first theorem is extremely important for our understanding of markets and social welfare, you can see that doesn't easily apply to the real world. Sometimes people — often policy wonks — try to build the case for "free markets" on the basis of this theorem. If you want to make a case for free markets, that's fine, but remember the first fundamental theorem doesn't make that case for you.

But what the first theorem of welfare economics *does* do is very interesting. It says that a market is continually trying to get the best outcome — trying in reality, succeeding in textbooks — and is driven by the following three conditions defining equilibrium:

- ✔ No one can be worse off than her initial endowment (otherwise she'd simply refuse to trade).

- ✔ No one can be made better off without someone else being worse off — otherwise gains could be made by trading their way to equilibrium, which they can't.

- ✔ No overall excess demand or supply can exist.

If you make these three things hold and solve for the allocation you would, given the four assumptions mentioned earlier, achieve a Pareto efficient outcome through the market alone. That's enough to ask the question of whether someone planning could *necessarily* do any better. The answer is quite probably not, because the market will continually be processing more information about people's desires, wants, and needs than someone trying to centrally plan an economy, even given that you may not have a perfect economy that satisfies our four assumptions.

The second fundamental theorem: Any efficient outcome will do

From Walras's argument, you can derive the *second fundamental theorem:* Given well-behaved preferences, any Pareto efficient outcome is also a market equilibrium.

To see why, start with the first theorem from the preceding section: remembering that a Pareto efficient outcome doesn't mean an equal one; Buttercup getting all of both goods is still Pareto efficient. Now, all outcomes that are market equilibria must be on the contract curve, because in a market equilibrium, each person's MRS is equal to the same price ratio and hence their indifference curves are tangent to each other. But does that mean that all points on the contract curve could be market equilibria? The answer is that they must be. Here's why:

✔ Along the contract curve, every point is a tangent between two indifference curves:

  • The tangency point corresponds to the price ratio.

  • The price ratio can exist and coordinate trades as long as preferences are well behaved, which means that indifference curves are bow shaped and do not cross.

✔ That price ratio is therefore the ratio of prices that must support a Pareto efficient equilibrium.

Putting the two theorems together: Equity and efficiency trade-offs

Put simply, the first fundamental theorem says that a free market will lead to an outcome that is efficient and the overall size of the pie to be traded will be as big as possible — if it weren't, it couldn't be Pareto efficient because by making the pie bigger you could make both parties better off without making one party worse off. The second theorem says that if you have a Pareto efficient outcome, it can be sustained by a market equilibrium. The two theorems separate out the question of efficiency (the first) from the question of distribution (the second).

This result is another startling point, in itself. In essence, the second theorem tells us that you can achieve any distribution you desire through a market system, as long as the distribution is Pareto efficient. The first theorem tells us that the market will lead to an efficient allocation, but not necessarily the one that corresponds to the desired distribution. Market mechanisms are neutral with regard to distributions, so in principle you can have any distribution you like or consider fair.

The result comes with some pretty big caveats, though. The most important is that you're better off trying to achieve an equitable distribution — in our example, the distribution is in terms of fish and shoes — by lump sum redistribution than by doing anything that distorts or interferes with the market-determined ratio of prices. The reason is that if prices are competitively set, every buyer consumes up to the point where the price ratio is a measure of the marginal benefit to that consumer. If you change the ratio of prices, you change the decisions of the consumer, and you may not get to a Pareto efficient outcome at all.

Instead, if a government wants to make some people better off, it would be better taxing or taking from the endowment of one person and giving it to the other. That at least would be Pareto optimal and leave the important allocative role of prices alone.

In practice, of course, things are rarely as simple as this intuition supposes. Take a tax on someone's labor, for example. A person's endowment of labor is actually the total amount of labor that she *might have* provided, not the total amount that she *does* provide. You can know the latter — it's how income taxes work — but can never know the former.

In reality, taxes are set for many reasons, from the noble to the downright awful. At some level, they're all fudges and compromises, sometimes because you can't work out the right thing to tax and sometimes because taxing the right things is unpalatable to an electorate.

Understanding why markets tend toward one price

Economists talk about the implications of a general equilibrium framework in terms of welfare. And you don't need to go very far before you can see some interesting real-world applications. One is the observation that the price of a good in any one market tends to be the same across all markets for that good. You can use the general equilibrium framework to get into the logic of why this must be the case.

This is known as the *law of one price,* and interestingly (unlike much of the general equilibrium framework), you can test it in practice. Suppose you grow apples in Massachusetts and sell them in Massachusetts and New York. If the law of one price is true, the price of an apple in New York can be no higher than the price in Massachusetts plus the cost of transporting those delicious apples to New York. If the prices in New York were higher, someone could make money by buying apples in Massachusetts and driving them up to Albany to sell them.

This is called *arbitrage:* buying something at a lower price in one market and selling it for a higher price in another market. Opportunities for arbitrage are the drivers of the law of one price. If arbitrage can take place, entrepreneurs will engage in it, and the supply of apples in the more expensive market will increase, lowering the price, leading eventually to the two markets being in equilibrium with each other. The law of one price rules!

Of course, in certain circumstances arbitrage may not be possible, for example, if people can't get ahold of information about the prices or transactions costs are involved. In those cases, the law of one price may fail to hold.

In a remarkable study, economist Robert Jensen looked at the availability of information in the market for fish in Kerala, a coastal state in southwest India. He found that the law of one price only started to hold after 1997. What changed to allow this to happen? The introduction of mobile phones meant that information about prices in all the local markets became much more available. As a result, the arbitrage process kicked in, and eventually all markets in the area converged on one price for each type of fish. When convergence between these markets occurred, no further arbitrage opportunities were possible, and arbitrage stopped working — people could no longer buy in a cheaper market and sell in a more expensive one.

Chapter 13

The Monopoly Game

*Y*ou can relax — despite its title, this chapter has nothing to do with the board game Monopoly and so you don't have to pick whether to be the dog or the car or whatever. You don't even have to explain why you didn't choose the iron (no one ever does). You may, however, come away with some better ideas for how to win the game, if you ever find yourself playing it.

The kind of monopoly we're interested in is the opposite of a competitive market (which contains many firms, none of whom has a significant market share): In a *monopoly,* one firm supplies the entire market. As you can imagine, when the production of a good is under monopoly control, there are plenty of consequences, most of which make economists quake in their boots.

In this chapter, we show you that a monopolist behaves differently from a firm in a competitive market and consumers lose out as a result. We also have a word or two about some of the other consequences of monopolies and how to deal with them in the real world. Plus, we describe the case of when a natural monopoly arises.

This chapter discusses a monopoly that is 100 percent a monopoly, the type of monopoly that economists use to compare to perfect competition. When you hear about the Department of Justice or the Federal Trade Commission investigating a monopoly, they're almost certainly not dealing with a monopoly as we describe here, but with what economists call *market dominance.* For example, a dominant firm may have only 40 percent of a given market, while each competitor has at most 5 percent. Although the media often refer to this situation as a monopoly, the monopoly of this chapter has 100 percent of the market all to itself.

But forgive us for, ahem, monopolizing your attention. We now get right into monopolies.

Entering the World of the Monopoly

For a producer, a monopoly is a good thing to have. The absence of competition means you can make long-run profits — which would get competed away in a markets that had competition. If you supply the entire market, you can raise price higher than a competitive firm would without fear of being undercut. You may also get lazy and stop innovating when you're not under any threat of an innovative competitor making a better product.

But consumers keenly feel the downsides of monopoly: They have to pay a higher price for goods, and society as a whole loses welfare because a monopoly doesn't have to be productively efficient. That's a problem and it's one reason why economists are keen to recommend that markets be made competitive.

When you understand why profits are zero, and consumers get all the surplus in perfect competition (see Chapter 10), you will also see how monopolies do the opposite. Monopolies are better for the producer at the expense of the consumer and society as a whole.

Monopoly and competitive markets: The case of the missing supply curve

In a competitive market, you use the structure of the supply and demand model in Chapter 9 to investigate the way prices, quantities, and equilibrium change in a given market. When you have perfect competition, you focus on the marginal company — as in Chapter 10 — because it helps to see how prices affect each firm's decision and then you aggregate up to the industry level. In contrast, a monopoly firm supplies the whole market, and that means you want to look at its decisions in a slightly different way.

One thing that's different is that you aren't looking at the aggregate of many firms' decisions: You're looking at just one firm. Therefore, you have to analyze how the monopoly supplies the market in a slightly different way. This section takes you through that process.

Here's a conundrum for you: *Equilibrium* is usually identified as the point where demand and supply curves cross (as discussed in Chapter 9). But if you look at Figure 13-1, which describes the same equilibrium features in a monopoly, you can see that the supply curve has disappeared. We deal with this situation now.

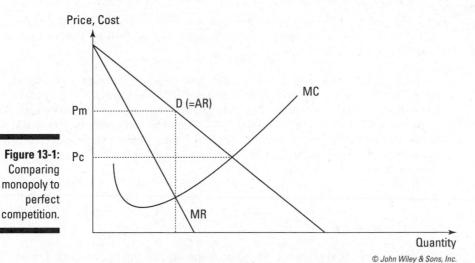

Price, Cost

Pm

Pc

D (=AR)

MC

MR

Quantity

Figure 13-1:
Comparing
monopoly to
perfect
competition.

P_c = Marginal cost price in a perfectly competitive industry, P_m = Monopoly price, D (=AR) = Demand (= Average revenue), MC = Marginal cost, MR = Marginal revenue. MR= MC determines monopoly output.

The supply curve for a "normal" (that is, not monopolized) market comes from adding up the marginal costs of producing outputs for each of the individual firms in the market at each quantity of output.

But for a monopoly, only one firm is supplying the market, so the supply curve for that market is the same as the marginal cost curve of the monopoly. Therefore, instead of looking at the equilibrium supply and demand for the market, you can just look at the cost of supplying the market for the one firm. In a monopoly market, there is no need to construct a supply curve.

Thinking like a monopolist: "It's mine . . . all mine! Bwa-ha-ha!"

We now think about what the monopolist is doing and how this mindset compares to a company in a competitive market. Again, economists are focusing on decisions of the firm — what it will want to produce at what price and how much it will make for doing it. Let's go through an example now.

Looking at a monopoly model

To start, we assume that the monopolist, just like all the firms in this book, wants to maximize profits. With that in mind, let's identify the profit-maximizing equilibrium for the monopoly. Figure 13-1 shows average and marginal cost curves looking more or less the way they do for a competitive firm (we define these curves in Chapter 7).

But what's that? The demand (or average revenue, AR) curve and the marginal revenue (MR) curve are no longer identical — something that has some important implications.

The monopolist is the only firm supplying this good, so the market demand curve (derived by adding up all the consumer demand curves) is the same as the firm's demand curve. So, the demand or average revenue curve for the monopolist is downward sloping. How much this firm sells on the market affects market price. That's of course not true for a perfectly competitive firm whose output choice does not affect market. This demand (or AR) curve can be expressed by the following formula:

$$AR = 10 - 2Q$$

where Q is quantity.

This means that as Q goes up, AR goes down, and so the curve slopes downwards as we would expect normal market demand curves do.

Now multiply both sides of the equation by Q to turn it into total revenues (TR):

$$TR = 10Q - 2Q^2$$

Now the *marginal revenue curve,* the contribution made by selling each additional unit, is going to be the change in TR as quantity, Q, changes. In other words, marginal revenue (MR) is the slope of the total revenue (TR) curve.

You can find the slope in a lot of ways. Probably the easiest is to work it out on a diagram, but we're going to use a little bit of calculus here and find the slope of TR by *differentiating it* with respect to Q:

$$MR = 10 - 4Q$$

Look at the resulting equation. The 10 (the *intercept* — the place where it crosses the axis) is the same on both the AR and MR equations, telling you that it crosses the vertical axis at the same place.

But the important difference is when you look at the change in MR and AR when Q changes: This is captured by the bit after the minus sign. The minus sign indicates that both curves slope downwards, but the *coefficient* in this case says that the marginal revenue curve slopes down twice as fast as the average revenue or demand curve. At this point, you may ask what does all this have to do with the price of beans? Well, provided the beans are supplied by a monopoly, quite a bit.

Remember the profit-maximizing condition: MC = MR. Here, the evil bean monopolies (and the evil bean counters who presumably work out how many beans they should produce) set their output to maximize profits and then read off the demand curve the price (which, remember, equals average revenue) that the beans command in the marketplace. Looking at Figure 13-1, you can see the big difference between the marginal cost price (P_c) that you'd get in a perfectly competitive industry and the monopoly price (P_m) that you see here. So, a profit-maximizing monopoly supplies less output at a higher price.

Using quantity over price

You may want to call shenanigans on the way we look at this issue; after all, we do everything in terms of *quantity* and only mention *price* right at the very end. Well, we do so for a very sensible reason.

Even the most evil monopolists in the world can't choose the quantity they make *and* the price the market is willing to pay for it. They have to choose one or the other, as follows:

- ✔ Set the price and allow the market (that is, consumers) to decide what quantity will be bought.
- ✔ Set the quantity and allow the market to determine the price consumers will pay for it — the price that clears the market.

Unless a monopolist can force price and quantity at the point of a gun, which in a marketplace they generally can't, it must choose to work with either price or quantity, not both. In this case, we prefer to model monopolists as quantity setters to make comparisons across different types of market, so that we can use the same type of calculations to compare them.

Considering profits

So, the evil bean monopoly (picture a baked bean with a dismissive smirk on its face) is making the same type of decision but getting a higher price for its beans. Now, we look at its profits.

Again, remember that a firm in perfect competition makes in the long run economic profits of zero, and so the *marginal* firm is *indifferent* between being in the market and being out of it.

A monopoly, though, is alone in the market and stays a monopolist as long as there are *barriers to entry*. This means that if you're making profits in that industry, you no longer face the threat of a new competitor coming in and competing away those profits. Figure 13-2 illustrates the profits a monopoly makes when it behaves rationally.

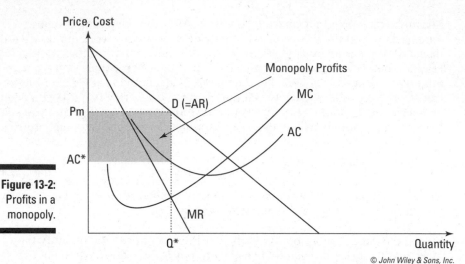

Figure 13-2:
Profits in a
monopoly.

© John Wiley & Sons, Inc.

P_m = Monopoly price, O = Average cost at monopoly output, D (= AR) = Demand (= Average revenue),
MC = Marginal cost, MR = Marginal revenue, Q = Quantity, AC = average cost.

Remember profit are equal to total revenue less total cost.

$$Profit = total\ revenue - total\ cost$$

And total revenue equals price multiplied by quantity. That means that we can rejig our equation a little by taking the quantity out of it. Total revenue divided by quantity is just price, and total costs divided by quantity are therefore average costs. So, to go through the stages:

$$Profit = (price \times quantity) - total\ cost$$

Factor the terms on the right by quantity so that you can write Q out of the brackets:

$$Profit = Quantity(price - average\ cost)$$

If you take the *markup* on the right-hand side (price – average cost) and multiply it by quantity, you get the total level of profit, above zero, made by the monopoly.

Look at Figure 13-2 again. The area between AC*, Pm, Q*, and the demand curve gives the profits made by the monopoly.

Stretching a point: Elastic demand

We want to deal with one final implication of the model of a monopolist's profit-maximizing choices here.

Monopolists produce only where the demand curve is *elastic* (see Chapter 9 for more on the elasticity of demand). The demand curve is inelastic when the elasticity of demand is between 0 and 1. On the inelastic part of its demand curve, the monopolist has an incentive to raise price.

To see why, consider quickly the relationship between marginal revenue and demand (discussed in the earlier section "Thinking like a monopolist: It's mine . . . all mine! Bwa-ha-ha!"). The marginal revenue curve crosses the quantity axis at exactly halfway down the demand curve.

At the point where demand is exactly *unit elastic,* that is, where the marginal revenue is zero, any change in price leads to an exactly counterbalancing effect on quantity demanded. Below this point, demand is inelastic, and marginal revenue is less than zero, and so at no point where demand is inelastic can marginal revenue equal marginal cost. The fact to remember is that the monopoly only ever produces where demand is elastic.

In the messy world of reality, monopoly is constrained by antitrust laws enforced by the Department of Justice and/or the Federal Trade Commission. The law doesn't deal with the consequences of pure monopoly as described in the textbooks, but with market dominance. The courts are treating almost no cases of a monopoly as we describe it in this chapter.

We say a little more about how this works in the later section "Tackling Monopoly in the Real World," but for the moment, just bear in mind that *legal monopoly* (that is, the way in which the legal system defines a monopoly) and *economic monopoly* (what we talk about in this chapter) are related but distinct concepts.

Counting the Costs of Monopolies

In any particular market, welfare can be measured by the sum of producer and consumer surplus — see Chapter 9 for the definitions and an example of how this works. A monopoly is no exception.

What is important about a monopoly is that it causes a welfare loss to society as a whole, because it produces a lower quantity at a higher price. The monopolist does this to gain relatively more of the potential surplus that in a perfectly competitive market would have gone to consumers. If a monopoly could charge different prices to each consumer, it would do so and try and gain even more surplus at the expense of consumers. This is called *price discrimination*, and being able to price discriminate across consumers will reduce what we call the *deadweight loss of surplus.*

The next section shows you what the deadweight loss is and three ways monopolies can get some of it back.

Carrying a deadweight

One of the costs of monopoly is the deadweight loss that results from monopolists producing less output compared to competitive firms.

In Figure 13-3, we make a little comparison between the two cases.

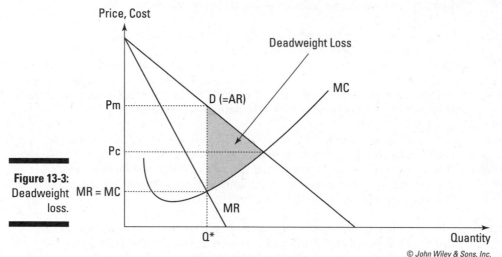

Figure 13-3:
Deadweight
loss.

© John Wiley & Sons, Inc.

P_c = Marginal cost price in a perfectly competitive industry, P_m = Monopoly price, D (= AR) = Demand
(= Average revenue), MC = Marginal cost, MR = Marginal revenue, Q = Quantity.

Worrying about the deadweight loss

In a competitive market, equilibrium is achieved where demand and supply cross. Because the supply curve is the sum of marginal cost curves, you know that the market price is equal to the marginal cost of output at each firm. Fine!

But look at the evil bean monopoly mentioned earlier and see the difference. The bean monopoly produces an output level where MC = MR, which is less than in a competitive marketplace, which would produce up to the point where the marginal cost curve crosses the demand curve, where P = MC.

In Figure 13-3, the area bounded by P_m and MR=MC (on the vertical axis) and the place where the marginal cost curve crosses the demand curve represents losses in *welfare* (that is, the sum of consumer and producer surpluses — as in Chapter 9) that are not realized in the economy due to the monopolist producing less output. Economists call this the deadweight loss caused by monopoly. Note that it consists of lost *consumer surplus* and lost *producer surplus*.

For economists, this deadweight loss is a troubling issue. They aim to see more produced for less resources overall, which happens in competitive markets. Economists can accept competition not being perfect, but when the monopoly makes higher profits *and* everyone loses out as a result, they start to get a little nervous. As a result, pretty much every economist since the days of Adam Smith has tried to find ways of preventing the monopoly situation from arising.

Using three degrees of price discrimination

In competitive markets, firms sell at the same price — any attempt to raise price or charge consumers different prices is undermined by arbitrage. This restriction doesn't hold for a monopolist, though. A monopolist can use three cunning ruses to grab some of the potential surplus in the market.

These methods, collectively known as *price discrimination,* all have the end result of allowing a monopolist (or, in the real world, a firm with a significantly dominant position) to appropriate more surplus from consumers. The methods differ as to how many different prices a monopolist is able to charge for the same good, and so economists distinguish them by *degrees,* just like a prosecutor distinguishes crimes by seriousness in an episode of *Law and Order.*

We start at the top with the case when a monopolist is able to charge every consumer a unique price for its product.

First degree (or perfect) price discrimination

In this case, the evil bean (monopoly) company sells the same product (standard beans) at a different price to each consumer, such that each bean is sold to that consumer who values that bean most.

Figure 13-4 illustrates this scenario using a greatly simplified version of the earlier diagram (Figure 13-3). Here, the monopolist charges any consumer at the maximum price that they're willing to pay for that good. As a result, the monopolist wants to sell to consumers as long as the price a consumer is willing to pay for that unit is greater than the marginal cost of that unit. The monopolist will produce up to where P = MC and extract every penny of consumer surplus. This means the consumer surplus that was lost when it charges a single price is now regained and goes to the monopolist. This eliminates the deadweight loss; but the real kicker is that all the welfare goes to the monopolist as producer surplus.

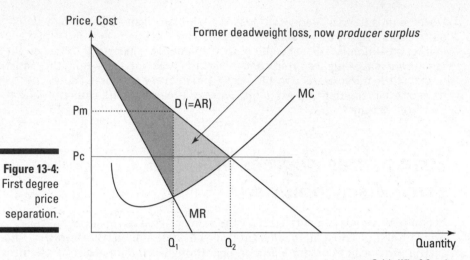

Price, Cost

Former deadweight loss, now *producer surplus*

D (=AR)

MC

Pm

Pc

MR

Q_1 Q_2 Quantity

© John Wiley & Sons, Inc.

*D (= AR) = Demand (= Average revenue), MC = Marginal cost, P_c = Marginal cost,
P_m = Monopoly price, MR = Marginal revenue.*

Figure 13-4:
First degree
price
separation.

First degree price discrimination was considered to be exceptional or very rare indeed, to the extent that it only existed in textbooks, largely because when you think about the practicalities of charging everybody different prices you realize how difficult it would be. You would have to identify "who is who" on the demand curve and prevent arbitrage among consumers who could buy at a low price and resell at a higher price.

These challenges are less daunting with the advent of online transactions, big data, and auction-style markets. Now first degree price discrimination is much simpler. Firms can now track customers and learn a lot about their willingness to pay — and in the case of services like airlines, you can easily prevent resale of the ticket.

Just because charging everybody different prices may be technically possible, please don't get the idea that it's always feasible in practice. Amazon, among other companies, has fallen afoul of customer complaints when customers noticed different prices being quoted to different customers and judged this to be an unfair practice.

Second degree price discrimination: Non-linear pricing

In second degree price discrimination, the price per unit paid by a consumer depends upon how much of the good (how many beans) the consumer buys.

Bulk discounts are an example. Here, the general principle is that the largest purchaser pays a lower per unit price because he buys a large quantity, whereas a consumer who buys a small quantity is charged a higher per unit price. The packaging of the goods makes it difficult for arbitrage — that is, difficult for the large purchaser to unbundle the package and resell it in smaller packages at a profit. Under second degree price discrimination, if two different consumers buy the same amount of the good, they pay the same amount. Differential pricing is based on quantity purchased by the consumer.

In contrast to first degree price discrimination, second degree price discrimination is relatively commonplace. Think for a moment about the market for soft drinks, typically sold by the wholesaler in cases of 24 cans. Suppose you operate a corner shop and sell, say, 5 cases a week, and charge a retail price of $1 per can. The wholesaler charges you $12 a case, making the cost to you equal to 50 cents per can. But now suppose the new supermarket around the corner is one branch of a large chain ordering 5,000 cases a week, and as a result the wholesaler is willing to charge only $5 a case. The cost to the supermarket of a can of soda is less than half yours. The supermarket can now undercut you while still making more money per can.

Second degree price discrimination in the form of bulk discounts like this is often why, in order to survive competition from the big box stores, small specialty stores must sell either different kinds of goods or the same goods at different times and places.

Third degree price discrimination: The student discount

In third degree price discrimination the monopolist segments consumers into different groups, and while consumers in one group pay the same price as each other, the individual groups pay different prices from each other.

To dig a bit deeper, the monopolist charges a higher price to the group with the less elastic demand (who reveal themselves as willing to pay a little bit more). Our example here comes from our experience with students, who often tell us that they don't have much money. Not having resources makes them a little more willing to shop around for better prices, which leads us to suspect that their demand is more elastic.

A monopolist supplier can therefore offer a lower price to students, who need to show their student ID when making the purchase, and a higher price to its other customers. Movie theaters and entertainment venues routinely do this. Similar cases exist with senior bus passes, or with mobile network services where the business market has a less elastic demand and correspondingly is charged more for services.

Tweaking the product

The real world has many examples of firms with some degree of market power doing something that isn't exactly covered by the three cases in the preceding section but is related to them. These firms offer fundamentally the same product in different versions with different features enabled in the higher price version — in one case, a printer manufacturer offered exactly the same product but with a cable cut in the cheaper version, causing the higher value features to be disabled!

This practice is common in the software industry, called *versioning,* where you often find the more expensive product labeled "Pro" even when it's not particularly sold to professional markets.

Playing with time and space

Another form of third degree price discrimination is to segment consumers in different geographic markets and sell the same product at different prices in different areas, capturing more of the value from the inelastic market.

A variant of this practice is common in the film and video entertainment industry, where a film is released in different *windows*. In the first window — or exhibition — the film is delivered to cinemas where those people who are most willing to pay go and see it earlier. Those who don't want to take the distributor up on the offer have the option of waiting for the DVD window, where they can view the same film at a lower cost per view. At the ultimate end of the chain is exhibition via TV where people can eventually view the same film for nothing. In this case, the distributor passes through each window, selling the product for a slightly lower price each time until the market is fully served.

This strategy, often known as *cream skimming,* also exists in the video game consoles market, where a high launch price is set and slowly allowed to fall over the lifetime of the console.

Tackling Monopolies in the Real World

In a pure monopoly, and compared to a competitive firm, the quantity a monopoly supplies is lower and the price higher (see the preceding section for details). If the monopoly charges only one price, the monopoly results in a deadweight loss, because producer and consumer surplus are lost.

But if by charging different prices to each consumer or group of consumers, the monopolist supplies more output, this mitigates against the efficiency loss. However, the surplus typically goes to the monopolist in terms of higher profits. In addition, if barriers to enter the industry are high, monopolies are also likely to be less innovative because they aren't subject to pressure from competitors.

Economists consider all these features of monopoly to be undesirable. The question is what to do about them.

Appreciating a complex problem

Tackling monopolies is a little tricky, because the solution depends crucially on how a monopoly comes about.

Nowhere in U.S. antitrust law is having a monopoly considered to be against the law. Although this seems counterintuitive, you can see why when you consider that in certain situations it may be the forces of competition that allow one firm to emerge much bigger than all its competitors.

For instance, Google search gets better the more people use it, because using it gives Google more data about what people search for and how, and this helps Google refine their algorithm. More users beget more users, leading to a situation where Google is the dominant search engine in the market.

Another type of legal monopoly is when intellectual property, such as patents or copyrights, have been granted. In this case, a person or firm is permitted to have a temporary monopoly in order to give people an incentive to do expensive research and development.

Understanding the legal response

The U.S. courts have interpreted antitrust law to mean that monopoly is not unlawful *per se,* but is unlawful if acquired through prohibited conduct that is seen as anticompetitive. So, a firm simply operating more efficiently than everyone else and therefore getting bigger than all its rivals is fine. But when in a dominant position, the firm can't engage in behavior that disadvantages other smaller rivals from competing. These behaviors include the following:

- ✔ **Full line forcing:** The firm, typically a manufacturer, is not permitted to require a dealer of one of its products to stock its whole line of products with a minimum inventory requirement that effectively blocks or forecloses other competitors from selling through the dealer.

✔ **Pricing below cost:** If a firm has a dominant position, then it may be able to cut its prices below cost in the short run in order to drive a rival out of the market (with, naturally, the intention of raising prices after it has removed the rival). This action is called *predatory pricing* and is illegal, although it is often difficult to prove in practice.

✔ **Making restrictive or exclusive agreements:** For example, favoring some purchasers over others. For example, if you own a port, you aren't allowed to charge your own boats less to use it than those of rivals. This example is highly relevant to Internet providers such as Comcast and content providers such as NBC — which is owned by Comcast.

The intention isn't to prevent monopoly, but to prevent monopolizing markets. In other words, the monopoly can exist but it can't go around throwing its monopoly weight around.

Taking companies to court

De minimis non curat lex means "The law does not concern itself with the trivial." This is a fundamental principle applicable to the enforcement of antitrust laws. Because antitrust investigations into firm conduct can be long running and expensive, good policy makers want to investigate the evidence carefully before charging a company with anti-competitive behavior in violation of antitrust law. The case of Standard Oil v. U.S. is one of the most important ones in antitrust case law. In 1909, the U.S. Department of Justice sued Standard Oil under federal antitrust law, the Sherman Antitrust Act of 1890, for exercising monopoly power through unfair practices against competitors, including predatory pricing, exclusive contracting, and preferential pricing practices. The case, resolved in 1911, led to the breakup of this highly profitable corporation into 34 separate, competing companies. The Supreme Court's decision to apply and uphold the Sherman Act created a key precedent in American case law. Moreover, the Standard Oil case was an impetus for the creation of the Clayton Anti-Trust Act, which was seen by many as a vast improvement and refinement of U.S. antitrust law. (The Clayton Act is ten times larger than the Sherman Act in length.)

Another famous case includes the eventual breakup of AT&T. Challenged as a monopoly through the years by potential entrants into the telecommunications industry, AT&T was long seen, however, as a "natural monopoly" by the U.S. government. Indeed, a monopoly can quite happily exist when it is considered a natural monopoly.

"You Make Me Feel Like a Natural Monopoly"

Okay, we admit that this heading's phrasing scans much better with Carole King and Gerry Goffin's original words, but in this section we describe how a monopoly can come about simply because it is efficient to have only one company serve a market. Water and wastewater networks and sewage treatment plants are natural monopolies and as a result run as public utilities typically owned by local government. Few persuasive arguments can be made that a community would be better off if government broke it up.

The key to understanding this point is to consider the *long run average costs* (LRAC) of the monopoly and, in particular, the minimum point of LRAC, referred to as the *minimum efficient scale* (or MES). Two cases apply here, depending on whether the MES is small relative to the total size of the market or close to it. Figure 13-5 shows both scenarios.

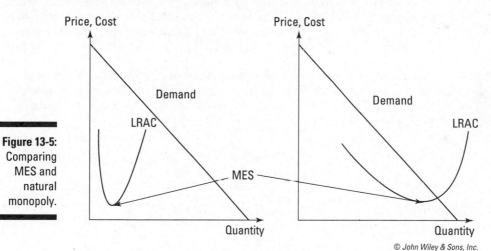

Figure 13-5: Comparing MES and natural monopoly.

© John Wiley & Sons, Inc.

LRAC = Long run average cost. (a) MES small fraction of total demand, market competitively supplied, (b) MES close to market demand, natural monopoly.

When the MES of the firm serving that market is small, firms can operate at their most efficient scale when holding only a small fraction of the market. Therefore you're likely to see the market as being competitively supplied. If, however, MES is very close to or even greater than the total demand in that market, that market is only ever likely to be supplied by one firm.

The question for economists is what to do about this situation, given that they don't like monopolies very much. One option for dealing with natural monopoly, where you don't expect much benefit to result from breaking the firm up, is to set up a system of regulation instead.

In practice, regulation tends to work in one of two ways:

- ✓ **Rate of return regulation:** The regulator oversees the pricing of goods and services so that the company makes a "fair" rate of return on its investments. In practice, however, this approach has drawbacks because it requires the regulator to have a lot of knowledge about the cost and the revenue side of the company. Despite its success in regulating public utilities for much of the 20th century, it has become replaced by price-cap regulation.

- ✓ **Price-cap regulation:** The regulator oversees a firm's prices according to an index that reflects the overall inflation rate, the inflation of the firm's inputs relative to the average firm in the economy, and the specific efficiencies this firm is able to realize relative to the average firm in the economy. It is often called CPI-X, where CPI is the Consumer Price Index or rate of inflation, and X is the expected efficiency savings. Price cap is intended to provide incentives for efficiency savings, as any savings above the predicted rate X can be passed on to shareholders of the firm.

Economists seldom expect the world to be perfect, even though the ideal is perfect competition. They do, however, prefer that monopoly be treated pro-actively. Where this is impossible, they may look for ways to regulate markets to make them work better.

Chapter 14

Examining Market Failure: Pollution and Parks

● ●

In This Chapter

▶ Identifying why the market fails to produce what people want

▶ Figuring out how to get the market to produce what people like

● ●

The well-known economist Nicholas Stern wrote in 2007 in a report commissioned by the U.K. government that climate change "is the greatest market failure the world has ever seen." He estimated that the costs of climate change if not addressed would be equivalent to losing between 5 and 20 percent of global gross domestic product each year, now and forever. Those are more than stern (no pun intended) words. Environmental damage is a market failure and we need to understand how the market is failing us.

On a cheerier environmental note, Grand Teton National Park is a pristine ecosystem enjoyed by people from across the United States and beyond. However, such a natural treasure owes its heritage not to the marketplace but to the intervention of the Rockefeller family (who did well in the market). In the 1920s, John D. Rockefeller established a blind trust and spent $1.5 million secretly buying ranches in the valley with the intention of creating a park to be enjoyed by everyone. The Rockefeller family has a long tradition of supporting national parks through philanthropy. They've established or enhanced more than 20 national parks from Maine to Wyoming, including Grand Teton, Acadia, Virgin Islands, Shenandoah, and Great Smoky Mountains. Why is it philanthropy and not the market that creates parks?

To economists, these two cases are linked by the concept of *market failure,* which comes in two types:

- ✔ **Where a market provides in equilibrium something in excess of what society wants:** Pollution.

- ✔ **When a market fails to provide in equilibrium the quantity of something that society does want:** In the case of public parks, a bias exists against producing goods for which the market has difficulty charging.

Economists spent a lot of time looking at these two types of market failure and came up with a library of ways to categorize the problems and find methods of solving them. In this chapter, we lead you through some of the simpler cases, so that you can see how economists approach the issue of market failure and what steps policy makers can take to solve it.

Coming to Grips with Externality: Too Much of a Bad Thing

Sometimes, as a result of trading, markets produce byproducts that society doesn't want or like, such as pollution from industrial processes. While looking at the specific problem of pollution, economists came up with a definition of the problem that makes sense more generally about the use of markets.

When two people make a trade and some part of the costs (or benefits) of that trade falls on a third party, that third party experiences an *external cost (benefit)*. The general existence of external costs (benefits) is called an *externality*.

Here's an illustration. In a market, two people — Molly, homeowner, and Nick, a fence builder — make a contract. In this contract, Molly decides that she wants Nick to build a fence that faces the front of a neighboring house. Molly hands over her money, and Nick builds a fence.

On the surface, all appears fine. But suppose Molly's and Nick's trade places a cost (or benefit) on the third party — the neighbor Olivia — who wasn't part of that trade. The cost (benefit) that falls on Olivia is the external cost (benefit).

Externalities can be one of two types:

- ✔ **Positive externalities:** Benefits conferred on a third party.
- ✔ **Negative externalities:** Costs that a third party incurs.

When economists look at externalities, they try to be careful about remedying them. For instance, Molly's and Nick's trade creates value and benefits to both Molly and Nick. A cost falls upon Olivia if the fence is undesirable from her perspective because it blocks her view — that's the bit economists want to remedy. However, they don't want to impose a ban on Molly and Nick trading if they can avoid doing so.

Instead they want to find mechanisms that reduce the degree to which an external cost falls upon Olivia without using legal prohibitions. This section discusses two of the approaches that economists advocate: one involving taxes and the other negotiation and contracts.

Both these solutions, however, depend on feasibility. For example, imagine an airline trying to negotiate with every single person affected by its landing noise. Ultimately, if you can't negotiate or work out a social-cost calculation (that is, a tax), your last resort may be legal prohibition.

Reducing externalities with taxes

Pigovian taxes, so named after Arthur Pigou, an early 20th century economist, are one method for tackling the issue of externalities. The idea is quite simple and is based on identifying the following two sets of benefits and costs:

- ✔ **Private:** Benefits and costs gained or incurred by the two main parties in a trade.
- ✔ **Social:** Benefits and costs from the trade that fall upon everyone.

The key is to align the private cost to the social cost, which a government can do by taxing the private transaction.

Pigovian taxes in action

Here's how Pigou's method works. When a person is trying to get the maximum benefit from doing something, he does so up to the point where marginal benefit equals marginal cost (see Chapter 3 for a refresher). Thus, without a tax, the equilibrium in a perfectly competitive market is where marginal benefit is equal to price is equal to marginal cost. If you measure the marginal benefit by marginal revenue equal to price — which works for a private transaction — you can derive a simple model (see Figure 14-1).

Note the presence in the figure of two possible equilibria:

- ✔ **Market equilibrium:** Marginal private cost is equal to marginal revenue equal to price.
- ✔ **Social equilibrium:** Marginal social cost equals marginal revenue equal to price.

Assuming that the transactions themselves are costless, the government can add the Pigovian tax to each unit of the good whose private cost is less than the social cost. For example, think of coal-powered electricity that causes pollution. Taxing the production of coal-powered electricity reduces the quantity traded and therefore reduces the quantity of the "bad" — that is, pollution — produced.

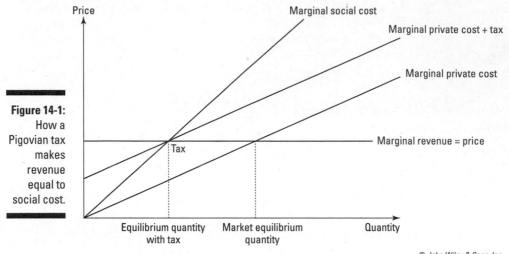

Figure 14-1:
How a
Pigovian tax
makes
revenue
equal to
social cost.

The difficulty of taxing

Economists often study what they call *wicked* problems, meaning that they tend to have no solutions or have solutions that themselves are subject to widespread disagreement. The case of taxing production to reduce a "bad" is just one of many such problems.

In particular, a number of problems exist with Pigou's approach:

- **Measurement:** Measuring and determining the social cost of something isn't easy and therefore neither is determining the right level of tax. Even Pigou found this to be a wicked problem in and of itself. For instance, some part of the cost may not be easily measurable because it's borne psychologically by the people subject to the external cost, and so doesn't readily show up in any data you can use for calculating the cost.

- **Gaming:** The level of the tax can be influenced by lobbying on behalf of the industry whose output production produces the externality, such as pollution. Lobbying is a form of gaming that consumes resources and can lead to losses for society.

- **Reciprocity:** In a society, all people are interconnected to a varying degree. Where do you draw the line of when one person's trade is another's external cost? If you move into an area knowing that, for instance, an extremely loud nightclub is nearby that could be a nuisance, to what extent can you hold the nightclub owner responsible? After all, you chose to live there.

Compensating the affected party through contracts

The problems mentioned in the preceding section don't invalidate the Pigovian approach, but they do indicate some problems with using it in practice. Therefore, economists have considered other ways for reducing negative externalities.

One such approach is based on people contracting with each other, instead of getting the government involved via taxes. This method is a contrasting way of looking at the problem compared to Pigou's and is often used as a basis for developing policy on big societal problems such as climate change.

Coase theorem

Ronald Coase looked at the problem of the divergence of social cost from private cost in a famous paper in 1960. His analysis became a famous result called the Coase theorem.

The *Coase theorem* is based on the following two related points:

- ✔ When property rights are completely assigned and parties can negotiate costlessly, the parties can always negotiate an efficient outcome; the legal framework just determines the payer of the cost.

- ✔ Negotiation is sufficient to solve the problem *unless* property rights are incomplete or negotiating is too costly.

The first point about property rights is a key observation. In many of the most challenging environmental problems that economics has been asked to solve, the issue is that no one has a property right over the resource. For example, consider who owns the air: either no one does, in which case the first problem exists of not being able to assign the property rights completely; or everyone does, in which case negotiation between every citizen is unfeasible and costly.

Whereas Pigou's model implies that social cost can be known and measured, Coase's focus is on cases of unremedied externalities in situations where property rights aren't fully assigned.

He uses a thought experiment about a doctor and a baker who work next door to each other. The doctor needs quiet to treat patients, but the baker's kneading and pounding of dough makes a noise that's essential to the baker's work. The prevailing logic was that the baker should therefore have to compensate the doctor.

Coase begins by pointing out the reciprocal problem. You can equally well frame the doctor as moving to a place where a bakery exists and then demanding that the baker bake in silence. Now suppose that the wise town mayor is fed up with being harangued over the argument of who's responsible for the noise. He points out that the baker could install quieter machinery for $500 and the doctor install soundproofing for $1,000. The cheapest or most efficient solution is therefore that the baker installs quieter machinery.

So that solves that, right? Well, not quite. In fact, two different possibilities exist depending on who has a property right over the ability to make — or be free from — noise:

- ✔ **If the doctor has the "sound rights" over the building:** The baker has to pay the $500 for quieter machinery.

- ✔ **If the baker has the "sound rights" over the building:** The doctor has to pay to reduce the noise. He could soundproof his own office for $1,000, although paying $500 to the baker for quieter machinery makes more sense because it's a far cheaper option.

Therefore, you can arrive at the best or efficient solution through negotiation, regardless of who's responsible for the noise, as long as property rights are completely assigned and people can negotiate. Here, the cost of remedying the externality is $500, the most efficient outcome regardless of who has the "sound rights" — the only difference is who ultimately pays the $500.

Coase is interested in why parties don't negotiate when they can and in what to do when property rights aren't assigned.

One thing that the Coase theorem absolutely does not do is say that the market can solve all externalities; that's an incorrect interpretation of the argument. Instead, the Coase theorem says that if you can completely assign property rights and you can negotiate, then the market *may* solve the externality. However, there may be cases where the solution may be unfeasible to implement.

Coase theorem in practice

Economists use Coase's reasoning when thinking about emissions — particularly of carbon — on a global scale; the idea spawned the approach that led to *cap and trade* policies for climate change. Regarding a carbon tax, no doubt you can envisage all kinds of difficulties with implementing the tax on very different nations — should a rich nation like Norway have the same taxes as a poorer one like Burkina Faso?

Instead, the carbon-market approach assigns each nation a tradable property right over its own emissions. If one country or region emits less than its property right allows, it can sell its spare capacity to a country or region that is less able to reduce its emissions. If it can't (or won't) reduce its emissions, instead of paying a tax the country or region, can buy "emission certificates" from regions that are not using their full allocation. The hope is that after trading, everyone is made as happy as possible.

Making the Market Produce What Otherwise It Would Not: Public Goods

The market is not able to produce every good that society wants.

Earlier we mentioned the Grand Teton National Park. What's remarkable about much of America's national park lands is that they are gifts to local, state, and federal governments by wealthy industrialists.

Public parks are almost never provided by a market system because they are what we call public goods, which are a type of goods with the following features:

- ✔ **Non-rival:** One person's consumption of a public good doesn't affect another person also enjoying the good, which means that the marginal cost (see Chapter 3) of supplying the good to one additional person is zero.

- ✔ **Non-excludable:** It is not feasible to prevent people from enjoying the good, even if they haven't paid for it.

This special set of economic circumstances means that the market doesn't provide these goods. If the marginal cost is zero and the good is non-excludable, price tends to fall to the marginal cost, which is zero. Market systems therefore have incredible difficulty pricing a public good and covering the costs of its provision.

We discuss some suggested ways of remedying the situation in this section. As you read what follows, though, bear in mind that not everything that looks like a public good up front turns out to be one, and some things that you'd think aren't turn out to be very similar to public goods.

Defining goods by rivalry and excludability

You can categorize goods in all sorts of ways, but here we're interested in thinking through whether the good is *rival* (the marginal cost is higher than zero) or *excludable* (you can keep out someone who hasn't paid from consuming the good), or both.

Four options exist:

- ✓ **Normal good:** One that's rival and excludable, which constitutes most things the market provides.

- ✓ **Public good:** One that's non-rival and non-excludable, such as street lighting or radio broadcasts.

- ✓ **Club good:** One that's non-rival but excludable. Some pay TV services fall into this category, though you can argue that technology has eroded some of the excludability of the services by enabling people to get them by illegal means.

- ✓ **Common good:** One that's rival but non-excludable. Think about grazing rights on common land: no one owns the land and so it's non-excludable, but because grazing affects the amount of grass available to another cow or sheep, it's definitely rival. We discuss a special economic problem that affects these goods in the later section "Considering a common (goods) tragedy."

A few really tough cases are tricky to place in one category. One of the most difficult is the case of pure information, such as TV, software, music, ebooks and audiobooks, and other digitally transmitted material, which is non-rival — when you've written a song it doesn't matter whether one person or a billion hear it, the cost was the fixed cost of writing the song, not the transmission cost — but partially excludable and often charged for.

Viewing a screen test

Pricing information was a wicked problem for the founders of the broadcast TV industry. TV programs are non-rival and not easily excludable, because they're easy to pick up and view. Broadly, the industry has come up with three solutions for the problem:

- ✓ In the United States, TV programming provides content that people want to watch and as such is valuable to advertisers who want to reach those viewers. Advertisers fund much of the programming on television.

- ✓ In Canada and in much of Europe, the government uses taxes to fund public television alone, and private television is funded through advertising.

- ✓ In the UK, instead of taxes funding television programming, there is a subscription model backed up by a legally mandated legal fee.

All these solutions have advantages and drawbacks, but all — more or less — worked until digital distribution made everyone rethink the economics of the industry.

Seeing spillovers, considering public benefits, and providing public goods

When you get down to the simplest definitions, a market makes the marginal cost of something equal to its marginal benefit. A trade gets made when someone agrees to pay a cost for a given benefit. In the case of goods with public benefits, though, a difficulty exists in equating the price with the marginal benefit. This problem is similar to the difficulty of setting Pigovian taxes — social costs and social benefits are difficult to calculate (check out the earlier section "Reducing externalities with taxes").

A public benefit is actually another kind of externality, one that gives a benefit to a party not involved in the transaction. In this case, the person gaining the benefit can be seen as a *free rider* — which, perhaps slightly unfairly, compares him to a person riding a train without paying.

A challenging problem is that almost no one exactly knows what the public benefit is and, because the marginal benefit can't be easily measured, no one really knows how to price it in a market through negotiation. The practical result is that a market almost never provides goods that fall into the public good categorization.

So how are these goods provided, and what can the public do to get more of them? Well, several mechanisms have been used over the centuries:

- **Patronage:** In the past, many composers of music — which has public-good aspects — benefitted from patrons. These rich supporters of the arts decided what to give based on their estimation of how valuable a composer's work and how their funding of it added to their social standing.

- **Philanthropy:** In this approach, wealthy individuals or groups bequeath items to society as a social good that fits with their view of their roles as "good" people. This is a bit like Blanche Dubois in *A Streetcar Named Desire* depending "on the kindness of strangers." Economists are reluctant to depend on it.

- **Public provision:** Of course, the government can also be the patron or philanthropist from general public spending. This is one of the ways that cities and counties get essentials such as parks and street lights. The disadvantage is that it takes provision into the political realm, and things get a little murky — too murky for some economists.

✔ **Crowdfunding:** This modern approach is a grass-roots variant of the philanthropy or patronage models. Here, the Internet makes it cheap enough to allow a large number of people to be patrons, each contributing a small slice of revenue. The research into the effectiveness of this solution is still new, but it has already brought products that the market system was unwilling to develop to the public. Many enjoyed the movie *Veronica Mars,* a result of the Kickstarter mechanism.

None of these systems is perfect. Crowdfunding can fail, patronage can result in too much control over the thing funded, and public provision can make everything a political battle. With a little help — for example, a tax break to induce philanthropists to part with their money — you can get more of the provision, but all these mechanisms can still fail to produce what society wants.

Considering a common (goods) tragedy

Common goods create contention wherever you go, because although they're rival, they're also non-excludable.

This specific issue, called the *Tragedy of the Commons,* is contentious because when a good is common, every user has an incentive to overuse the resource.

To see why, think about cod stocks. No one owns the sea, and so it's non-excludable. But because the stocks of cod in the sea are rival, overusing the resource leads to depletion. Overuse is exactly what happened in reality, leading to the collapse of cod populations such as those on the Grand Banks in the North Atlantic (people used to say that they were so full of cod that you could walk straight over them — though you'd need to watch your step).

Over the years, the Tragedy of the Commons has been refined, mainly in thinking about it in terms of poor management of a common resource. In particular, Elinor Ostrom, the first woman Nobel Prize winner in Economics, did a lot of research into how indigenous people, such as the Masai in Kenya, managed common land. She found that the dimensions of the Tragedy of the Commons were overstated and relied on people not using a common framework.

Ostrom's main point is that when people can agree upon a common framework for managing the commons, they can eliminate or at least lessen the tragedy. She describes four conditions that can achieve this goal:

- ✔ **Resources with definable boundaries are easier to preserve:** International waters, for example, are one of the harder cases, because the boundary definition is imprecise.

- ✔ **Communities find managing the resource easier with the threat of resource depletion and a lack of substitutes:** The fear of resource depletion is an incentive to preserve the resource.

- ✔ **The presence of a community helps manage the resource:** In particular, a strong, stable economy has a collective interest in preserving the resource.

- ✔ **The community needs a set of rules and procedures:** These can include dealing with individual overuse and agreeing on common use.

In essence, when you put these four conditions together, you end up with a community treating the common good *as if* the community holds a property right over the resource, which means that people in the community are willing to invest time and effort into maintaining it.

Preventing good things: Anti-commons

The flipside of the Tragedy of the Commons is the *anti-commons,* which reflects situations where too many private property rights prevent the development of a common benefit.

Think about the difficulties of negotiating with all the people affected by building a new road in town. At some point, because all property owners want to be compensated up to their estimation of their value of their property, the required buyouts can be prohibitively expensive, and necessary common projects fail to take place.

One answer is the power conferred to the government called eminent domain. Essentially, this power can force landowners to sell their property, typically for public projects like highways, when a "fair" price is met.

That way, society gets its product, and property owners get compensation — though not so much that it imperils the project. This system isn't perfect by any stretch of the imagination — court cases can go on for years — but it does at least prevent holdouts from stopping projects going ahead.

"I can't hear you!"

One interesting case of the anti-commons effect is the issue of clearing music rights for DVDs. When broadcasts use music, a compulsory license scheme giving standard compensation works, so that broadcasting the shows isn't prohibitively expensive. But this scheme doesn't apply to DVDs — they're not covered. So when the producers of the show want to release a DVD of the show, they have to make a separate arrangement with the music's license holders.

In the case of the successful 1990s TV series *Northern Exposure,* many individual rights holders had to clear, and all wanted full compensation. The result was that the producers abandoned the deal, and commissioned license-free music for the bulk of the re-release. To this day — and to the dismay of fans — the show has never been released with its original music on DVD.

Another serious problem of the anti-commons effect is in the area of pharmaceuticals. Many medicines depend on prior discoveries for at least part of their formulas, and patents still cover some of them. If the patent holders demand the best possible fee, and you can't negotiate it down, investing in developing the new medicine can become unprofitable In these cases, society loses through the excessive ability of owners of the properties to extract the highest possible price for their work.

The general remedy to this situation is compulsory or pooled licensing. In these situations, the government negotiates a standard fee with patent holders to prevent them from stopping the new product.

Chapter 15

Understanding the Dangers of Asymmetric Information

During the banking crisis of 2008–9, one of the key financial markets — the interbank lending market — screeched to a halt. The problem was that any bank needing to borrow had become a signal to a lender that the bank was in a poor financial state. A bank trying to engage in the routine behavior of borrowing from another bank was telling the potential lender that it needed credit, and so inadvertently identified itself as a risk. As a result, until more normal trading conditions returned to the market, no one would risk lending to anyone else.

The only lenders left in the game at that point were the central banks. Amid cries for bailouts, the central bankers had to ponder a difficult question: If you establish the principle that a central bank will bail out a bank in distress, aren't you saying to those banks that they can always count on you? And doesn't that mean that banks will have less incentive to keep themselves honest and healthy, financially speaking? After all, if they don't, they can always come to the central bank for a bailout.

These two cases — signaling that you're risky by your need to borrow and giving someone a bad incentive by bailing them out — are aspects of an important economic problem called *asymmetric information,* where one side in a trade has more information than the other side. The first case is an example of *adverse selection:* The ones who want to borrow the most are the bad risks for lenders. The second is an example of *moral hazard:* The terms of the bailout provide an incentive to behave badly. Whereas previous models (for instance, the ones in Chapters 9–14) assume perfect information on both sides of a deal, sellers and buyers, asymmetric information in a trade can make markets break down and "fail," leading to no trading taking place at all.

Asymmetric information can be a problem every time a seller knows more about the quality of her product than a buyer can pre-sale. It also lies at the heart of labor market problems — when candidates know more about their abilities than hirers. And insurance problems — when buyers know their own risk levels better than insurers. They're also the bane of gambling industries, which rely on betters not knowing more about the market than bookies.

In the case of asymmetric information, what you don't know *can* hurt you — which is why you need to read this chapter.

Seeing the Effects of Asymmetric Information

The market models developed in Chapters 9–14 are built on the assumptions that both parties to a trade have full knowledge of all information relevant to the trade or, alternatively, that they're equally ignorant. When you change this core assumption, things start to look very different indeed, as this section makes clear.

Visiting the market for lemons and plums

One way in which asymmetric information can lead to market failure is when it creates a negative *externality* (a cost imposed on a third party not included in the transaction — check out Chapter 14 for more about externalities).

In 1970, George Akerlof published an extremely important article on the economics of asymmetric information. "The Market for Lemons" shows very simply how asymmetric information affects markets — even shutting them down because bad trades drive out good.

We begin by assuming that a used car market has two kinds of car:

- **Lemons:** Real clunkers — cars of poor quality.
- **Plums:** Cars of good quality.

Suppose 100 people are selling their cars, and all that buyers know is that 50 of the cars are plums and 50 are lemons. Each seller knows the quality of its car, but the buyers don't know until they buy. *Caveat emptor,* folks. ("Let the buyer beware.")

Now we put in some prices. Suppose the sellers are willing to sell a plum for $2,000 and a lemon for $1,000. That would, fairly, show that their price is related to the quality. Imagine that the buyers are willing to pay a little more than that: $2,400 for a plum and $1,200 for a lemon. What's the equilibrium for this market?

Well, if you could immediately tell whether you're buying a plum or a lemon, you'd just have two separate equilibria for each kind of car where a plum went for $2,000–2,400 and a lemon for $1,000–1,200.

But buyers can't tell here. So their best strategy is to offer the expected value of the car — which you get by multiplying the buyers' offer by the probability of getting that type of car. If they know that 50 percent of the cars are lemons, then the expected value (EV) of a used car is as follows:

$$EV = (0.5 \times 2,400) + (0.5 \times 1,200) = \$1,800$$

That's the maximum that a buyer would bid for a car of unknown — some may say dubious! — quality. But now suppose the sellers know that buyers would only pay $1,800 for a used car. What do they do?

Sellers of plums leave the market, because buyers are willing to pay only $1,800 for a car, and plum sellers won't sell for less than $2,000. But wait, it gets worse. Now buyers know that only lemons are left in the market. They won't pay more than $1,200 for a car that is a lemon, so the market equilibrium drives out good cars and leaves only the market for lemons. The externality makes bad cars drive out good, and the market for plums fails.

Signaling your risk by buying cover: Adverse selection

Sometimes the externality arising from asymmetric information gets so bad, it can destroy an entire market. In the case of interbank lending during the financial crisis, it very nearly did. If lending banks *knew* that the only borrowers were poor risks, they couldn't very well lend at the prevailing rate. The problem was that some banks were in real trouble, and as long as they had enough effect on the lenders' view of the average likelihood of failure in the market as a whole, the lenders couldn't lend to them.

This problem relates to hidden information: The lenders were unable to directly observe the quality of the borrowers, but they could read the need for capital borrowing as a *signal* (Chapter 19 talks more about signals). Alarming signals eventually made lenders almost disappear from the market.

Demonstrating adverse selection with a quality-selection model

A simple way of seeing adverse selection is with a quality-selection model in which producers must choose whether to produce a high-quality item as opposed to a low-quality item. They choose high quality with a probability q, and what you want to know is what size of q will keep the market working.

We start by putting some prices into the model so that you can see it in action. Suppose the product is a tradable good (that is, rival and excludable — see Chapter 14 for definitions), such as a basic cellphone. A better-quality one would cost you $100, and a lower-quality one $64. Suppose for now that manufacturers can make either type of phone for $85. We make everything nice and easy by assuming that the industry is in perfect competition — so that the phones aren't differentiated by obvious features, and the price equals marginal cost.

Starting off with that information, three things can happen:

✔ **If high-quality manufacturers are the only ones in the market,** the trades will occur somewhere between $85 and $100, but perfect competition means that the price gets competed down to $85.

✔ **If low-quality manufacturers are the only ones in the market,** customers are willing to pay only $64. The manufacturing cost is $85, so no phones are produced, and no market exists.

✔ **If high- and low-quality manufacturers are in the market,** the market clears only if q is big enough to ensure that the expected value (EV) of customers is also higher than the cost of production. So you need to know what value of q leads to EV being $85.

Finding the value of q that clears the market therefore means solving the expected value equation:

$$\$85 = (\$100q) + (\$64(1-q))$$

The answer is 7/12.

Graphing the equilibrium result allows you to see how this market failure manifests (check out Figure 15-1). Putting price on the vertical axis and q on the horizontal, you can show the market failure as a blank area where no items are sold. The supply is horizontal, as in perfect competition, but only above $q = 7/12$. Above that, the diagonal shows consumers' willingness to pay — that is, the expected value as q goes up (it can't be bigger than 1). Between the two is a shaded area of consumer surplus — excess benefit the consumers get when they're willing to pay more than the $85 that producers end up charging under perfect competition.

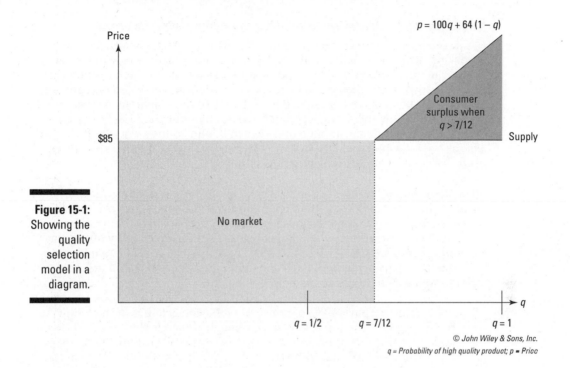

$p = 100q + 64 (1 - q)$

Price

Consumer
surplus when
$q > 7/12$

$85   Supply

No market

Figure 15-1:
Showing the
quality
selection
model in a
diagram.

$q = 1/2$ $q = 7/12$ $q = 1$ q

© John Wiley & Sons, Inc.

q = Probability of high quality product; p = Price

Note that the shaded oblong — no market equilibrium — reflects the external cost of producers not producing a high quality product. If enough of
them exist, they destroy the entire market. But if each individual producer
doesn't believe that they, individually, contribute to the average quality in
the marketplace, they have an incentive not to choose to produce at a high
quality. Thus, poorer products tend to drive out better ones, and consumers lose out.

Seeing what happens when producers choose product quality

Adapting the model to allow producers to choose the quality of the product
they'll produce shows how adverse selection can destroy both high- and low-
quality markets. Suppose now that the cost of making a high-quality phone is
a little more — say, $90 — and the manufacturer can choose which to make.

Consider the position of a high-quality manufacturer. It knows that it has
only a small fraction of the market, and so it too has an incentive to produce
a lower-quality phone. Unfortunately, the same reasoning is true of all the
higher-quality manufacturers. Because a consumer will pay only $64 for a
low-quality phone, no equilibrium exists, and high-and low-quality markets
disappear.

Dealing with adverse selection through compulsory coverage

In practice, adverse selection is generally associated with health insurance markets, where consumers differ according to the risk they face of requiring costly medical treatment. If one population has a higher risk than another, and the insurance company does not know who is in which risk category, it faces a problem of adverse selection. If it tries to price insurance (that is, set premiums) using the average risk in the overall population, lower-risk consumers may not find insurance to be worth it, and so they wouldn't buy, and higher-risk people would make more claims. Therefore, the bad risks drive out the good — adverse selection in action, again.

The provision of health insurance is such an important policy issue, it is worthwhile spending some time understanding the economics of health insurance. As an example, suppose each consumer belongs to one of four different risk categories, where a risk category is the probability of needing a medical treatment that costs $10,000. There are a large and equal number of consumers in each group. Each consumer knows her risk, but insurers cannot tell which group a consumer belongs to.

The willingness to pay (WTP) of consumers in each group is in the following table. We also give the actuarially fair premium, which is the expected loss a company faces when it insures a consumer. It is equal to $10,000 times the risk or probability of needing treatment, and it is always lower than the willingness to pay since consumers exhibit risk aversion.

Risk	20%	40%	60%	80%
WTP	2,500	5,200	6,800	8,500
Actuarially fair premium	2,000	4,000	6,000	8,000
Potential surplus	500	1,200	800	500

If everyone has insurance, then the company would face a 50% chance of a loss in the population and would have to charge at least $5,000 to avoid a loss. In a competitive market, this would be the price of health insurance. However, at this price, consumers in the lowest-risk 20% category would not buy insurance because they would find the premium too high. However, if only the 40%, 60%, 80% risks are in the market, then the chance of a loss is 60%, and a company would need to charge $6,000 to avoid losses. If the price is $6,000, only the 60% and 80% risks will want to buy insurance, but then the overall risk rises to 70%. A company would need to raise the premium to $7,000, driving out the 60% group and hence the equilibrium premium for insurance will be $8,000, and only the highest-risk agents will insure.

This is not an efficient outcome — if insurance could be provided on actuarially fair terms to each group individually, this would generate a surplus for each group. However, the adverse selection problem leads to the collapse of the insurance market, leaving many consumers uninsured.

Could we do any better? If there is no way to obtain the private information, then the policy maker faces the same constraints as the market, and the insurance market creates only $500 of surplus per high-risk person.

Making participation mandatory can create more total surplus. In this case, insurers would know that the aggregate risk is 50%, and the competitive price of insurance would be 5,000. At this price, the surplus of the agents would look like this:

Risk	20	40	60	80
WTP	2,500	5,200	6,800	8,500
Actuarially fair premium	2,000	4,000	6,000	8,000
Pooled premium	5,000	5,000	5,000	5,000
Surplus	–2,500	200	1,800	3,500

Note, however, that even though the total surplus has increased, *this is not a Pareto improvement* — the low-risk consumers are worse off with mandatory participation, and there is no way to compensate them because that would require that we can somehow identify them, which by the assumption of private information is impossible.

One way of dealing with the problem of health insurance is to require everyone to buy a product with the average-risk profile:

✔ High-risk people are better off, because they can get insurance that they'd have otherwise been priced out of getting.

✔ Lower-risk people are better off only insofar as they can get an insurance policy that they wouldn't otherwise be offered.

Changing Your Behavior because of Asymmetric Information

In October 2008, recapitalizing the banks by providing huge amounts of capital was part of the policy makers' solution to the crisis in the financial markets. The principal aim was to prevent the financial system from descending into an even greater crisis. One side effect of this policy, however, was the need to manage moral hazard.

Moral hazard, as mentioned earlier, is a situation that gives an incentive to someone to behave "badly." Suppose, for instance, that you have superb all-coverage home insurance. You may not have an incentive to fit a good-quality lock on your back door, because you know that if someone gets into your house, the insurer, and not you, is going to pay for the loss.

In the case of the bank bailouts, many commentators saw the bailouts as an invitation for banks to lend recklessly. If the banks knew that the government would pick up the bill, they had no incentive to stop lending recklessly — when things worked out well, they made large profits, and when they didn't, they weren't taking the losses.

Managing moral hazard

Policy makers and companies seek to manage moral hazard in different ways, including the following:

- ✔ **Banking:** The U.S. government has confronted the problem of moral hazard in the recent financial crisis. The government introduced the Troubled Asset Relief Program (TARP) as a mechanism for purchasing the assets of troubled financial institutions and putting them on the path to recovery. Other bailout programs included the federal takeover of Fannie Mae and Freddie Mac and the public ownership of GM and AIG. Whether bailing out the banks and other institutions will rise to the problem of "too big to fail" is still an open moral hazard question.

- ✔ **Insurance:** Companies cover perhaps only 90 percent of the losses to ensure that the insured customer bears some of the risk. The risk born by the customer is the deductible in the plan and provides at least *some* incentive to take care.

If an insurer could observe accurately how much care a customer would take, no moral hazard problem would exist, and the market would work as efficiently as it should. But because the insurer doesn't know, the outcome of moral hazard is under-insurance — each consumer would like to buy more insurance, but the insurance companies would be less likely to provide it because rational customers who would buy the full insurance product would have the incentive to take less care. That's why insurers insist on the type of deductible clauses just mentioned.

Incentivizing: Asymmetric information in contracts

One classic problem where asymmetric information and moral hazard pop up is when you want to get someone to do something for you and the other person knows more about whether she's going to do it or not.

Considering the principal-agent problem

One problem of this kind is the *principal-agent problem*. It concerns a principal wanting to get an agent to do something for him and an agent having her own interests that she wants to take care of too.

A good example is a Hollywood agent who gets a percentage of the fees paid to an actor she represents. The actor — the *principal* here — has an interest in maximizing his lifetime career standing and is therefore particular about what kind of jobs he wants to take. The agent, however, just wants to maximize her percentage and tries to get the actor signed up for as many jobs as possible, regardless of quality.

More seriously, the principal-agent problem also exists in the structure of an ordinary company. Shareholders own the company and are the principals, but managers are their agents. Management may want to act in their own interests — manage a big company instead of a smaller one — rather than in the principals' interests. Thus shareholders need a scheme for making the management act in their interests. The simplest, though not always most effective way, is to pay managers in company stock, so that they take the same risks and gain the same benefits as do the owners. But that too may not always work.

Modeling incentives for contracts

In a contract, an owner (the principal) wants a manager (the agent) to put in an effort or care level, x^*, which is known to the manager but not the owner. The manager wants to choose her own utility-maximizing level of x. What should the owner do?

Simple: The profit-maximizing level of x has to be the level where the marginal product to using x amount of effort is equal to the cost of performing the effort. So the owner wants to choose x^* on that basis.

The owner needs to get this level of effort into an *incentive-compatible contract* — one that assures that the utility to the manager of doing anything other than x^* is less than the utility of doing x^*.

Here are three methods the owner can use to achieve this aim:

- **Lump sum fee:** The owner can charge the manager a lump sum fee, R, so that after the manager has paid R — you might think of this amount as a franchise fee — any profit belongs to the manager. In that way, the manager chooses x^* in the same way as if she were the owner.

- **Wages:** Set wages so that the marginal product of the manager's work equals the wage, and the manager will want to choose the level of effort that maximizes this relationship.

- **Fixed fee:** The owner can pay the manager a bonus if x^* is achieved and nothing if it's not.

What won't work is a share scheme where manager and owner divvy up the output. The manager won't be trying to maximize marginal product but only the share of the product that she gets. Calling that share α, the manager would be trying to set α times the marginal product equal to marginal cost, and that won't give the optimal output x^*.

Now suppose because of random events the owner is never able to infer from the output whether the manager has put in the correct amount of effort. This certainly makes the model more realistic and in that case, we can deduce that

- ✔ If the manager is more risk averse than the owner, and output is random, the lump sum franchise fee must be reduced so that the manager is willing to bear the risk of uncertain output. (This is generally a problem with franchises.)

- ✔ Wage setting depends on owners being able to assess the amount of labor input. If the owner can't do that, using wages becomes inefficient.

- ✔ In a take-it-or-leave-it case, the manager is at risk of losing everything if the output can't be controlled from her desk, which places all the risk on the manager and is unlikely to be agreed to as a contract.

- ✔ If the output fluctuates, the profit-sharing solution means both parties take on some of the risk, though not all. In turn, the manager has the incentive to produce some output but isn't carrying all the risk.

The value of an incentive contract depends crucially on the degree to which the principal is able to monitor the efforts of the agent. If the principal can find out at some point, even if not up front, what the agent is doing, then franchising, wages, and bonus payments will ultimately all lead to the same outcome. If risk is present, so that neither the principal nor agent knows how things will turn out, or if the principal is never able to monitor the activity of the agent, profit-sharing may be the most efficient solution.

Part V
Thinking Strategically: Life Is Just a Game!

	ROCK	PAPER	SCISSORS
ROCK	0,0	−1,1	1,−1
PAPER	1,−1	0,0	−1,1
SCISSORS	−1,1	1,−1	0,0

Find what you need to know at www.dummies.com.

In this part . . .

✔ Use game theory to understand economic problems.

✔ Realize why the Nash equilibrium is such an important concept.

✔ Understand the way auction design affects strategy.

✔ Decipher people's signals that reveal their intentions.

Chapter 16

Playing Games with Economic Theory

Game theory provides a powerful set of tools for probing into and modeling situations from an economist's perspective. It's a way to think about strategic behavior and help clarify how outcomes affect behavior, and vice versa. Economists have used game theory to look at problems as diverse as nuclear deterrence, how animals display dominance, and even the best way for a striker and a goalkeeper to act in a penalty shootout in soccer. You can approach these problems using an underlying model that takes into account the behavior of more than one decision-maker at a time and considers what they may do in a situation where the benefits — and of course the costs — depend on everyone's actions.

Game theory is one of the most popular areas of microeconomics. When you know some of the models, you begin to recognize that game-theoretic situations feature in many films and TV shows, from *The Godfather* and *The Wire* to *Dr. Strangelove*. The famous Prisoner's Dilemma game (discussed later in this chapter) is a staple of cop and detective dramas.

All these situations feature participants or decision makers who want to maximize their own benefits given that another participant is trying to do exactly the same thing for him or herself. What emerges, generally, is an equilibrium that balances the interests of the parties, though not necessarily so that they get exactly what they want.

In this chapter, we walk you through some of the basic concepts of game theory. We show you three cornerstone one-shot models and how dealing with these situations has led to — for good and for ill — some of the institutions people live with today. We also describe some of the ways in which you can apply game theory, sometimes all too practically, to real-world situations, and how things change when a game is repeated. We explore strategy through game theory, describe how cooperation and competition shape outcomes, and see what "the best you can do" means when someone else is doing his or her best as well. Let the games begin!

Setting Up the Game: Mechanism Design

One of the key uses of game theory in the real world is called *mechanism design* — setting up games so that a particular or desired behavior becomes the best strategy for a player to choose.

To show you what we mean, consider this example: You've been left with the demanding job of ensuring that two hyped-up five-year-olds cut a cake fairly between the two of them. You can frame their decision, but you can't make the decision itself for either child (that has to be up to them). How do you do it?

Mechanisms are very useful tools in economic policy, especially when it is the case (as it usually is) that the mechanism designer has less knowledge about the relative valuations and optimal choices of the parties who are competing or bargaining. For example, there are government auctions of radio spectrums, where the government is the mechanism designer and does not know the market values of the spectrums, whereas the bidders in the auction do know them.

The government would like to implement the best allocation of the resource, in this case the spectrum, but not know the value of the resource to the players of the game. Therefore, the government wants to design its auction in such a way that players with the highest valuation will self-select a bidding strategy that allocates them the resource. In this way, the government makes consistent individual optimal choices with its own objectives.

The following are some core terms used in game theory:

- ✔ **Hawk:** The party acting strictly in his own interests.

- ✔ **Dove:** The party acting in the collective interest of the group. It's important to recognize though, that the Dove is doing so because its own individual interests lead it to do so.

- ✔ **Payoff:** The outcome to a player of following any particular strategy.

Locking Horns with the Prisoner's Dilemma

The *Prisoner's Dilemma* scenario is a common starting point for exploring game theory because it's a simple but insightful game. It involves only two participants or players and an easily understood setting, which you'll recognize if you've ever read or watched a detective story.

The setup of the Prisoner's Dilemma is designed to give a police investigator the best chance of getting a confession from a suspect. As a result, the structure of the payoffs or the incentives of the game are designed so that police have to do the least work in getting a suspect to play the Hawk. In other words, the police engineer a situation, by offering penalties and rewards, to extract a confession. During questioning, the police offers one suspect a lighter sentence or even freedom if he confesses. The police can use the confession as evidence to nail the other suspect. Each suspect is interrogated separately and made the offer. When you find yourself being made an offer in a Prisoner's Dilemma game, you're likely already in a precarious situation.

The Prisoner's Dilemma allows economists to think about the behavior that goes on when there is a conflict between cooperation (Dove) and self-interest (Hawk). For example, another way of looking at oligopoly (see Chapter 11) is to see it as a type of Prisoner's Dilemma where firms have to decide whether to play hawks and produce more, or play doves and produce less.

Reading the plot of the Prisoner's Dilemma

The story goes like this. A bookmaker is robbed, and the police apprehend two suspects for the crime. The detective investigating the robbery puts the two suspects in separate rooms — so that they can't communicate — and makes each of them a one-time offer of a deal:

- ✔ **If neither participant confesses:** Both get six months in the slammer.

- ✔ **If one participant confesses and the other doesn't:** The participant who confesses is released, while the one who doesn't confess gets a five-year sentence.

- ✔ **If both participants confess:** They both go to jail for two years.

The question is: When the suspects are presented individually and separately with the same deal, what happens?

On the face of it, you may think this is a no-brainer for the suspects. Obviously, the best outcome is that neither of them confess and they each end up serving six months. After all, this means that the total time served by the two suspects is the least. Obviously, they'd be crazy to take any other action. So neither suspect should confess, right?

If you are thinking like that (and many do before they investigate the scenario), alas, you'd be wrong. To see this, suppose the first suspect, whom we'll call Mr. Pink, thinks like you did and decides he doesn't want to confess. He doesn't know what Mr. Blue (his partner in crime) has decided. Mr. Pink would like to think that Mr. Blue hasn't already taken a deal that puts Pink in prison for five years. However, on second thought, Mr. Pink realizes that Mr. Blue has a big incentive to rat on him if Mr. Blue thinks for a moment that Mr. Pink won't confess. And of course, if Mr. Pink does confess, Mr. Blue is better off confessing too. Similarly, locked away from Mr. Pink, Mr. Blue doesn't know whether or not Mr. Pink has decided to rat him out too, sending Mr. Blue to prison for five years. Because neither suspect can take the chance that the other person isn't a stool pigeon cooperating with the police to cut himself a better deal, neither can rely on the other not confessing. So both confess and get a two-year sentence each — game over.

The key to understanding this result is that both suspects (players) are considered economically rational agents (as defined in Chapter 2), and therefore each player wants to do the best for him, given what he anticipates the other player will do. Both players need to think through what is the best action to take given their best guess about what the other player will do. The reasoning goes like this: "If my partner is not going to confess, then I'm better off confessing. If my partner is going to confess, then I'm better off confessing as well. So no matter what my partner does, I should confess." Both players reason like this and both confess. The incentive to confess or the payoffs from confessing are key to this game, and that is why they make the police's job easy.

Solving the Prisoner's Dilemma with a payoff matrix

Economists look at the Prisoner's Dilemma through some of the tools of game theory. The first and perhaps clearest way to do so is with a *payoff matrix* — a simple chart that shows what the payoffs are to both participants given their choices in the game. In Figure 16-1, we label the two participants as Mr. Pink and Mr. Blue, and the two actions they can perform in this setting as "Confess" and "Don't confess."

Figure 16-1:
Payoff
matrix for
the
Prisoner's
Dilemma.

Mr Pink's moves		Mr Blue's moves	
		Confess	Don't confess
	Confess	−2 −2	−5 0
	Don't confess	0 −5	−0.5 −0.5

© John Wiley & Sons, Inc.
Bolded payoffs go to Blue, and shaded go to Pink.

When you read down the columns, the payoffs to Mr. Blue's actions (or *moves,* in game terminology) are shown against the payoffs to Mr. Pink's moves. For example, in the situation where Mr. Blue doesn't confess but Mr. Pink does, the payoffs are no loss of time in jail for Mr. Pink and a loss of five hard years for Mr. Blue. Similarly, when you read along the rows, the same pair of moves gives the payoffs a loss of nothing for Mr. Pink and a loss of five years for Mr. Blue.

The payoffs are dependent on the actions of both participants. For instance, although confessing lets Mr. Pink out of serving jail time, it does so *only if Mr. Blue doesn't confess.* If Mr. Blue also confesses, the advantage Mr. Pink gets from being the only one to confess is wiped out.

This sort of matrix is called the *strategic form* or *normal form* of the game, and its purpose is to clarify how the payoffs depend on the strategies chosen so that you can see clearly which strategies wouldn't be chosen and which would be. Most importantly, it helps you to see one of the most important concepts in game theory: the Nash equilibrium.

Finding the best outcome: The Nash equilibrium

Named after the celebrated mathematician John Nash (played by Russell Crowe in the biopic *A Beautiful Mind*), the *Nash equilibrium* has a special role in game theory. It's defined as that set of strategies where no player has an incentive to change. Or less formally, the combination of strategies where players are doing the best they can, given what other players are doing.

In the Prisoner's Dilemma, the Nash equilibrium is a pair of strategies — in this case, one for Blue and one for Pink — such that playing that strategy makes the player as well off as he or she can be given the other player's strategy. The outcomes for the Nash equilibrium are in the top left corner of Figure 16-2. This pair of strategies make each player as well off as he or she can be, given each other's options.

		Mr Blue's moves	
Mr Pink's moves		Confess	Don't confess
	Confess	−2 −2	−5 0
	Don't confess	0 −5	−0.5 −0.5

Figure 16-2: Nash equilibrium in the Prisoner's Dilemma.

Nash equilibrium

© John Wiley & Sons, Inc.
Bolded payoffs go to Blue, and shaded go to Pink.

The Nash equilibrium does not lead to the payoff where any given player is *best* off, nor does it lead to the best outcome for both participants collectively. Instead, it takes into account that both players want to do the best for themselves, not knowing what the other player is going to do. Chapter 17 talks more about the Nash equilibrium's special properties.

Applying the Prisoner's Dilemma: The problem of cartels

In economics, a *cartel* is a collection of organizations that act collectively to get the best deal for themselves. The most famous example is the oil and petroleum exporters' group OPEC, which attempts to restrict the supply of oil to the market in order to get as high a price as possible for its exports. Cartels in the U.S. are illegal under the Sherman Act. The collusive agreement to raise prices is a *restrictive trade practice* that operates in their members' interests and against the public good. Therefore, the fines for being a cartel or secretly operating one are extremely high. The U.S. Department of Justice has already imposed $2.7 billion in cartel fines this year, representing more than 85 per cent of the total fines handed down across the world. (OPEC, by the way, is not an illegal cartel because it is made up of countries, rather than companies, and U.S. competition law doesn't make it illegal for countries to form cartels.)

The fact that cartels are illegal means that cartel members can't rely on an enforceable contract to ensure that everyone acts in the collective best interests of the cartel. Even if all the members of the cartel do agree, for a period of time, to forego the best individual outcome in favor of the collective best, they always have an incentive to return to doing their individual best. If one does, the other members can't go to court and sue the defecting member for breach of contract — because that would mean admitting being part of a criminal conspiracy. (OPEC is an interesting exception. See the nearby sidebar "Oiling the wheels: The OPEC cartel.")

Let's think of the cartel's dilemma as a Prisoner's Dilemma and look at it using the strategic form of the game. We begin by walking through the payoff matrix in Figure 16-3 as representing an agreement between two companies, (Blue PLC and Pink, Ltd.). Either company has a choice of playing Hawk or Dove (refer back to the section "Setting the Game: Mechanism Design" for a definition of these terms).

		Blue PLC	
Pink Ltd		Hawk	Dove
	Hawk	5 5	–50 130
	Dove	130 –50	100 100

Figure 16-3: Applying the Prisoner's Dilemma to a cartel.

Nash equilibrium

© John Wiley & Sons, Inc.
Bolded payoffs go to Blue, and shaded go to Pink.

Looking at the payoffs in Figure 16-3 (which are all in millions of dollars), you can see that the collective best, which the cartel or collusive agreement wants to achieve, is in the bottom right corner, where both Blue and Pink are playing Dove. But if one plays Hawk while the other plays Dove, the Hawk (which means cutting prices and selling more) gets a higher return ($130 million in this case) by stealing market share from the other, who in this case takes a loss being the high price seller (top right corner).

Oiling the wheels: The OPEC cartel

Interestingly, the OPEC cartel seems to have bucked the trend about cartels not lasting. Here are two reasons why:

✔ **Repeated games establish possibilities for more cooperation.** The Prisoner's Dilemma model as we use it here is played only once.

✔ **The role of Saudi Arabia distorts the picture.** Saudi Arabia's big oil reserves mean that it can play Hawk longer than any other nation can play Hawk against it. Therefore, as soon as Saudi Arabia plays Hawk, the other members have reason to return to the negotiating table.

Neither party can trust the other to stay in line with the agreement, and so they both default to playing Hawk, and acting in their own best interests. As a result, the Nash equilibrium is (Hawk, Hawk) in the top left corner, and the cartel falls apart.

This is one reason why cartels don't tend to be long-lasting, irrespective of whether a regulator is able to use legal action to keep them in line. As the saying goes, there's no honor among thieves, and the logic of the Prisoner's Dilemma bears that out to some extent.

Of course, regulators also help cartels break down and get to the Nash equilibrium — as the police do in the earlier section "Reading the plot of the Prisoner's Dilemma" by giving the parties an extra incentive, such as shorter prison terms, to give in evidence. In the case of competition law, the practice is to give a free pass to the first party who talks to the authorities. That way, any party that thinks it may get caught has an incentive to come forward and tell tales on its former cartel partners.

Escaping the Prisoner's Dilemma

An alternative heading for this section could be "How to form an organized crime syndicate without really trying." Game theory has investigated one particularly interesting example of cartel behavior: that of organized crime syndicates, when they operate a cartel that tends to work for the benefit of those under its influence, although not generally for society as a whole.

In Chicago during the reign of Al Capone, for instance, the local mafia had a monopoly on the supply of pasta-making machines, which were an essential piece of physical capital for any Italian restaurant in the city. However, the restaurants benefitted from Capone's patronage. Sure, they had to pay him fees, but they could rely on him to take care of any competition that threatened to undercut them. Thus, the mob ended up as a way of enforcing a cartel agreement *and* guaranteeing higher profits for its favored establishments.

An organized crime syndicate can achieve a similar outcome by changing the payoffs for its members. When you look at the syndicate as a cartel and understand its payoffs, you can see that, in essence, it changes the payoff for confessing to a crime from whatever offer the police make to the easily understood *dead.* So if you're a member of a syndicate, and you're offered a deal that tempts you to confess, you don't choose it — unless you feel like sleeping with the fishes.

In Figure 16-4, we summarize the strategic form of the Prisoner's Dilemma when a crime syndicate can change the payoffs. As you can see, the payoff to any actions involving confessing are now "Dead" (which you can interpret as infinitely large and negative). Thus the Nash equilibrium is now *not* to confess.

		Mr Blue's moves	
Mr Pink's moves		Confess	Don't confess
	Confess	Dead Dead	−5 Dead
	Don't confess	Dead −5	−0.5 −0.5

Figure 16-4: Payoffs for an organized crime syndicate enforcing the cartel.

Nash equilibrium

© John Wiley & Sons, Inc.
Bolded payoffs go to Blue, and shaded go to Pink.

This change in the Nash equilibrium provides the rationale for the formation of syndicates. If you can't get criminals to cooperate with each other, change the payoffs so that it's in their interests at least not to confess. Capone, Corleone, and several others took that lesson to heart.

Looking at Collective Action: The Stag Hunt

Game theorists have turned their attention to many different situations, ranging far and wide and covering many issues. One of these is the problem of collective action, where a bigger prize is available only to those who can coordinate their actions.

Collective action is a problem the world over. People can often make a gain by acting individually, but the best gains are made by coordinating actions so that they can get a prize bigger than they can attain individually. One way to consider these situations is by using a game known as the Stag Hunt. (Don't worry, no animals are harmed in the playing of this game.)

Designing the Stag Hunt

The Stag Hunt is set somewhere around the dawn of time. Littlenose and Bigfoot set out from their village one morning to go hunting. They can choose from two possible locations: One field contains a population of hares, and the other field has stags. Any hunter on his own can capture a hare, but to capture a stag, both hunters must work together. The model assumes that they must both make their decisions with no idea of whether the other is going to make the same choice or a different one.

We give names to the two possible strategies for Littlenose and Bigfoot:

- **Hawk:** They strike out individually looking for hares.

- **Dove:** They turn up independently at the same field as the stags, hoping to coordinate their actions so that they can bring home a bigger meal for the village.

Next we assign values to the potential meals:

- **Hare:** As the smaller creature, the hare gets a smaller value. Call that a value of 1.

- **Stag:** To the larger stag, we assign a larger value of 4. Any number larger than 1 will do, but we'll use 4 to keep things clear.

We want to compare possibilities and solve for a Nash equilibrium, so we put up the payoffs in strategic form, as in Figure 16-5. Now look at the possible strategies and outcomes to see where the Nash equilibrium lies. Can you spot it?

		Littlenose	
Bigfoot		Dove	Hawk
	Dove	4 4	1 0
	Hawk	0 1	1 1

Figure 16-5:
The Stag hunt payoffs.

Sorry, that was a sly question, because in fact two Nash equilibria exist: one that maximizes payoffs (top left) and one that minimizes risk (bottom right). To see why, we think through Littlenose's decisions:

✔ **Littlenose plays Dove:** He goes to the field where the stags reside and hopes that Bigfoot makes the same decision to play Dove. If Bigfoot doesn't, Littlenose will have an incentive to change. But if Bigfoot does, they successfully get a stag and the higher payoff, and neither has an incentive to change.

✔ **Littlenose plays Hawk:** He goes to the hare field and whatever happens, he gets something to eat. If Bigfoot also plays Hawk, they bring home a nice hare each and are in equilibrium. If not, and Bigfoot plays Dove, it has no effect on Littlenose, although he could've brought home a far bigger meal if he had also played Dove and visited the stag field.

Therefore, Dove, Dove is the payoff-maximizing equilibrium (a stag). Hawk, Hawk is a risk-minimizing equilibrium (at minimum, a hare each). But neither Hawk, Dove nor Dove, Hawk can be an equilibrium, because given what the other player chose, a player could make himself better off by changing to the same strategy as the other player (hence the game being seen as a *coordination game*).

Economists use the Stag Hunt game in situations where both parties can gain by taking an action, but because each party also has a defensive strategy and because they don't know what the other party will do, they play their defensive strategy to avoid losses. This case often applies in international negotiations where a treaty is the collective best, but the risk-minimizing strategy is to act in your own immediate interests.

Examining the Stag Hunt in action

To our great delight, a Stag Hunt came to light in an economics class at an American university, where a poor choice of mechanism design led to students being able to exploit the system.

The students in a microeconomics course were to be graded to a *curve* — that is, by their relative position in the class instead of by the raw results that they themselves would achieve on the final exam. The students were upset about this, but they knew a bit of game theory and used it to their advantage to ensure that everyone got the top mark in the class. If no one sits the exam, a zero grade is the top grade in the course and every student gets it (that is, no one must sit the final exam to get it). We immediately gave them a long-distance standing ovation for brilliant use of game theory.

The key to this problem lies in two points:

✔ Analyzing this situation, an economist would use the Stag Hunt model to see where the benefit of collective action is.

✔ The corollary of a ranking system is that if everyone is equally terrible, then everyone is equally good. Another way of looking at it is that if everyone gets last place, they all tie for first.

Suppose that the exact marking scheme gives the first-place student 90 percent, the second 89, the third 88, and so on. Call that scheme the "teacher's offer" and denote it M:

✔ **If all students play Hawk:** They play by the test scheme and their mark at the end is M_i.

✔ **If all students play Dove, don't play by the test rules, and instead submit blank papers:** They all receive the payoff for first place: a mark of 90.

Hawk and Dove refer to the strategies of players in cooperating with *each other* and not the teacher.

✔ **If *some* of the players play Hawk and some play Dove:** The Hawks take the test and get the teacher's offer based on their place in class, M. The Doves don't take the test and get a mark that reflects their worse performance; call it W (for this to work the offer, W, must be worse than any given possible mark M).

Figure 16-6 shows the strategic form of the game. As in the traditional Stag Hunt in the preceding section, two Nash equilibria exist:

✔ **Hawk, Hawk equilibrium:** Every student goes along and takes the exam as normal and is placed on the curve.

✔ **Dove, Dove equilibrium:** Every student submits a blank paper and guarantees themselves 90 per cent.

Any given set of other players		Any given player	
		Dove	Hawk
	Dove	90 90	M W
	Hawk	W M	M M

© John Wiley & Sons, Inc.

Figure 16-6: Strategic form of the Stag Hunt for the class economics exam.

The coordination problem is how to coordinate students' decisions so that they all end up playing Dove. This particular class solved it by waiting outside the exam room so that they were able to monitor anyone going in to the room. If they saw someone go in, they rushed after the person eager to get started on the exam with the hope that they'd get M (rather than W) at least. In fact, no one walked into the room and all students got 90!

A better mechanism for assessing and grading performance would have been to spring the test on the students, or to tell them the grading scheme after the test, or even to set the test in different rooms so that no one could monitor whether anyone else was cooperating. That way, the students would have then been unable to solve the game's coordination problem.

Annoying People with the Ultimatum Game

Sometimes the value of a game is in illustrating the difference between people who act according to the microeconomic model of rationality and those who don't. A classic example of a game that can be used to test rationality is the ultimatum game. Many forms of this game exist, but we show you a simple version that characterizes the problem.

In this version Polly starts with $100. She makes an offer to Quentin that she'll split some of the $100 with him, and if Quentin accepts the offer, they'll both take home their respective shares of the $100. If, however, Quentin doesn't accept the offer, they both get zero. How much do you think Polly should offer? (To make it easy, the offer has to be in whole numbers of dollars.)

The answer is for Polly to offer Quentin $1. After all, if Quentin is economically rational, he'll realize that $1 is better than nothing, which is what he would get if he doesn't accept the offer. However, this is not what is observed when the game is played. In fact, more often than not, people reject any offer that doesn't give them a fair — their definition of fair, of course — share of the sum of money.

You can try this game yourself with a friend (or someone you really want to annoy) by adopting Polly's strategy and seeing what happens.

Getting out of the Dilemma by Repeating a Game

In all the models discussed so far, the game is *one shot* — that is, it's played only once. Think of this as being tantamount to a forced deadline (often used in negotiations to get a deal, especially when one party is holding out for a better deal). The key thing is that the Nash equilibria we've found are all based on the fact that both parties participate only once (check out the earlier section "Finding the best outcome: The Nash equilibrium").

But what happens if the players are in a game that's repeated over many rounds, such as in the Prisoner's Dilemma, where neither party can be sure whether the other's going to cooperate?

Well, certainly, the players' previous histories in playing the Prisoner's Dilemma game matter. For instance, suppose one player has a reputation for never ratting. As a result, his fellow wise guys trust him not to confess, and so he has no shortage of accomplices for his nefarious deeds because they understand that as partners in crime they will cooperate in the Dove, Dove Nash equilibrium.

But you may say, hang on a sec: what about where you said that the Nash equilibrium for the Prisoner's Dilemma is Hawk, Hawk? Yes, but the difference between the two situations is whether the parties get to play the game again. If you play a Prisoner's Dilemma repeatedly, it turns out many behaviors can lead to a Nash equilibrium — a result that in fact can help game design and play.

To distill this point into a bit of folk wisdom, that great economist Marx — Groucho, not Karl — said that the key to success in life is honesty and fair play: "If you can fake that, you got it made." In the case of a repeated game, signaling honesty may confer the advantage of making it more likely that you'll move to the Dove, Dove outcome and avoid being stuck in Hawk, Hawk.

Investigating a repeated game using the extensive form

The *strategic* or *normal form* of a two-player game is a technical way of saying that the payoffs are arranged in a matrix, where player 1 is the Row player, and player 2 the Column player. The Nash equilibrium for a one-shot game can be found by elimination of worse or dominated strategies. Games that are repeated or go on over many rounds are often better understood by looking at them as if they were a set of sequential decisions. This representation of the game is called the *extensive* or *tree* form of the game.

We do this for the Prisoner's Dilemma in Figure 16-7. The important thing to notice is that the payoffs at the end of the tree are the same as the payoffs in the strategic form of the game. We've done this for a one-shot game because it keeps everything simpler for now — the key point to note is that the payoffs at the end of the extensive form should be the same as the payoffs in the strategic form we used up until now.

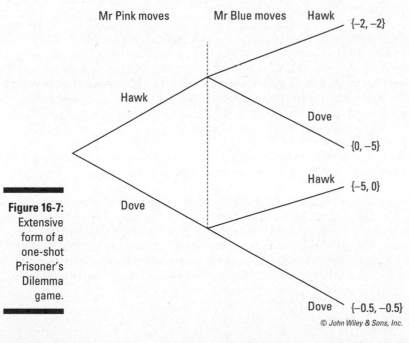

Figure 16-7: Extensive form of a one-shot Prisoner's Dilemma game.

Mr Pink moves — Mr Blue moves — Hawk {–2, –2}

Hawk — Dove {0, –5}

Dove — Hawk {–5, 0}

Dove {–0.5, –0.5}

© *John Wiley & Sons, Inc.*

The extensive form and the strategic form are equivalent ways of depicting a game, in the sense that the final payoffs have to be the same. The key advantage of the extensive form is that it can make the sequence of moves clearer where that's something that matters in the game. In these one-shot games where players move at the same time, we don't really need the extensive form all that much to tell you about the equilibrium. As games get more fiendish, however, the extensive form yields more information about the underlying structures of the game.

Mixing signals: Looking at pure and mixed strategies

In many games — especially sporting matches — a player gains by being unpredictable. To understand why a tennis player or a quarterback wants to keep their opponent guessing, game theorists make a distinction between a pure and a mixed strategy for a player:

- **Pure strategy:** Describes what the player will do, with probability 1 at each point in the game in the game. In the Prisoner's Dilemma, both Hawk and Dove strategies are pure strategies.

- **Mixed strategy:** Describes what the player will do, with some probability at each point. Imagine that the two players from the Prisoner's Dilemma example toss a coin in order to decide whether to play Hawk or Dove. In this case, each plays Hawk with 50 percent probability and Dove with 50 percent probability.

As a general rule, for a player to want to "mix" her moves — that is, play Dove if heads or play Hawk if tails — she has to be indifferent between playing Hawk and playing Dove. For if she weren't indifferent, she could do better by playing Hawk (or Dove) against her opponent, in which case she shouldn't be mixing. When playing sports, you typically want to keep your opponent guessing about what you are going to do. A mixed strategy can tell you what is the best way to keep your opponent guessing.

Game theory can help us look at the best strategy for a penalty taker in a soccer match, as mentioned at the beginning of this chapter.

Another example is what is called the *madman strategy*. This game makes it clear how "mixing" strategies is a way to play a repeated game. Here a player deliberately tries to confuse the other player into making a sub-optimal move by switching between moves unpredictably. In a repeated Prisoner's Dilemma, a player using the madman strategy switches between Hawk and Dove in such a way that the other player can't extract rhyme or reason from his moves, sometimes confessing and sometimes not confessing. The effect is to create uncertainty in the other player, who's deprived of information about what the first player may do and therefore has less knowledge upon which to base his actions.

The madman strategy isn't very good for getting cooperation. There is an important difference in economics between the type of game in which one party can make a gain over the other player and a more cooperative game where both parties gain from achieving cooperation. In a competitive market setting, holding an advantage over the other party in a repeated game can be desirable. But if cooperation is the desired goal, building trust is often the first stage, and you will have difficulty trusting someone who keeps changing his moves on a seeming whim.

Chapter 17

Keeping Things Stable: The Nash Equilibrium

As we explain in Chapter 16 on game theory, the Nash equilibrium is a combination of strategies whereby each player is doing the best she possibly can given the strategies of the other players. Read the nearby sidebar "A Nash equilibrium aids human survival" for a somewhat chilling example.

Knowing about a Nash equilibrium and how you find one are important for understanding how economists go about looking at issues of competition and cooperation. As we describe in this chapter, economists use the concept of a Nash equilibrium to go beyond exchanges in markets and into wider questions of organizational behavior, bargaining, and even international negotiations, without giving up economic rationality.

A Nash equilibrium is a situation where no one has an incentive to change behavior. In that sense, Nash equilibria tend to be stable as long as the conditions around them stay stable. For instance, in the sidebar example, the peace between the nuclear powers was maintained for as long as nuclear weapons stayed out of the hands of rogue nations — ones that might not act "rationally." If, for example, North Korea suddenly got the bomb, then the stability of the arrangement would have changed, perhaps catastrophically.

You might find the same thing looking at an oligopoly, as in Chapter 11. The equilibrium described between the two firms in Cournot's model is a Nash equilibrium. However, if a third, more innovative firm enters the market, things will change. It would change the decisions of the firms in the market and eventually lead to a new Nash equilibrium.

A Nash equilibrium aids human survival

During the Cold War — which lasted approximately from 1945 to 1989 — the NATO powers and the Warsaw Pact nations found themselves committed to spending astronomical sums of money on nuclear weapons, which were never (and indeed probably could never be) used. Looking at this period of history through the lens of game theory, the strategy of building a nuclear arsenal and *not* using it is a Nash equilibrium, because no party had any incentive to move from that position. Thus, the fact that the world made it through this period is no surprise to a game theorist.

The two powers could have chosen to disarm or to use their weapons against each other, but

✔ The party that disarmed when the other didn't would have handed an incentive to the other side to use its weapons knowing that retaliation couldn't happen.

✔ The party that used its weapons would invite instant and fatal retaliation.

So, the best any of the players could achieve was to have the weapons but not use them. It may sound crazy to someone not versed in game theory, but nuclear weapons have arguably been an investment in securing peace.

So, finding the Nash equilibrium can be a useful tool for understanding market dynamics and market stability.

If you're unfamiliar with game theoretical reasoning, we suggest that you read Chapter 16 before proceeding with this one.

Defining the Nash Equilibrium Informally

The Nash equilibrium does have a formal definition (and proof) but it requires some highly advanced math. Mercifully, this section only provides three *informal* definitions that amount to the same thing without having to dip into the really hard stuff:

✔ A Nash equilibrium is a set of strategies, one for each player, such that when these strategies are played, no one player has an incentive to change strategy. The Cournot, Bertrand, and Stackelberg equilibria in Chapter 11 are Nash equilibria.

✔ A Nash equilibrium exists when each player is maximizing her payoff in response to what she anticipates the other players will do given that the other players are also choosing strategies that maximize their payoffs. Again, this applies very clearly to Oligopoly models, and situations such as a when a monopoly buyer is negotiating with a monopoly seller — the Department of Defense, for example, negotiating with Boeing.

✔ A Nash equilibrium is an outcome in which adopting a strategy or making a move that makes a player better off is impossible without making other players worse off.

The last definition ties the Nash equilibrium to the concept of *Pareto efficiency*, often used when looking at how people can be made better off. Economists describe an allocation of resources as Pareto efficient when no party can be made better off without making another party worse off. If those conditions hold at the Nash equilibrium, the payoffs are a Pareto efficient distribution. (Chapter 18 discusses Pareto efficiency more deeply.)

Looking for Balance: Where a Nash Equilibrium Must Apply

If you like, you can think of a Nash equilibrium as being a point of balance. At a Nash equilibrium, no participants have any incentive to change their behavior. You might imagine it as being like balancing on a seesaw — both people at either end could move the seesaw down, but they'd rather stay exactly as they are.

To see where a Nash equilibrium has to exist, we start by pointing out that not every game has one. In many games, if a player is restricted to choose a pure strategy (that is, choose a strategy with a probability of 1 — see Chapter 16 for more on that), it may not be possible to find a Nash equilibrium.

Consider, for example, the game Rock, Paper, Scissors as played by many a child in the playground. Each choice of rock, paper, or scissors is defeated by exactly one opponent's move — rock smashes scissors, paper wraps rock, scissors cut paper — and also defeats exactly one opponent's move. Thus the payoff matrix or strategic form of the game (flip to Chapter 16 for a definition) looks like Figure 17-1. (You'll have to work out the matrix for Sheldon Cooper's far more complicated version of Rock, Paper, Scissors, Lizard, Spock for yourself.)

	ROCK	PAPER	SCISSORS
ROCK	0,0	–1,1	1,–1
PAPER	1,–1	0,0	–1,1
SCISSORS	–1,1	1,–1	0,0

Figure 17-1: Payoff matrix for pure form of Rock, Paper, Scissors.

© John Wiley & Sons, Inc.

No Nash equilibrium (in pure strategies) exists for Rock, Paper, Scissors because for any outcome a player can make themselves better off by changing strategy. Consider the three possible outcomes when Karen plays rock in a game against Kevin:

✔ If Kevin also plays rock, Karen would've been better off playing paper.

✔ If Kevin plays paper, he wins that round and Karen would be better off switching.

✔ If Kevin plays scissors, he loses and would've been better off changing his choice.

So, no point exists where both players are going to stay happy with their moves. Irrespective of where you start with Rock, Paper, Scissors, you always end up in a situation where at least one player can be made better off by doing something different. Hence, no Nash equilibrium.

Recognizing that a Nash equilibrium must exist in mixed-strategy games

The pure strategy version of Rock, Paper, Scissors has no Nash equilibrium. But if the strategies were used with a given probability — for example, Karen played rock with probability 1/3 — then you'd see a very different outcome. What does it mean to play a strategy with probability 1/3? It's as if Karen had a pie chart divided into thirds: one third for rock, one third for scissors, and one third for paper. Before choosing, she spins a pointer on the pie chart, and where it lands is the move or action that she makes. When players mix their strategies, we can show that at least one Nash equilibrium must exist in any finite game. The equilibrium strategies in this case are probability mixes that no player has an incentive to change.

Finding a Nash equilibrium by elimination

The typical way of finding a Nash equilibrium in the strategic form of a game is by eliminating any strategies that can't be optimal to play. This method relies on the concept of *a dominant strategy*.

A strategy is dominant if, regardless of what any other player does, playing that strategy results in a higher payoff. A strategy can be dominant in two ways:

- ✔ **Weakly dominant:** If it's always at least as good as any other given strategy in terms of payoff the player gets
- ✔ **Strongly dominant:** If it always gives a higher payoff than any other possible strategy the player could choose

A good way to solve a game is to look at its strategic form and eliminate any strategies that are *dominated*. This approach involves looking at the reverse of a dominant strategy, that is, eliminating any strategy that you know a rational player *won't* play, because it is dominated irrespective of the moves of another player by another strategy.

Figure 17-2 shows an example of a strategic form of game. The method just described is called the *iterated elimination of dominated strategies*. It means, very simply, that you go eliminate one by one any strategy that wouldn't be chosen by a player, because playing another strategy would lead to higher payoffs no matter what the other player does. If you arrive to a point where no player has any incentive to change strategy, then you've "solved" the game. You found the Nash equilibrium. In the game in Figure 17-2, start by eliminating Right for the Colm player (she always does better playing Middle than Right). Once Right is eliminated for Colm, then we can eliminate Down for Rowe. Once Down is eliminated, then we can eliminate Left for Colm, and voila we have found the Nash Equilibrium (Up, Middle) and you can award yourself a gold star.

Colm

		Left	Middle	Right
	Up	**1**, 0	**1**, 2	0, **1**
Rowe	Down	0, **3**	0, 1	**2**, 0

Figure 17-2:
Finding a
Nash
equilibrium
by elimina-
tion of
dominated
strategies.

© John Wiley & Sons, Inc.

Solving a repeated game by backward induction

A *repeated game,* such as a repeated version of the Prisoner's Dilemma (described in detail in Chapter 16) takes place over many rounds, and the overall payoffs are computed at the end of the game. The matrix you get by looking at the payoffs for one round is the strategic form of the game from the last chapter.

The best way to find out which of the payoffs for the repeated game corresponds to a Nash equilibrium is to solve by *backward induction*. This technique means starting at the payoffs for the last round of the game and looking for the Nash equilibrium for that final round. Then you work backwards and see what players would do at the second-to-last round, knowing what will happen in the final round. Keep rolling back to the beginning or first round of the game. As you roll back through the game, you eliminate paths that don't lead to an outcome that would have been chosen.

As an example, consider the *trust game*, which has been applied to the relationship between managers and workers or to the "trust but verify" strategies in disarmament. In the trust game, two participants have to decide whether or not to trust each other. In the first round, the first player, Yvonne, has to decide between trusting the second player, Zak, or not trusting him. After Yvonne makes her choice, Zak has to choose in the second round between honoring Yvonne's trust or betraying it. We set up the game and see how to solve it.

Start with Yvonne:

> ✔ If Yvonne decides not to trust Zak, the relationship is over, and both parties gain zero.
>
> ✔ If Yvonne does trust Zak, he makes the next choice:
>
> > • If Zak chooses to honor this trust, he gets 1 and Yvonne gets 1.
> >
> > • If Zak cheats, he gets 2 and Yvonne gets –1.
>
> ✔ If Yvonne knows this, what should she do?

To solve the game using backward induction, you start by writing the game down in *extensive form* as a tree. (Or take a look at Figure 17-3, which does this for you.)

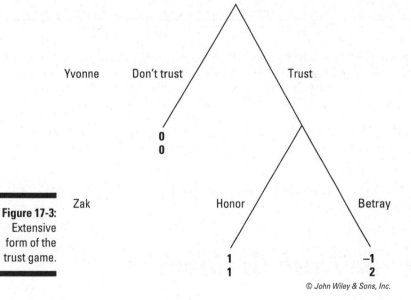

Figure 17-3: Extensive form of the trust game.

© *John Wiley & Sons, Inc.*

The payoff numbers can be equally well represented on a *strategic form* matrix, and so you can use the method in the preceding section to find the Nash equilibrium — and if you don't trust us, you can verify the results by doing so!

Working backwards from the very end, Zak's round, note that Zak has a dominant strategy: Starting from this part of the tree, Zak does better, getting 2 (as opposed to 1) when he betrays Yvonne. Thus Zak will betray Yvonne.

Scoundrels don't profit in the long run

One application of backward induction is to ask about the ability of the financial market to police itself. Trust will be important to that answer since financial transactions involve the credibility of promises to pay. Backward induction using the trust game tells us that if the financial market is significantly infected with distrust, it will have fewer trades going on in it. This suggests that self-regulation may be workable because even though playing dishonorably may seem like a profitable strategy, it poisons the whole business environment, reducing the amount of business you do and worsening your eventual payoff. The role of government should be to support institutions and contract enforcement that fosters trust. When the near-collapse happened in the wake of the Lehman Brothers bankruptcy in 2008, both trust and credit nearly vanished from the market.

Now go roll back to Yvonne's move. If she knows what Zak's payoffs to cheating are, then she can anticipate that he's going to cheat, and so she chooses not to trust. Thus, the business relationship terminates before it has a chance to be poisoned.

You can say that solving this game for a Nash equilibrium finds that Yvonne and Zak do their best given each other's payoffs by staying well away from each other.

Check out the nearby sidebar "Scoundrels don't profit in the long run" for a timely financial example.

Applying the Nash Equilibrium in Economics

Microeconomists use game theory to investigate many issues in economics — ranging from bargaining to imperfect competition to choice of political affiliation. Here are two classic examples of how economists use game theory — first to look at what a monopoly might do to defend its dominant share of a market, and then to look at what happens to societies over the long run when members of that society have different strategies for dealing with people who would do them wrong.

Deterring entry: A monopolist's last resort

If a company has been successful enough to gain a dominant share of a market, it often wants to prevent a rival from coming in and stealing that market away.

Entry deterrence is a key concept in antitrust policy. The main antitrust statute in the United States, the Sherman Act, makes it clear that exploiting monopoly power to impede competition is illegal. So, for example, it is illegal to temporarily price below cost to prevent a competing firm from surviving in the market. If the competing firm is a would-be entrant, it would not be able to afford to enter the industry.

In Figure 17-4 we set up the situation as a game between a monopolist and an entrant. The entrant chooses to enter or not, and the monopolist chooses to retaliate (fight the entrant) or not. The monopolist wants to make the payoffs turn out so that the Nash equilibrium has the entrant choosing "Don't enter." When you analyze the game, you will see that it is a variant of the trust game in the earlier section "Solving a repeated game by backward induction."

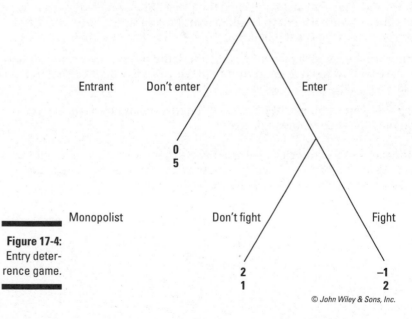

Figure 17-4: Entry deterrence game.

© John Wiley & Sons, Inc.

Analyzing society with economic reasoning

Economists have come a long way from merely studying markets and often look for ways of applying economic reasoning to difficult problems in other areas. One of these is the evolution of social institutions. Economists are able to use the insights of game theory to consider how cooperation and competition shape the strategies people use to punish those who cross them.

In society people have two ways of dealing with those who act against others: forgiving them or punishing them. If you think of society as a set of repeated Prisoner's Dilemma games (see Chapter 16), you can develop a model that looks at punishing and forgiving as two different strategies. If the repeated games have different Nash equilibria, you can then think about how to characterize the different ways of behaving and compare the equilibria, telling you over the long run which strategy would be preferred from society's point of view.

Typically, economists compare and contrast three strategies for playing a repeated Prisoner's Dilemma (if you're unfamiliar with the roles of Hawks and Doves, check out Chapter 16):

- ✔ **Tit for Tat:** Players start by playing the Dove. When one plays a Hawk, the other players default to Hawk too until the first player to play Hawk returns to playing Dove. Then, everyone else reverts to Dove.

- ✔ **Grim Trigger:** After a player has defaulted, the other players punish her by playing Hawk and never return to playing Dove, whatever the original defaulter's subsequent moves.

- ✔ **Firm but Fair:** A bit like tit for tat, but the first default to Hawk is forgiven, and only the second one punished.

The evidence is that strategies like Firm but Fair tend to do better in simulations than Grim Triggers — providing evidence that though nice guys may finish last, nice societies tend to be better in the long run.

Chapter 18

Knowing How to Win at Auctions

· ·

· ·

*P*eople often associate auctions with the sale of antiques and artworks, often sold in specialist auctions run by famous auction houses such as Christie's or Sotheby's. For example, in June 2006 Christie's in New York auctioned Vincent van Gogh's painting *Portrait of Dr. Gachet* for $82 million (which, allowing for inflation over the last ten years, amounts to $152 million in today's prices — not bad for a man who sold only one painting during his lifetime). Or they think of auction sites on the Internet, like eBay, where you can bid on just about anything imaginable.

But all sorts of other things can be auctioned, too, and they don't need to be physical objects. The U.S. Federal Communications Commission auctions off valuable parts of the radio spectrum to mobile phone networks. Since 1994, it has conducted more than 85 auctions and raised roughly $60 billion for the U.S. Treasury.

In an auction, the seller tries to maximize the value of the assets that it wants to sell. More potential buyers exist than assets, so the seller attempts to use the mechanism design of an auction to reveal the value that buyers ascribe to the asset in order to get the highest price possible.

Auctions can be devilishly tricky things to participate in, with sellers and bidders using all sorts of tactics and maneuvers. In this chapter, we talk you through some of the features of auctions and introduce you to the underlying theory behind auctions from the seller's, the bidder's, and the auctioneer's perspective. We show you why auctions are such a useful tool for allocating assets, and that despite their positive features, they also have some limitations and downsides — even for the auction winner.

Spotting Different Kinds of Auction

The term *auction* is a category rather than a specific thing. Many different types of auction exist, each with advantages and disadvantages depending on whether you take a seller's, a buyer's, or even society's perspective. They all have a mechanism in which an auctioneer solicits bids for the item under the hammer, but they vary in the means they take to get to the final sale price.

Economists have explored many existing types of auction using economic theory and discovered that the results vary from auction to auction. They've found that being specific about the design pays off when describing individual types of auction.

An auction can be considered a refinement of the conditions of a monopoly, with only one seller and several buyers. When only one buyer exists, the condition is a *bilateral* monopoly, and the good is more likely to be disbursed by negotiation than auction. The price that buyers pay is likely to be above the marginal cost of the item, and so auctions do mean that surplus tends to go to the seller.

Knowing the type of auction you're in

Here are the most common attributes of the many types of auction. Often these types aren't mutually exclusive, so you can talk about a sealed bid, second price, English auction (flip to the later section "Making bidders honest with a Vickrey auction" for more on this type of auction):

- **English auction:** The most familiar type, from auction scenes in films and on TV. The auctioneer starts at a floor price — a minimum price below which the good won't be sold, usually selected by the auctioneer who represents the seller — and successive bids raise the price until the item is eventually sold to the highest bidder.

- **Dutch auction:** The price starts at a price ceiling and each successive round consists of the auctioneer dropping the price until someone takes the item.

- **Open outcry:** Each bidder reveals his bid to all other bidders by calling out the sum he wants to pay to receive the lot.

- **Sealed bid:** Bidders submit their bids in sealed envelopes, so that other bidders don't know the bids. Variants can include different degrees of disclosure required of bidders or the auctioneer.

- **First price:** The winning bid is the highest declared bid when the auctioneer finally says, "Sold!"

✔ **Second price:** The winning bidder pays the second-highest declared bid. So, if you'd bid $100 and the winner had bid $110, the winner finally pays $100 (your second-highest bid) when he comes to take the goods home. This refinement gives bidders the incentives to bid how much the item is worth to them, and not to misrepresent their valuation of the good.

✔ **Reservation (or reserve) price:** A variant with a floor price, below which the item isn't sold (check out the later section "Setting a reservation price wisely" for more details).

✔ **Online auctions:** Sometimes these allow the seller to set a price at which the auction ends and the item goes to the first bidder to meet the "buy it now" price.

The other major distinction that economists make between auctions concerns what's being sold:

✔ **Private-value auctions:** Every bidder may have a different valuation for the good in question, as is the case for art auctions.

✔ **Common-value auctions:** The good has the same value for every participant, but because of uncertainty their estimations of that value may differ. This case applies for some mineral-rights auctions, where the rights have the same value, and bidders differ by belief.

Suppose, for example, that 10 billion barrels of oil are under Dallas Airport, and the rights to drill are being allocated in an auction. Every potential bidder would get the same amount of oil if they win the auction. However, the amount that they're willing to pay depends on their belief about how much that oil would be worth to them; the amount may vary wildly among the bidders if they have different costs of extracting the oil or different beliefs about how much they'd make from selling it.

Designing an auction to get (most of) what you want

Economists are often asked to give their opinions on which particular kind of auction is best for a particular situation. They usually express their answer in terms of two criteria:

✔ **Pareto efficiency (or optimality):** The outcome of the auction should be *Pareto efficient,* meaning that making one party better off without making another party worse off isn't possible.

✔ **Profit maximization:** The auction should yield the highest expected profit to the seller.

Given these criteria, as the economist you can examine some of the auction types and score reasons to prefer one or another in a particular context.

An auction is a type of *mechanism design* and is similar to designing a game that players play. When you design a mechanism, you're assuming that players have privileged information over their own strategies but that the expected payoffs are known to the designer. We discuss mechanism design more fully in Chapter 16.

Meeting an auction's two core criteria

For the mechanism to be Pareto efficient, the good must go to the bidder with the highest bid. To see why, suppose two bidders bid for a good. Bridgette bids $100 and Brian bids $80, but suppose for some reason Brian gets the good. If he then sells the good to Bridgette for $90 both parties make themselves better off without making anyone worse off. So the result of the auction couldn't have been Pareto efficient. (The seller, by the way, is part of the original auction, not the subsequent transaction, and here the focus is on whether the allocation between the bidders is Pareto efficient.)

When you know every bidder's valuation exactly, profit maximization for the seller is easy. The question is what to do when the auctioneer or seller doesn't know their valuations. Here, examining the different types of auctions with economic theory helps. But the answer can only "help" rather than "exactly predict," for the simple reason that the behavior of the bidders depends on their true beliefs about the value of the good, which the auctioneer doesn't know.

Setting a reservation price wisely

One way to increase the likelihood of maximizing profits in an auction is to set a reservation price — a minimum price lower than which the good won't be sold. Sometimes the reservation isn't met, but in all other cases, the auctioneer is certain of getting a level of profit above the reservation.

On the online auction site eBay, there are over 81 million active users and billions of goods are auctioned off annually. Minimum reserve price or minimum starting bids are common in eBay auctions, and evidence from eBay suggests that higher reserve prices decrease the number of bidders and increase the likelihood that the good is sold. Conditional on a sale occurring, setting a higher minimum reserve price does increase the expected revenue of that sale.

When you set a reservation price, sometimes you'll fail to sell the item, meaning that Pareto efficiency is not achieved. Having a reservation price still maximizes expected profit even though sometimes the auction fails. In this case, you're trading off between Pareto optimality and profit maximization.

Bidding for Beginners

The most important piece of advice that economists have for bidders in an auction is: *Read the rules carefully*. Optimal bidding strategy varies wildly among the different auctions, and because some types (check out the earlier section "Knowing the type of auction you're in") can be significantly more complex — especially in awarding huge procurement contracts — make sure that you have all the small print covered.

Modeling a simple auction

Despite the warning that opens this section, some of the simpler types of auction are easy to model.

Lawrence Friedman's analysis of a lowest-price, sealed-bid, common-value auction provides one such framework. Suppose there are a number of painters, say N, bidding on a contract to paint a historic home. Each painter bids an amount of what they want for doing the job — say b_i — where i is the number of the bidder. The lowest bid wins the job. If a bid b wins, the yield is $b - c$, where c is the cost incurred by each of the painters to do the job.

The probability that painter i's bid b_i is lower than the bid b is equal to

$$F_i(b) = \text{Prob}(b_i \le b)$$

F indicates the likelihood of any individual bidder bidding less than the bid, b.

If the winning bid is b, that means that the other bidders $N - 1$ have submitted a bid that has a winning probability of $1 - F_i(b)$. Because probabilities must sum to 1, the probability of something not happening for a bidder is $1 - F$.

The probability of winning the bid is equal to the probability of the other $N - 1$ bidders not winning, so we can expand the expression for winning in terms of all other participants losing. For $N - 1$ other bidders, it must equal

$$P(b) = \left(\left(1 - F_1(b)\right) \ldots \left(1 - F_{N-1}(b)\right) \right)$$

Expected profit of the winning bidder is

$$P(b)(b - c)$$

where $P(b)$ indicates the probability of winning the bid. This is the expression that Friedman recommends maximizing.

To do that, you want to have as much information as possible about other bidders' past bidding behavior.

One challenge for contractors bidding on a job in a sealed-bid auction is knowing what their costs of doing the job will be. Contractors have a best guess at what a contract will cost without really knowing what's going to happen to costs over that period. For instance, when bidding for the contract to repair the Enterprise Canal Bridge in Idaho, a company may have a plan and some guesses on how much the contract will cost, but the firm can't know exactly and thus may still get caught out bidding too low because costs turn out to be higher.

Providing advice on a bidding strategy means you may have to make assumptions about the costs and/or benefits of the future value of the item.

For instance, if you know that Mondrian's reputation in the art world is about to take a tumble — hey, art is a rough world! — then the rational decision is to bid a lower price in an upcoming auction, because the value of the option to resell the item is going to be lower. Of course, as a Mondrian fan, the art value received from the item may be enough for you to contemplate bidding sub-optimally high for the item. If the auction is a private-value auction, this is all that matters to you — whether you personally value the item at the bid price. For a common-value case, on the other hand, the expectation of what will happen to the value of the item is important.

Bidding late: The Internet auction phenomenon

An open-outcry, English auction allows successive rounds of bidding to reveal more information about the valuations of successive bidders, which isn't the case in — for instance — a Dutch auction (see the definitions given earlier). It definitely is the case, though, in an Internet auction, which is generally structured as a *Vickrey auction* (more on these in the later section "Making bidders honest with a Vickrey auction").

An Internet auction goes through successive rounds of bidding up to a final deadline. What's interesting is that a high percentage of bids are made close to the deadline — around 37 per cent in the last minute. The Internet auction house eBay calls this strategy *sniping*.

Economists have come up with two explanations for sniping:

✔ **Bidders don't want to tip their hand to other bidders:** If you're an expert on, say, rare guitars, and the auction site is designed to display your profile with your bid, then you may want to delay bidding to prevent other people from knowing of your interest in, say, that rare Gretsch White Falcon.

✔ **Implicit collusion between buyers:** In the case of an auction, collusion means that the bidders have coordinated their strategies by waiting until the last few moments before the auction ends (of waiting until the last few moments before bidding), so there is less time for bidders to bid up the price.

Imagine a *second-price* auction, where the prize is a White Falcon guitar worth $6,000, with a reserve price of $2,000. If two bidders start their bids early and both honestly state their true value as $6,000, they'll end up with one receiving the guitar for $6,000 — great for the seller, but the buyer gets no consumer surplus. Suppose instead that they wait until the last second. Now only one of those bids may get through, and by the second-price rule of the auction, that bidder ends up paying the reservation price of $2,000!

Gaming an auction

Auctions are useful for revealing the value that a buyer is willing to pay for an item. Sometimes, though, auctions fail to work out the way the auctioneer or the buyers want. Dodgy behavior can take place on both sides of the deal, with buyer and seller possibly having incentives to take the process away from a true and fair auction, just as they may do in a cartel (discussed in Chapter 16).

Although auction design can mitigate these "gaming" factors, you also need to be on the lookout for *bent* auctions, which occur when auction rules are broken or bent, like trying to learn what others are bidding in advance of making a bid. Authorities and regulators often are on the lookout and can get bent out of shape about it.

Trying to avoid an auction

In certain cases, forcing someone *not* to auction something can be a viable strategy.

When negotiating for the transfer of the talented Welsh soccer player Gareth Bale from Tottenham Hotspurs, the buying club Real Madrid — allegedly — tried everything to make sure another potential buyer wasn't found. Why? Well, Tottenham could've leveraged the two potential buyers against each other to get a higher price for the player. Eventually Real Madrid paid an undisclosed sum believed to be around 90 million euro ($99 million) for Bale's services. If another bidder had emerged, the final sum might well have been even higher.

Colluding

Sometimes bidders collude by not making competitive bids against each other or by pooling their bids and redistributing the returns after the auction.

Bidder collusion is illegal and is a potentially pervasive problem. Not surprisingly, it is a target for antitrust enforcement. In 1990, the U.S. General Accounting Office reported that from 1982 to 1988, more than half of the criminal restraint of trade cases filed by the U.S. Department of Justice's Antitrust Division involved auction markets. If a cartel is operative, then it is easy to see how it could instruct its highest-valuing member to bid a value while all other cartel members bid some amount below the auctioneer's reserve price.

Summoning buyers

An auctioneer can receive a higher price for a good by summoning a *phantom* buyer. Imagine an art auction where a phone bidder is in cahoots with the auctioneer and keeps phoning in a bid increment until the auctioneer guesses that he isn't going to get away with raising the price any higher. More potential buyers are therefore kept in the game (even if one isn't real), competing against each other to raise the price.

This situation — again, allegedly — was encountered in a soccer transfer where the selling club "found" a bidder very late in the process who was willing to pay double the eventual buying club's initial bid. The buying club decided to bite the bullet and pay the fee. The selling club received double its expected compensation for the transfer.

In case you're wondering, transfers of star team players can often appear murky because of the amount of private information involved and the relatively low requirements for disclosure compared to many other industries.

Suffering from the Winner's Curse

Oscar Wilde famously identified two tragedies in life: not getting what you want and getting what you want. The winner's curse is a problem that comes from winning an auction.

Essentially, the problem is that in an English, first-price auction, bidders always have an incentive to bid more than they can afford to get an item — and, of course, the auctioneer has no knowledge of what they can afford and is unable to know this until the auction concludes.

This issue is primarily a problem with common-value auctions — where the true value of the item isn't known. In bidding for a sports franchise, airwave spectra, mineral rights, or broadcast licenses, it's a perennial problem, because the true monetary value of those items is never known in advance. Microeconomics is often used to look at the allocation of goods and services, and so this makes the incentive to bid too high a real economic problem — whether you're designing the auction or bidding in one.

Making bidders honest with a Vickrey auction

Auction houses can mitigate the bidding-more-than-you-can-afford problem in a number of ways. For instance, they can require a bank guarantee before someone enters the auction, so that if a person doesn't have evidence of being able to afford the good, he can't enter the race for the Gauguin.

But consider the problem of a government auction of a valuable license. In this case, the winner itself may not know that it has been cursed until some-time into the period of the license.

The International Olympic Committee (IOC) is an organization whose bidding contests attract a great deal of attention. Major cities see hosting the games as an opportunity to attract tourists and be the center of international attention. However, overbidding for hosting the winter or summer Olympic Games may not be revealed until well after the last gold medal has been won. The host city that overbids for the games may be left with a debt burden, often in the billions of dollars, that taxpayers will have to foot the bill for. The fear of overbidding was a motivating force in the 2015 No Boston Olympics, a volunteer-based group that was persistent and successful in spreading its message that hosting the 2024 Summer games in Boston would be risky and expensive and would leave taxpayers on the hook with no economic gains. The city's quest to host the games soon came to an end when the U.S. Olympic Committee pulled the plug on its bid.

Meeting the Vickrey auction

One of the auction designs that doesn't have an incentive to overbid is the sealed-bid, second-price, English auction, better known as a *Vickrey auction* after celebrated Canadian economist William Vickrey.

In a Vickrey auction, the item under the hammer goes to the bidder who submitted the highest bid, but at the price bid by the second-highest bidder. This design removes the incentive to bid too high, because the price that's eventually accepted is the second bid.

In an English auction, the good goes to the highest bidder at the price that bidder was willing to pay. The result is therefore Pareto optimal (as explained in the earlier section "Designing an auction to get (most of) what you want"). In a Vickrey auction, participants make sealed bids, which gives them an incentive to bid a value that honestly reflects their valuation of the bid. But in a standard English sealed-bid auction, this isn't necessarily the case. How does changing from a standard auction to a Vickrey auction change things?

Seeing the Vickrey auction in action

Suppose two bidders, bidder 1 and bidder 2, have valuations for a good, v_1 and v_2 respectively, and bid b_1 and b_2 for it. The expected payoff for bidder 1 is

$$\text{Prob}\left(b_1 \geq b_2\right)\left(v_1 - b_2\right)$$

You don't need to consider the case where b_2 is bigger than b_1, because in that case bidder 1 receives 0, and the expected payoff is zero.

Two possible bidding cases exist that get the best payoff:

- **When v_1 is bigger than b_2:** In this case, bidder 1 is best off when making the probability of a winning bid as high as possible. Thus, given that his valuation of the item is v_1, he makes b_1 as high as makes sense and so he sets $b_1 = v_1$, his true valuation of the item.

- **When $v_1 < b_2$ and bidder 1 wants to make the possibility of winning as small as possible:** How would bidder 1 best do that? Well, by bidding v_1. That way, bidder 1 is unlikely to win the auction and would get the best possible value by bidding less than the valuation of the person who wants it most, which would be bidder 2.

The key point here is that in either case, the incentive for the bidder is to declare his true valuation of the bid. In both the cases, the most important factor is that if the auction is set up in this way, no one has any incentive to bid other than his true valuation of the good.

Perusing the curse in public procurement

When the government auctions to bidders a license to operate some activity, it's trying to do the best for the public purse by maximizing the value it gets for the license under auction. The problem is that because the government and the bidder don't know what the costs or the expected revenues of the winning bid will be, public procurement contracts are often subject to winner's curse problems.

Stamping approval for the Vickrey auction

Vickrey noticed how the sealed-bid, second-price auction affected bidders' behavior while studying the market for collectible stamps. These were sold at conventions using an open-outcry, English auction and by mail order using a sealed-bid, second-price auction — now called a Vickrey auction.

Vickrey noticed that the two auctions showed the same results, although the sealed-bid, second-price auction did so over only one round of bidding. Thus, the open-outcry, English auction's tendency to equate price with the true value of an item could be found in a sealed-bid auction, as long as the second-highest price was eventually what was paid.

Typically, a public procurement auction tends to be a sealed-bid, lowest-price auction. Bidders bid for the lowest possible contract fee they can get from the government, the one with the lowest fee getting the franchise.

Even if the auction is completed at the second price, however, because winners don't know exactly how the revenues and costs of the franchise will work out, situations still exist in which the franchise may prove to be too expensive to operate. Typically, these issues are mitigated through the contractual system, so that the franchise may be conditional, and the government or bidder can cancel the agreement (often subject to penalties).

Clearly, therefore, the ability of mechanism design to bring order to an uncertain world is limited. Often both designer and bidder are subject to significant uncertainties, and more importantly, they both have a rationale for measuring the uncertainties and a technique for mitigating the penalties of getting things wrong. A bid is always an estimate, in these cases, of the value of the contract rather than a direct valuation of the contract, so don't be too hard on parties that make errors. Being wrong about uncertain futures is easy — people ever getting such things right is more surprising.

Chapter 19

Understanding the Game: Credible Threats and Signals

In This Chapter

▶ Seeking an equilibrium concept that removes non-credible threats

▶ Finding and using an equilibrium for positive signals

*O*ne *wicked* problem (as we use the term in Chapter 14) is that people rarely have perfect information, particularly when making strategic decisions in a game-like situation. Sometimes information is *asymmetric* — one party or player knowing more than another, as discussed in Chapter 15). Sometimes a player is unable to figure out the other's best moves because the player is unsure about the type of opponent it faces in the game. In the Prisoner's Dilemma from Chapter 16, for instance, neither party *knows* what the other one will do, but *infers* what is in the player's interest from their payoffs. But what if a player is unsure about the payoffs of the other player because the other player could be a *good guy* with one set or a *bad guy* with another set of payoffs?

In reality, people typically do have imperfect or limited information. In a game-like situation they don't know entirely what the other party will do, and so they look for information to go on in order to work out the right bargain or the right move.

Suppose, for example, you're deciding whether or not to employ someone. Taking a look at her resume, you notice that she worked for a prestigious employer. You see that information as a sign that the person is a good bet to take on, and so you decide to call her in for an interview. A candidate with a less prestigious history may not fare so well.

Economists call the type of information in a resume a *signal.* It's an imperfect piece of information about a person's productivity in a new job, but it can be helpful to you in figuring out your next move.

In this chapter, we discuss signaling games where a player wants to signal or convey information to the other player about what type of player they are. In other words, these are games of asymmetric information, where one player knows their type but the other player does not. In each case, game theory looks at the signal and sees what payoffs you can infer from it.

Refining the Nash Equilibrium to Deal with Threats

In general, game theory looks at threats by dividing them into two categories: credible and non-credible. Distinguishing the two types of threat is difficult in real life, because it depends on you knowing quite a bit about the other party and what they might do.

In using a game theoretic model, we work from the assumption that the player issuing the threat of a future move is rational and plays the game in a way to secure the best payoff for that player. Therefore, you can evaluate a threat to see whether it leaves the player worse off — in terms of payoff — if carried out than not carrying out the threat. If so, we say the threat is non-credible.

In turn, this approach means using a stronger definition of the Nash equilibrium from Chapter 17 that eliminates non-credible threats: This equilibrium concept is called a *subgame-perfect Nash equilibrium*. If, after eliminating any non-credible threats, you still have a Nash equilibrium, it's subgame perfect.

Finding a subgame-perfect Nash equilibrium by elimination

The best way to check whether a Nash equilibrium is subgame perfect is by backward induction (as explained in Chapter 17). To do so, it is best to write out the game in its extensive or tree form and work backwards from the end, eliminating any branch that a player has no incentive to move down.

If a rational person or entity wouldn't do something, that action or behavior is non-credible from the standpoint of game theory.

A non-credible threat is a threat in a sequential game that a *rational* player would actually not carry out, because it would not be in their best interest to do so. For example, a frustrated parent driving the family to a summer vacation destination may threaten the kids quarrelling in the car by saying, "If you don't start behaving, I am going to turn around the car and cancel the vacation." The game-theoretic–savvy kids may reason that it is most unlikely that the parent would turn around and cancel the vacation — lose the deposit and so on. A better threat would be no dessert at lunch.

A non-credible threat is made in the hope that it will be believed, and therefore the threatening undesirable action will not have to be carried out. For a threat to be credible, it is one that should the occasion arise it will be fulfilled. In solving a game, we eliminate non-credible threats through backward induction, and the remaining equilibria are subgame-perfect Nash equilibria.

Exploring subgame perfection in an entry deterrence game

Here we explore a simple game and discuss how to eliminate non-credible actions. A common application of subgame perfection in economics is within games of *entry deterrence* — for instance, when a competitor in a market is trying to prevent an aggressive entrant from coming into that market. This game is appropriate in such a case because the working assumption about a business is that it is rational (otherwise it's unlikely to stay a business very long), so weeding out irrational strategies is relatively easy.

In this game, NewCo is deciding whether to enter a market currently held by the monopolist OldStuff. NewCo gets to move first, deciding whether or not to enter the market — if it does, OldStuff decides whether or not to retaliate. Given the payoffs in the tree (see Figure 19-1), what's the Nash equilibrium? In the figure, the numbers give the payoffs to the two companies from following the strategies in each branch of the tree.

One Nash equilibrium is for NewCo not to enter, because if it does, OldStuff has threatened to cut its prices and punish NewCo. But is this threat credible? No, because it would leave OldStuff worse off, so the equilibrium isn't subgame perfect; therefore, NewCo can see that it's not credible — and therefore, NewCo can enter knowing that OldStuff can't punish it without hurting itself.

In Chapter 13 (on monopoly), we say that a monopolist may decide to take losses in the short run to keep a competitor out. This could happen because the entrant may not know what kind of incumbent firm it will face if it enters — a high-cost one or a low-cost one. This is a situation in which one player does not know the payoff matrix of its opponent. Taking losses in the short run can be a way to convince the entrant that it is a low-cost rival and to keep out. We explore this strategy in the next section.

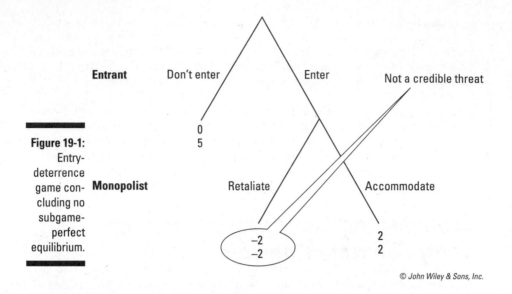

Figure 19-1:
Entry-
deterrence
game con-
cluding no
subgame-
perfect
equilibrium.

© John Wiley & Sons, Inc.

Employing game-theoretic reasoning in real-world situations can be challenging. You may not know all the necessary information. What if a company is deploying the madman strategy described in Chapter 16 to confuse a potential purchaser? Or what if you are dealing with an entity that does not behave rationally, such as a rogue nation or terrorist group?

Deterring entry: A guide to the dark arts

Given that we rule out strategies that involve taking a loss — because they're non-credible threats — let's dig deeper to see how a firm with a dominant position in a market could signal to a would-be entrant that it should stay out.

Firms can use a number of deterrent strategies in the real world, some of which may be illegal for larger companies under competition or antitrust laws. All these strategies have their basis in the entry-deterrence game, and so they all provide some reason to believe that they may signal a retaliatory action:

✔ **Limit pricing:** A monopolist can price below its profit-maximizing monopoly price and make lower profits in the short run in order to deter entry in the longer run. This pricing behavior signals to an entrant that if it tries to grab market share, it's going to be up against a low-cost competitor that can support lower prices, and it's therefore unlikely to enter the market profitably.

Two problems exist with this tactic:

- Although economically sensible, it might attract the attention of regulators — who could be on the lookout for entry-deterring strategies. If you went as far as pricing below your average variable costs, you'd be acting illegally.

- The entrant may not interpret the pricing signal unless it's accompanied by a statement of commitment to continue that pricing when it enters. Low prices means selling more output, so a commitment could be an investment in a new factory to support limit pricing.

✔ **Creation of brand loyalty, and advertising:** Investment in creating a brand name is a type of sunk cost — when the money is spent, it's unrecoverable whether the investment is successful or not. The intention is to make the entrant see the cost of entry as including the cost of making a comparable effort in advertising, branding, and marketing. If the effort seems sufficiently high, the entrant stays away.

✔ **Raising the cost of exit:** Again, the way to achieve this is by creating a market environment that requires investments incurring large sunk costs. In that case, leaving the market will be costly — an entrant will have to think carefully about whether entering it is worthwhile because those investments will be lost if it leaves the market. The issue for policy makers is whether those investments benefit consumers or just raise rivals' costs.

All these strategies require some degree of *pre-commitment* to be effective — that is, committing yourself to a course of action, usually by making an investment. The value in strategic terms is that it signals to another party that you've eliminated other possibilities, so that you can be sure you're committed to whatever action you're likely to take. If that action is costly to a rival, it acts as a deterrent signal.

The legendary Chinese strategist Sun Tzu recommended that if you want your army to win, you should burn your ships after landing. The idea is that if you cut off your own retreat, you're signaling your determination to your opponent and therefore helping to break their morale — this is a very strong example of pre-commitment.

Signaling your good intentions

Of course, signals of pre-commitment aren't always negative in the sense that they deter or limit competition — although the main examples used in the preceding sections are. Perhaps two economic agents want to facilitate market transactions and use signals positively, such as is often the case with product quality. A mark or certification of product quality can be a signal to the customer that your product is of superior value, for example.

The value of this type of mark to a consumer depends on how many sellers are able to fake a similar mark:

- **If faking is hard:** The quality guarantee helps to avoid the adverse selection problem detailed in Chapter 15.

- **If faking is easy:** The quality guarantee, if anything, supports the adverse selection problem and helps eliminate the market. This provides one other rationale for companies making strenuous efforts to defend the value of their brand. If the brands are fakeable, any quality signal is lost, and bad competitors drive out good ones.

If that isn't sufficient, signaling quality by offering an expensive warranty program does the trick. The key thing that makes it doubly effective is for the warranty to be expensive. That way, the signal works in the right way and less scrupulous competitors are deterred from trying to fake it. (If in doubt, pull up the Groucho Marx quote from Chapter 16 for some sage advice.)

Responding to Positive Economic Signals

One of the important features of a market is that decision-makers respond to conditions without knowing for certain how things may turn out. As a result, participants in markets are often looking for information — to give them a sign of how things are going to be as much as for knowledge of how markets are right now.

Signals become most important when people and firms are looking for some guide to others' intended actions. Often the best guide to deciding what to do for yourself is to look for something that gives you a sign that you may be making the right choice. In predicting markets, for instance, people look for signs of what direction prices may move in; in assessing unknowns, people look for any information that confirms their view of that unknown.

The decision whether to hire someone is a classic example of this problem. Only in retrospect do you know for sure what contribution a person is able to make to your firm's value. When hiring, you have some information to go on, but there are a lot of unknowns about whether you are making the right hire.

Consider the level of an applicant's education. You hope that it includes all kinds of useful skills to indicate that hiring the person will enhance your company's profitability, but you don't know for certain until you hire the person. But even if you assume the worst — that education gives little or no benefit — looking at the applicant's education level and choosing the candidate with the most completed years may still be worthwhile.

Why? Completing a certain number of years of education is a *signal* that the person has a certain amount of stickability in the job — that she won't bail when the work looks too hard — and that she's reliable, as her continued attendance in education demonstrates.

This section describes a model and equilibrium to show you how signaling a person's ability to stick at a job would affect wages for two different groups. This is, if you like, a use of a positive signal — a signal of employability. (We could, in fact, reverse some of the assumptions and use a similar model to show how, for instance, a criminal record signals poorer ability.) In this case, though, we use a classic model to show you how signals affect a market and how the use of these positive signals may not lead to an outcome that's better for society.

Investigating signaling with a model

Economists use a framework developed in the 1970s by Michael Spence to analyze many signaling problems, the most famous of which is looking at the value of a university degree. In Spence's model, asymmetric information exists (see Chapter 15 for more on that) because one party knows more about its value than another. In this case, the applicant knows more about her potential effort and ability or value than the hirer. The employer therefore looks for a signal — something that captures, albeit imperfectly, the ability of the applicant.

Spence's framework has two types of applicants who are distinguished by their marginal product — that is, the amount of value that they add to the organization, denoted by a:

- ✔ **Good workers** have a marginal product of a_2.
- ✔ **Bad workers** have a product of a_1 with the constraint that $a_2 > a_1$.

This framework provides a simple way of making a clear distinction between the workers, and also leads to a first intuition: If you can clearly differentiate between the workers, working out what wages each type will receive in a competitive market is easy. Competition will drive wages $w_1 = a_1$ for the poor workers and $w_2 = a_2$ for the good workers (where w = wages of any given worker). A wage equal to the marginal product of labor in the two groups is also efficient.

Setting up the basic model

We continue to assume a competitive labor market, but now a firm in that market cannot distinguish between the two groups of workers beforehand. But suppose the firm knows that the proportion of good workers in the population is b and the proportion of poor workers is $(1 - b)$. Here's what happens if it offers a wage relative to the average quality of the workers:

$$w = (1-b) \, a_1 + ba_2$$

This may look familiar to the problem from Chapter 15 — where a population or a product is of two types, most of which end in market failure. Here, though, the good workers may be able to find a way of telling the potential employer which group they're in — in other words, their positive signal.

The signal in this case is how much education they've undergone, and it's related to a cost of getting an education — and specifically to the opportunity cost to the two different types of workers. Suppose that type 1 workers incur a cost c_1 per level to acquire an e_1 level of education, and that the respective figures for type 2 workers are c_2 and e_2. That means the total cost incurred by a type 1 worker is e_1c_1. Firms can observe a worker's education level before hiring.

Now each party needs to make a decision:

✔ The firm needs to decide what to pay workers with different levels of education.

✔ The worker needs to decide what level of education to get.

To look at these decisions in the context of signaling, assume that there is no particular gain in productivity from any level of education. This seems ridiculous, we know, but the important part of the model at this point is the signal, not the productivity.

Supposing that the marginal cost of getting educated is lower for better workers means that $c_2 < c_1$. Also, $a_2 > a_1$, so a unique level of education e^* must exist that satisfies the following:

$$(a_2 - a_1)/c_1 < e^* < (a_2 - a_1)/c_2$$

Finding a signaling equilibrium

Assume that the signals hold perfectly and education is a perfect signal of the worker's marginal product. In that case, the wage must equal the marginal product, so a perfect signal is tantamount to the equilibrium where firms can observe workers directly. Now consider an outcome in which a poor worker chooses zero education, whereas a good worker chooses e^*.

Is this an equilibrium? For the firm, yes. It has a clear way, based on the choice of signal, to choose between workers, and can set a wage based on their marginal product.

What about for the poorer quality workers, those with product of a_1? Is it optimal for them to acquire e^* of education? The benefit would be $a_2 - a_1$ but the cost would be $c_1 e^*$. So a poor quality worker will have an incentive to get e^* levels of education only if

$$a_2 - a_1 > c_1 e^*$$

But you know from the choice of e^* that $c_1 e^*$ is bigger than $a_2 - a_1$. So, in this model, the benefits of getting e^* of education are less than the cost incurred, and so the poorer quality workers will choose equilibrium, zero education.

For the better quality workers, it's worth getting educated if $a_2 - a_1 > c_2 e^*$. The choice of e^* implies that this is true, so this logic works for better workers too.

Therefore, the equilibrium holds. Under these conditions, neither type of worker has any reason to change behavior.

This equilibrium is called a *separating equilibrium,* one based on subgroups of people within a population — whether producers or consumers — behaving differently from each other. The opposite, where they make the same choice, is called a *pooling equilibrium.* A pooling equilibrium would be if both types of workers acquire the same level of education e' and receive the pooling wage of $ba_2 + (1-b)a_1$, and no worker has an incentive to deviate and acquire a different level of education.

Evaluating the signaling equilibrium

The signaling equilibrium has some interesting implications for policy makers. The most important is that even if you believe that education has no effect on productivity, it's still worth getting if you're a high-productivity worker and want a higher wage.

In a Yale lecture, microeconomist Ben Polak describes the model as having a pessimistic conclusion. His points are as follows:

> ✔ For the signal to work, it has to be costly, and so $c_1 > c_2$. Within Spence's framework, that means that the cost of education is its key feature. So what you studied doesn't matter, only that you paid — in money or sweat — to study it.

✔ If that's the point of education, spending money on teachers' salaries is socially wasteful. (We prefer that you don't believe that conclusion.)

✔ Given that the value of the signal is related to its cost, a separating equilibrium like this one tends to exclude any high-productivity worker who starts out too poor to afford the opportunity cost c_2. So, signaling can hurt the poor and increases inequality.

Those conclusions are indeed pessimistic — for educators at least. Are they justified? Well, as long as you believe that the sole purpose of education is in signaling, you'd be entirely justified in holding those conclusions.

But education isn't only a signal. Many reasons exist for valuing education and they are not related to signaling. For instance, education can provide important skills that improve productivity. In addition, education confers social benefits such as active citizenship and better health outcomes. The signaling framework leaves these features of education out of the model.

So here's another lesson: Models can be *garbage in, garbage out*. If the thing you want to know about isn't built into the model, you're unlikely to be able to draw robust conclusions from it.

Part VI

The Part of Tens

Check out other great books at www.dummies.com.

In this part . . .

- Meet ten giants of the discipline.
- Consider ten microeconomic essentials.
- Get a grip on microeconomics terminology in a handy glossary.

Chapter 20

Meeting Ten Great Microeconomists

*I*n this chapter we introduce you to some great economists who inspired us to discover microeconomics. Microeconomics has become a broad and deep subject, and although we can't possibly do justice to all their work, we want to give you a flavor of some of their important results.

Many microeconomists have also made contributions to other subjects: macroeconomics, mathematics, sociology, law, and history being the most common. In fact, some people say that no such thing as a pure microeconomist exists! We have some agreement with that view, given the areas into which some of these greats have moved.

So what follows is a — perhaps slightly eccentric — list of inspiring and challenging thinkers. But they're just the tip of a huge iceberg, and we apologize — in some cases, sadly, posthumously — to all those we leave out. This job was as difficult as picking an all-time Fantasy Football team or the top ten greatest singles. We hope that given the scarcity of available places, you'll forgive the omissions.

Alfred Marshall (1842–1924)

The approach to microeconomics that we pursue in this book — which is the mainstream approach for the profession — is sometimes called *marginalism*, and much of it is due to Alfred Marshall. He started as a mathematician before switching to philosophy — this was before economics became a discipline in its own right. That change led him to look again at the work of the utilitarian philosophers and develop a theory based on their work that could improve the lives of the working classes.

Among his greatest achievements Marshall wrote *Principles of Economics,* which was a standard textbook for around 70 years, made economics a discipline in its own right at Cambridge, and invented the supply and demand graphs that economists know and love today.

Marshall's style was to try to communicate in the most understandable way, aiming much of his work outside the profession — with the meaty stuff going in technical appendices. Among the people he taught were John Maynard Keynes and Arthur Pigou, making him an important father figure to modern economics.

Joseph Alois Schumpeter (1883–1950)

Born in Triesch, in what's now the Czech Republic but was then part of Hapsburg Austria, Joseph Schumpeter made many great contributions to microeconomics, though not all were appreciated during his lifetime. He began his studies as a law student, but moved on into economics, eventually serving on the board of two private banks (both of which eventually ran into the ground) before moving to America to lecture at Harvard. There Schumpeter finally began to build the reputation that he has today.

Among Schumpeter's many contributions to economics was the idea of *creative destruction.* This applies theories of evolution to reasoning about the way firms innovate — over time. Old ideas, products, and firms may be destroyed by the way newer rivals create new ideas and businesses. In his great book *Capitalism, Socialism, and Democracy* (1942), he provided an account of how capitalism itself would come to an end, largely through its own successes — successful companies in capitalist societies would come to exert influence on politics, leading to demands for socialist policies and a falling rate of innovation instead of the revolutionary crises foreseen by Karl Marx. He was profoundly driven to understand the mysteries of entrepreneurship, producing two complementary accounts of how it happens — one as the result of heroic visionaries with a kind of spirit or outlook driving them and one as a result of large companies having the capital to invest.

Schumpeter was a famously devoted teacher and had a keen sense of humor. He wrote that he'd only had three goals: to be the greatest economist in the world, the best horseman in Austria, and the greatest lover in Vienna. He quipped that he'd only achieved two of the three, but never spelt out which two.

Gary S. Becker (1930–2014)

If you've seen articles in the popular press applying economic reasoning to all kinds of things — such as marriage, discrimination, or the political system — you've come across the work of Gary Becker, who held a chair at the famous department of Economics at the University of Chicago. He applied his rigorous understanding of the consumer behavior (introduced in Chapter 2) to all kinds of issues — generally things studied in sociology departments rather than economics ones.

Becker is famous, among other things, for his ground-breaking study of discrimination against minority groups. His analysis showed that the costs of discrimination tend also to fall upon people or firms who discriminate, meaning that they tend to incur higher production costs: Therefore, discrimination isn't really in the economic interests of a majority group. His insights into lobby groups and the democratic process are equally startling — showing that democratic and nondemocratic societies can both have a problem with the external costs imposed on other voters (in democracies) or other citizens (in nondemocratic societies) by overly successful lobbyists.

Most startlingly, Becker points out that utility maximization itself isn't necessarily selfish. If you place value on acting altruistically, it maximizes your utility to help others, and so criticisms of the utility model are misplaced and have more to do with framing than with reality.

Ronald Coase (1910–2013)

Ronald Coase was a British economist who spent much of his career as a professor at the University of Chicago, where he was practicing economics. He published his final book at the age of 102, long after most people have retired. Although Coase's career covered many areas of microeconomics, he's probably most famous for his analyses of law — he edited the famous *Journal of Law and Economics*.

Two papers of Coase's are considered absolute classics in microeconomics:

✔ **"The Nature of the Firm":** This essay from the 1930s looks at the motivations for forming companies. Speaking in the abstract, no real reason exists for having large complex companies do anything: Probably a lot of other structures could do the job. So why do these large companies get created?

His answer has to do with the costs of using the market itself — *transactions costs* — such as the cost of finding someone to do business with, the cost of getting the deal done, and the cost of enforcing the deal afterwards. An organization such as a company is a way to minimize these costs in one place so that they're easier to coordinate, and often it does so by making them internal to the company, where they become the costs of administration.

So you can see companies as a cycle: When transactions costs are high, companies form; and when the costs are fully internalized, the administrative burden can choke the company, leading to a breakup and the formation of new companies.

✔ **"The Problem of Social Cost":** This paper contributed to dealing with externality. Coase's insight was that without transactions costs, to whom or to which side of a deal a property right is allocated makes no difference to achieving an efficient outcome. But *with* transactions costs, it does matter: The rights should go to the person whose action will lead to the economically efficient outcome. Later, his reasoning became widely known as the basis for "the Coase theorem" — even though he never felt that it was truly based on his work. We discuss the theorem, externality, and property rights in Chapter 14.

Elinor Ostrom (1933–2012)

Any list of great scholars in the academy is likely to be dominated by men. In fact, historically, economics as a discipline has a male bias (don't worry, microeconomists are already studying why, of course). But of all the recent winners of the Nobel Prize in Economics, perhaps one of the most important is Elinor Ostrom, the only woman to win the prize so far.

Ostrom was a professor at Indiana University, working on *public choice economics* — the area that studies how people and institutions interact. On field trips to Africa and Himalayan Asia she codified an approach to dealing with the problems of looking after things that no one owns — what microeconomists call *common pool or property resources,* such as the ecosystem of the plains of the Serengeti.

By looking at how indigenous peoples did things, she advanced a strong criticism of many of the approaches people used to deal with the Tragedy of the Commons (discussed in Chapter 14). She pointed out that as long as people can agree on certain principles, indigenous societies are perfectly capable of managing the commons without ecological collapse. This result challenges most traditional schools of economic or political analysis.

Ostrom did much of her work on these kinds of problems, which meant that she studied areas such as reciprocity or trust that aren't immediately or obviously parts of the economist's toolkit. Along the way, she also co-wrote one of the most important textbooks on modeling cooperation using game theory (the subject of Chapter 16).

William Vickrey (1914–96)

Canadian economist William Vickrey was posthumously awarded the Nobel Prize in 1996, largely for his work applying game theory and incentive theory to situations with asymmetric information (see Chapter 15). He was a professor at Columbia University for much of his career, and in that role he turned out a stunning amount of work, stretching over many areas of economics — we wouldn't have even attempted Chapter 18 (on auctions) without his work. Vickrey's most famous paper was his study of stamp collector auctions in 1961, where he rediscovered and worked out the logic behind the traditional use of a second-price winner in auctions. He then showed how to use this insight to prevent winner's curse problems (again, see Chapter 18).

Vickrey's contribution to public economics, and his applied work looking at government, is also extremely important. For instance, levying a charge on drivers in congested traffic zones in London is based on some of the work that Vickrey did looking at road pricing.

A devout Quaker, Vickrey also believed that full employment in society was a moral question and devoted much of his other research time to proposing schemes to remedy idleness. In this aim, he was less successful.

George Akerlof (born 1940)

George Akerlof, currently a professor at Georgetown University, won his Nobel Prize in 2001 (together with Joseph Stigliz and Michael Spence) for his research on information problems or imperfect information in market trades. His famous "Market for Lemons" in Chapter 15 is a fine example and a classic paper to many microeconomists.

Akerlof's work on information problems extended to his work on signaling in labor markets (see Chapter 19). He points out that paying higher wages may not be sub-optimal if the threat of losing a wage premium when going to a rival company is enough to keep worker productivity higher in the higher-paying company. He co-wrote this paper with his substantially more famous wife, Janet Yellen, who's currently the Chair of the Board of Governors of the Federal Reserve System.

More recently, Akerlof looked at how psychology is central to decision making, exploring how people's sense of identity affects their decisions. People don't just have preferences on which they act, they also have to respect certain types of social norm, which conditions how markets behave in reality.

Joseph Stiglitz (born 1943)

Joe Stiglitz, a professor at Columbia University, is considered to be one of the most influential economists alive — in 2011, *Time* magazine named him one of the 100 most influential people in the world. Stiglitz's most famous work is on how markets work under imperfect and asymmetric information (Chapters 15 and 19) for which he shared the Nobel Prize in 2001 with George Akerlof and Michael Spence.

His research calls into question the efficiency of markets when information is imperfect and there is uninsured risk. Stiglitz makes the case for government intervention in the market much stronger and the case for the "invisible hand" much weaker. The policy debate today, informed by Stiglitz's research, is about finding the right balance between the market and government. Besides having written seminal academic papers in economics, Stiglitz is also the author of several books, his most recent being *The Great Divide: Unequal Societies and What We Can Do About Them* (W.W. Norton, 2015).

William Baumol (born 1922)

A professor of economics at New York University, William Baumol is one of the most prolific authors in the field of microeconomics. Perhaps his most important contribution is looking at entrepreneurship, bringing Joseph Schumpeter's insights into mainstream economics and coming up with ways of dealing with one of the most important gaps in the traditional microeconomic literature.

Microeconomics' problems in understanding innovation are many and being worked on as we write. One of the problems is captured in an old joke about how long it will take to pick up a $100 bill that is dropped in the middle of Wall Street. The punchline — "If there really were a bill, someone would've picked it up by now" — expresses a dilemma in entrepreneurship and innovation: If there was a new and profitable idea, then someone would have already invented it. Baumol drew on the Schumpeterian tradition by providing an account of what entrepreneurs do to begin new companies and how they make new kinds of business work. Baumol has also written about macroeconomics, the tendency of costs in service industries to rise without corresponding rises in productivity — often called Baumol's cost disease — and how the threat of entry can keep monopolies from raising their prices. He's also famous for his interest in the economics of the arts, writing a spectacular paper on the economics of composition in Mozart's Vienna.

Arthur Cecil Pigou (1877–1959)

Although we haven't gone through the enormous economic literature on the environment — yes, many economists have studied it — we do want to pay tribute to British economist Arthur Cecil Pigou. He was Alfred Marshall's successor as Professor of Political Economy at Cambridge University, and a friend — though you wouldn't believe it from their arguments — of John Maynard Keynes.

Pigou wrote about many subjects, including contributions on which modern labor economics is built. But perhaps his most enduring and best remembered work is on welfare (see Chapter 12) – his 1920 book *The Economics of Welfare* introduced the concept of externality to economics. He came up with the idea of using what are now called Pigovian taxes to remedy some of the social costs of private actions (check out Chapter 14 for details). His influence is still felt to this day in the existence of the Pigou Club, an informal and nonparty-aligned group of economists who want to see carbon taxes implemented.

A conscientious objector in the First World War, he spent his vacations from Cambridge serving with the Friends Ambulance Unit on the front line — volunteering for the most dangerous rescue and recovery missions.

Chapter 21

Top Ten Tips to Take Away

Microeconomics is a huge area of study, and no one can do the entire subject justice in one book — all of your authors are proud owners of entire shelves full of microeconomic textbooks. You can, however, take away many of the most important core ideas of microeconomics from this book.

So without more ado, here are ten important points to remember from this book.

Respecting Choice

All microeconomics is built on the idea that consumers and producers make choices about what to make or what to buy. As a result, economists tend to have a healthy respect for choice itself. People value things in different ways, and economists want to look at the consequences of, rather than the reasons for, those values. You only get to know what value people place on something after they choose it — or as economists say, you get to know people's preferences when they have chosen (they also say that there are as many valuations as people).

Trade is possible because people value things differently. The desire to trade creates the need for a means to trade things — a market.

In a famous paper, "The Economic Organization of a Prisoner of War Camp," Richard Radford, an economist interred in a POW camp, described the need for a means to trade in detail. Starting with Red Cross packages, prisoners traded allowances with each other to make themselves better off. For instance, Gurkhas, being strict Hindus, were only too happy to trade meat for other goods. At first, these trades were done by bartering goods directly, but eventually, through evolution and without anyone making an overall strategic decision, the camps alighted on using tobacco rations as currency — a simple form of money. At this point, very simply, the POWs had created a market.

The result of properly functioning markets is, over the long run, the betterment of everyone. The market relies on people choosing, and economists generally prefer an allocative mechanism that allows people to choose — for instance, by designing mechanisms that let people choose within a framework — as opposed to coming in and preventing or prescribing choice.

Pricing a Good: Difficult but not Impossible

In several situations, a market has difficulty pricing a good. One case is when the marginal cost of the good is at or near zero — a competitive market ends up with no one being able to price above zero and everyone scrambling around for other ways to make money. Public goods — such as street lighting, public parks, or even law enforcement — are another case, one made worse by the impossibility of excluding people who haven't paid for these services from using them (check out Chapter 14).

But just because a market finding a competitively sustainable solution is difficult, that doesn't mean it's impossible. For instance, television broadcasts can be distributed to an extra person at zero marginal cost. In this industry, firms found a way to price something else — advertising — effectively using programming as a lure to sell viewers' attention to advertisers. Another possibility is selling "membership" to a club as a way of getting access — in essence, a subscription model.

People are essentially creative in such situations. When they come up against an unfavorable economic situation, they try to find solutions to get around the problem. Economists have great respect for this creativity, which is one reason why they want to see what can be achieved without intervening, before coming up with ways to intervene.

Competing on Price or Quality

In a perfectly competitive market, competition is only ever on price, which is always forced down to the marginal cost of production for the marginal firm. But in many market structures, competing on price is tough, and firms have an incentive to focus on other dimensions of their product.

If you start in monopolistic competition (see Chapter 13) — which is a common market structure — you can see why. If you compete on price, over the long run, the price gets pushed down to average cost, and the firm doesn't make profits. The alternative is to change your focus and try to make your product different or distinctive from the other competitors and, in so doing, make nonzero profits. However, you need to invest to do that, and if you're investing in keeping the product different or better, you're using resources that you could've spent on getting costs down.

This problem is one reason why firms tend to choose either to be the lowest-cost competitor or a high-quality competitor. The alternative is generally pleasing neither to people who want things cheap nor to those who want good quality.

Seeking Real Markets' Unique Features

This book discusses lots of ways in which markets are structured, and the economic literature contains many more. What they all have in common are the basic assumptions about what people may do — whether deciding to produce or consume — in those markets. But in reality, markets do have unique and distinctive features — such as, for example, in health care — that often vary from place to place and product to product.

When economists come across distinctive features, they explore the differences between that market and a more generic one. Sometimes they propose ways to make such markets more productive or efficient. Most importantly, economists look very carefully at why a particular market exhibits those features before they rush in and call it a market failure. Instead, they ask a number of questions: Is the market like that because people value things in a particular way? Is a distortion involved, such as a tax or a subsidy? Are there very high sunk costs?

Generic models form a starting point for comparison. Economists aren't trying to say a given market should be exactly like this or that.

Beating the Market in the Long Run is Very Difficult

The phrase *you can't beat the market* is the kind of saying that drives economists to distraction. For a start, when transaction costs are high, a market in many cases is not the most efficient organizational design. Plus, it's just not realistic to suggest, for instance, that all firms should abandon management structures and replace them with internal markets. Firms are market-facing on the outside, but above a certain size, many of the jobs in a given company aren't involved in dealing with market transactions. Professors don't offer their classes at market-clearing prices. When economists say that you can't beat the market, they're pointing out that we know that markets can be shown to achieve the highest level of efficiency. In a general equilibrium model (see Chapter 12), for example, the contract curve of best choices relies on people being able to trade their way to their highest level of utility. But that doesn't mean that doing so is feasible — general equilibrium rests on some strong assumptions. Nor does it mean that a market in every instance is practical. In the Renaissance, Italian city-states hired private armies called *condottieri*. But they had great difficulty ensuring that condottieri followed orders — in some cases, the soldiers just came in and took over the city. The fact that few places would prefer a mercenary army today is no coincidence.

Having said all that, always be skeptical of people's claims that they can make long-run profits — and therefore, if you're an investor, returns — greater than the average of those in the market they're in. Why? Well, if they could, someone would come in and compete them away. If we can persuade you to take one piece of advice from us, it's this: *Watch your wallet when anyone claims to be able to beat the market in the long run.*

Knowing a Tradeoff Always Exists Somewhere

The economist's model of consumer behavior is called a *constrained optimization* — because ultimately you're trying to do your best given that you can't have everything (see Chapter 5). As a result, at some point you have to choose between one option and another because you can't have both.

As long as things are scarce, you have to make choices. To an economist, this is just a fact of life, and you may as well complain about gravity as about scarcity. That means that getting your best level of utility is always about trading off one thing for another.

A similar situation happens when you try to balance efficiency and fairness. Now, in the short run a society can be so far away from peak efficiency *and* complete fairness that a gain in both is possible. But if you're at the constraint or very near it, trying to prioritize equity leads to a fall in efficiency unless you can do it by lump-sum transfers — which again may not be practical.

A good rule for looking at the world is that if you see a free lunch, ask who's paying for it: If you're not, someone else probably is. When a product seems free — as it does for some Internet services, especially in social media, check whether the product is actually you — or more accurately, your personal information that has a value to whoever is offering the service "free."

Arguing about the Next Best Thing

Throughout the book, we look at the optimal decision for people or firms (Chapters 2–8) or society (Chapter 12 especially) to make. Here's a little problem though: As Mick Jagger sang, you can't always get what you want. Microeconomics has some advice for you though. An economic principle, the *Theory of the Second Best,* reminds us that if you can't get the optimal solution, then there may be second-best alternatives.

Suppose, for instance, that a polluting monopoly produces your electricity — imagine that electricity can only be made using smoggy coal. Then, if you're a policy maker and you act to counteract the monopoly, you increase output and produce more smog. So, your best choice under the circumstances isn't immediately clear. Should you increase production, by dealing with the market inefficiency of monopoly, or mitigate the pollution while keeping the monopoly in place?

 Although getting the optimal isn't possible, you can certainly argue about what the next best thing is. Economists recommend that you look carefully at the inefficiency and the external cost in this situation before coming up with a solution.

When you hear politicians arguing about what to do, remember that often the argument isn't about what the best thing is, but which of several "practical" options is the second best. You can then choose, on the basis of your investigations, and sometimes on which party you want to support.

Using Markets Isn't Always Costless

Even though economists generally prefer free exchange — and therefore markets — as their way of achieving goals, using those markets isn't always costless. Sometimes, an unaccounted cost falls upon another person — an *external cost* — and sometimes there are costs associated with just finding the person to trade with — *transactions costs.*

To an economist, the key question is what makes those costs as low as possible? The answer isn't as simple as just saying that a market inevitably keeps those costs at the lowest possible level, because using the market may not be as "free" as a standard textbook implies.

If, for instance, a hundred painters of varying quality work in your town, and you don't know any of them because you've just moved there, how can you know which one to hire to paint your house? You probably spend a fair amount of time looking for one, getting recommendations on their reliability, quality, and likelihood of leaving your house a mess. These activities are all costs, and they all come about precisely *because* you're using a market to find the person.

Economists have two pieces of advice here:

✔ Think carefully about where the inevitable costs of using a market fall.

✔ Seek out the opportunities that always exist for entrepreneurs with good ideas for reducing transactions costs for buyers and sellers.

Believing that Competition is Good — Usually

Any time a market isn't perfectly competitive, the firms in the industry are getting a greater share of the gains from trade. As a result, they always have an interest in preventing another firm from coming in and competing away the gains. They may erect barriers to do so — including advertising, investing in things that involve sunk costs, and making their product or brand different or unique in the consumer's eye.

These tactics can prevent a rival, even one producing at a lower cost, from competing and taking away some market share. Consumers lose out because the incumbent producers produce less, for higher cost, and take more of the surplus. For this reason, economists look carefully at barriers to market entry and work to get them down as low as possible in the long run.

But that isn't the whole story. There are times when economists give two cheers to markets that aren't competitive. For example, a monopolist doesn't compete with itself, which can mean that you can get a better range of product diversity when there is less competition.

Research in Australia, for instance, suggested that in order to get a different genre of television programming than the prevalent soaps in a prime-time slot, the market would require five TV channels, because the first four competing for viewers would find that making soaps was the best strategy. A monopolist, however, could instead produce a different genre for each channel, because that maximizes the profit from each "slice" of the market.

Suppose that 80 percent of Australia liked soaps in that time slot. Then the first channel would produce soaps, hoping to get 80 percent of the market. The second would also (two channels competing for 80 percent of the market would get around 40 percent each). So would the third and fourth (because 80 divided by 4 is 20 percent). It's not until you get to the fifth channel that the expected share of the market from producing something different matches the expected share from producing soaps.

In some markets, competition costs too much because it means that competitors can't produce at a big enough scale. In others — for example, Internet search — competition can't happen because the market has a winner-takes-all feature. The more people using a search engine, the better the search engine. But if a possibility exists of getting a result from a competitive market, many economists take it as the best option.

Getting Cooperation and Organization in the World

Economics often gets a bad rap because the assumed behavior of individuals in economics seems selfish, because the model of people and firms seems to make a priority of individual benefit, and even because the model of an individual making decisions doesn't try to reproduce many of the features people think of as essential. But in fact economists are the world's greatest optimists. Why? Well, economic models are built from no greater assumption than that people follow their own interests — and in so doing, create firms, organizations, production, and consumption, and all the things that make the world go round!

You may disagree that this world is ideal — many people do. But what's remarkable to the economist is that even if you don't expect people to follow what Abraham Lincoln called "the better angels of our nature," you still get cooperation as people get together and form companies, and people following their own interests create and trade in markets.

Glossary

● ●

Adverse selection: An outcome caused by *asymmetric information* where a product is selected only by the people who'll make the worst returns for a supplier — for example, only people with risky lifestyles buying life insurance. The typical effect is that the market fails.

Agent: (1) Anyone who acts in an economic model. (2) In the principal-agent model, anyone who acts on behalf of the principal.

Allocative efficiency: When a firm produces up to the point where *price* equals *marginal cost*. As a result, when firms are allocatively efficient, no deadweight loss exists because the price paid by consumers equals the marginal cost incurred.

Asymmetric information: A situation in which one side of a trade knows more relevant information than the other — for example, when sellers know more about the quality or performance of their product than buyers.

Auction: A way of selling a good where an auctioneer calls out prices and solicits bids from potential buyers. The good being auctioned goes to one buyer — usually the highest bidder.

Average cost: Total cost divided by the number of units of output produced — in other words, costs per unit output.

Backward induction: A method of solving dynamic games by starting at the end *payoffs* and working backwards, eliminating any move that would yield a lower payoff.

Barriers to entry: Anything that significantly raises the irrecoverable or sunk cost to a firm of entering a market and thus deters one from entering.

Bertrand oligopoly: A model of *oligopoly* where firms compete in price and react to each other's decisions on price.

Cartel: A group of firms acting together to maximize their collective *profits*. Cartels try to secure *monopoly* profits for their members and therefore impose *deadweight losses* on everyone else.

Coordination game: A type of *game theory* model where the best outcome depends on participants being able to coordinate their actions. The *stag hunt* is one such game.

Cournot oligopoly: A model of *oligopoly* where firms compete in quantities and react to each other's decisions on quantity.

Deadweight loss: A loss of *welfare* (producer plus consumer surpluses) that occurs because production isn't *allocatively efficient*. Deadweight losses are lost to producers and consumers and therefore to society as a whole.

Demand curve: In the *supply and demand* model, relates the quantity purchased to the price of the good — holding income, prices of other goods, and tastes constant. It generally slopes downwards: As price rises, quantity demanded goes down.

Demand function: Any mathematical description of quantity purchased in terms of prices.

Deterrence: In *game theory*, deterrent strategies are those whose purpose is to deter a rival from taking an action by signaling that the rival's *payoffs* will be lower if it takes that action. The word is often used in terms of preventing a firm from entering a market.

Dominant strategy: A *strategy* that gives higher *payoffs* no matter what the opponent does.

Duopoly: Any market supplied by only two firms.

Dutch auction: Where the auctioneer calls out descending prices until a bidder determines that the price is low enough to buy and calls "mine."

English auction: Where the auctioneer starts at a low price and in successive rounds of bidding raises the price until only one bidder is left.

Externality: A benefit or cost that falls on a third party not included in a transaction. Externalities can be negative — costs — or positive — benefits.

External cost: A cost that falls on a third party. If A and B trade and C, who isn't involved in the trade, gets burdened with some cost, C is experiencing an external cost.

Factor of production: The basic inputs of a firm — land, labor, and capital. The firm combines them using a *technology* to produce its output.

Fixed cost: Costs that don't depend on how many units of output a firm produces. For example, for a football team, the cost of constructing a stadium is a fixed cost, because it costs the same to build no matter how many games are played there. It is also a sunk cost if it has no resale value.

Game theory: A branch of mathematics relevant to understanding strategic interaction, modeling what strategy each player will take given the *payoff* to that strategy, given the strategies of other players, and investigating an equilibrium outcome for all players.

General equilibrium: A concept used to define an equilibrium in all markets in an economy. In a general equilibrium, all markets are simultaneously in equilibrium; in a *partial equilibrium*, only one market is in equilibrium.

Hotelling's law: An observation that under certain conditions, firms will in equilibrium choose to market products that are minimally differentiated from each other.

Indifference curve: Different bundles of goods that yield the same level of utility to an individual.

Isocost: A cost curve where the cost is the same at all combinations of inputs along the curve.

Isoquant: A curve that shows all the combinations of inputs that produce the same output at all points along the curve.

Iterated elimination of dominant strategies: A method for solving games by eliminating at each step strategies that a rational player motivated to maximize his or her payoff would never choose.

Marginal cost: The cost incurred by a firm for producing one additional unit of output.

Marginal revenue: The revenue a firm earns from selling one additional unit of a product.

Marginal social cost: The cost incurred to society (including the firm) when an additional unit of output is produced.

Mixed strategy: A *strategy* in which the player assigns a probability to each of the pure strategies available to the player. For instance, a mixed strategy in Rock, Paper, Scissors is playing rock, paper, and scissors each about 1/3 of the time.

Monopolistic competition: A type of market structure with free entry and exit but where competing firms each attempt to differentiate their brand of product. It yields some *welfare* losses because firms do not produce at the minimum of average cost.

Monopoly: A market served by only one firm and as a result the firm is able to set price higher than marginal cost and, if there are barriers to entry, can earn profit.

Moral hazard: A feature of a market in which there is *asymmetric information,* and someone takes on more risk because she knows that someone else will bear the costs of those risks — for instance, leaving your door unlocked because you have generous home insurance.

Nash equilibrium: In *game theory*, any outcome where each player is doing the best they can do, given other players' strategies. At a Nash equilibrium, no party has an incentive to change *strategy.*

Oligopoly: A market served by few firms with some barriers to entry and exit. Firms in an oligopoly interact strategically given each other's strategies.

Pareto efficiency: A distribution where making one party better off without making another party worse off is not feasible.

Partial equilibrium: An equilibrium where *supply and demand* are equal in a particular market, as opposed to *general equilibrium* where they're equal in all markets.

Payoff: The benefit or loss a player receives in the outcome of a game.

Perfect competition: An idealized market structure where a large number of producers are making the same product, each is small relative to the market, and their decisions cannot influence price. The result is that profit-maximization leads to price equal to *marginal cost*.

Pooled equilibrium: This occurs in a market with asymmetric information in which there are two types of traders with different characteristics, but in equilibrium choose the same action so that their uninformed trading partner cannot distinguish between them.

Prisoners' Dilemma: A *game theory* model where the two players rationally choose a strategy that leads them to an outcome that only could be achieved if the players can commit to cooperation.

Productive efficiency: Productive efficiency is achieved when firms are producing output at the lowest possible cost, at the minimum of the long-run average cost curve.

Profit: The residual left over after all relevant costs have been taken away from a firm's revenue.

Pure strategy: A *strategy* chosen by a player with probability equal to one. As a result, pure strategy equilibrium is a deterministic description of how a game will be played. In contrast, the outcome of a *mixed strategy* equilibrium is probabilistic.

Reaction function: A description of what is the profit-maximizing strategy of one firm in an *oligopoly* in reaction to its competitor's strategy.

Separating equilibrium: This occurs in a market with asymmetric information in which there are two types of traders with different characteristics, but in equilibrium they choose different actions so that their uninformed trading partner can by their actions distinguish between them.

Signal: The term used in a game with asymmetric information in which the action of a player reveals information to the other uninformed players.

Stackelberg oligopoly: A model of an *oligopoly* where one firm is the leader and moves first and in so doing is able to anticipate the reactions of other firms and take them into account when making its decision. A Stackelberg oligopoly outcome leads to more output produced than a *Cournot oligopoly*.

Stag hunt: A type of *coordination game* with two *Nash equilibria*, one that maximizes the *payoffs to players* and one that minimizes risk of a low payoff.

Strategy: A set of actions that describes how a player will move at each turn in a game. A strategy must describe each action at each possible point in the game regardless of whether that point will be arrived at in the course of the game.

Sunk costs: Costs that are unrecoverable after being incurred.

Supply curve: A curve that describes how much output will be produced in a perfectly competitive firm or industry at each possible price.

Supply and demand: A model macroeconomists use to look at prices and quantities in a perfectly competitive market. The equilibrium in the model is where supply equals demand, which is where the supply and demand curves cross.

Switching cost: The cost incurred by a consumer changing from one product to another — for example, in switching from one type of word processor to another. Switching costs may come from the *sunk cost* of learning how to use a product, from having to give up complements, or from loss of opportunities to trade with other consumers.

Technology: Any method for transforming inputs into outputs, most often used to describe the mix of capital and labor a firm chooses.

Tragedy of the Commons: A situation where a common resource is overexploited because no one owns it and access can't be controlled.

Transactions costs: The costs incurred by a firm using a market to make a trade, including the costs incurred searching for people to deal with, negotiating a trade with a partner, and enforcing a deal when made.

Trust game: A type of game where one player has to decide whether to trust another player, and if she does, the other player has to decide whether or not to betray that trust.

Utility function: A description of the utility a consumer gains from consuming a bundle of goods. Utility functions depend on consumers' preferences.

Variable cost: A cost that depends on the number of units of output that a firm produces.

Vickrey auction: A type of *auction* where the highest (or lowest) bidder gets the good (the contract) for the price bid by the second-highest (or second-lowest) bidder. Vickrey auctions are designed to avoid the incentive to overbid (or underbid).

Welfare: A measure of the value created across all consumers and producers in a market equilibrium. In a partial equilibrium model, it's the sum of consumer and producer surpluses. In a general equilibrium model, it's the sum of all utility and profits gained by all agents in the model.

Index

About the Author

Lynne Pepall is professor of economics at Tufts University in Medford, Massachusetts. Professor Pepall received her undergraduate degree in mathematics and economics from Trinity College, University of Toronto, and her PhD in economics from the University of Cambridge in England. She has written numerous papers in microeconomics and in industrial organization, appearing in *The Journal of Finance, The Journal of Industrial Economics, Economic Journal, Economica,* and other publications. She has taught industrial organization and microeconomics, with enthusiasm, at both the graduate and undergraduate levels, and is the co-author of a leading undergraduate textbook in industrial organization, *Industrial Organization: Contemporary Theory and Empirical Applications,* also published by Wiley. From 2007–2013 Professor Pepall served as Dean of the Graduate School of Arts and Sciences at Tufts University. She was a Visiting Economist in the Economic Analysis Group of the Antitrust Division, U.S. Department of Justice in 2013–2014. She lives in Newton, Massachusetts with her husband, sometimes one or two sons, and a lively golden retriever called Nelson.

Peter Antonioni is a senior teaching fellow in the Department of Management Science and Innovation at University College London, where he teaches strategy. His research interests are in the economic history of music production. If not working, he can usually be found crying over Tottenham Hotspurs' most recent performance or putting his angst into playing blues guitar.

Manzur Rashid read economics at Trinity College, Cambridge, where he graduated with a double first and was elected to junior, senior, and research scholarships. He completed his doctoral studies in economic theory at UCL, where he specialized in game theory, bounded rationality, and industrial organization, under the supervision of Martin Cripps. Manzur has taught economics at UCL, Cambridge University, New College of the Humanities, and Charterhouse.

Dedications

Lynne: To my partner in life and in economics, Dan, my sons Ben and Will, and my golden Nelson.

Peter: To Tanya, Mum, Dad, Paul, and Jen, who suffered most from me writing this.

Manzur: For Ilyas.

Author's Acknowledgments

Lynne: Thank you to Tufts University and my colleagues in economics for their academic inspirations and to the wonderful people at Wiley, Tracy Boggier and Corbin Collins, for their commitment and support. It takes a village!

Peter: With many thanks to the support of my colleagues at UCL, and to the many economists who once had to explain patiently all this material to me.

Manzur: I am grateful to all the people at Wiley — including Mike Baker, Simon Bell, Steve Edwards, Andy Finch, Annie Knight, and Kate O'Leary — who helped us to get this book into shape. I am also grateful to Ron Smith for his helpful suggestions and comments. Thanks to my friends and family for their endless support. Finally, thank you to my teachers: Martin Cripps, Hamish Low, Rupert Gatti, Steve Satchell, Gernot Doppelhofer, and Kevin Sheedy.

Publisher's Acknowledgments

Acquisitions Editor: Tracy Boggier

Editor: Corbin Collins

Project Coordinator: Kinson Raja

Cover Image: © SusaZoom/Shutterstock, Westend61/Getty Images, Inc.

Apple & Mac

iPad For Dummies,
6th Edition
978-1-118-72306-7

iPhone For Dummies,
7th Edition
978-1-118-69083-3

Macs All-in-One
For Dummies, 4th Edition
978-1-118-82210-4

OS X Mavericks
For Dummies
978-1-118-69188-5

Blogging & Social Media

Facebook For Dummies,
5th Edition
978-1-118-63312-0

Social Media Engagement
For Dummies
978-1-118-53019-1

WordPress For Dummies,
6th Edition
978-1-118-79161-5

Business

Stock Investing
For Dummies, 4th Edition
978-1-118-37678-2

Investing For Dummies,
6th Edition
978-0-470-90545-6

Personal Finance

Personal Finance
For Dummies, 7th Edition
978-1-118-11785-9

QuickBooks 2014
For Dummies
978-1-118-72005-9

Small Business Marketing
Kit For Dummies,
3rd Edition
978-1-118-31183-7

Careers

Job Interviews
For Dummies, 4th Edition
978-1-118-11290-8

Job Searching with Social
Media For Dummies,
2nd Edition
978-1-118-67856-5

Personal Branding
For Dummies
978-1-118-11792-7

Resumes For Dummies,
6th Edition
978-0-470-87361-8

Starting an Etsy Business
For Dummies, 2nd Edition
978-1-118-59024-9

Diet & Nutrition

Belly Fat Diet For Dummies
978-1-118-34585-6

Mediterranean Diet
For Dummies
978-1-118-71525-3

Nutrition For Dummies,
5th Edition
978-0-470-93231-5

Digital Photography

Digital SLR Photography
All-in-One For Dummies,
2nd Edition
978-1-118-59082-9

Digital SLR Video &
Filmmaking For Dummies
978-1-118-36598-4

Photoshop Elements 12
For Dummies
978-1-118-72714-0

Gardening

Herb Gardening
For Dummies, 2nd Edition
978-0-470-61778-6

Gardening with Free-Range
Chickens For Dummies
978-1-118-54754-0

Health

Boosting Your Immunity
For Dummies
978-1-118-40200-9

Diabetes For Dummies,
4th Edition
978-1-118-29447-5

Living Paleo For Dummies
978-1-118-29405-5

Big Data

Big Data For Dummies
978-1-118-50422-2

Data Visualization
For Dummies
978-1-118-50289-1

Hadoop For Dummies
978-1-118-60755-8

Language &
Foreign Language

500 Spanish Verbs
For Dummies
978-1-118-02382-2

English Grammar
For Dummies, 2nd Edition
978-0-470-54664-2

French All-In-One
For Dummies
978-1-118-22815-9

German Essentials
For Dummies
978-1-118-18422-6

Italian For Dummies,
2nd Edition
978-1-118-00465-4

𝑒 Available in print and e-book formats.

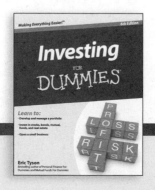

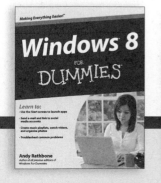

Available wherever books are sold. **For more information or to order direct visit www.dummies.com**

Math & Science

Algebra I For Dummies,
2nd Edition
978-0-470-55964-2

Anatomy and Physiology
For Dummies, 2nd Edition
978-0-470-92326-9

Astronomy For Dummies,
3rd Edition
978-1-118-37697-3

Biology For Dummies,
2nd Edition
978-0-470-59875-7

Chemistry For Dummies,
2nd Edition
978-1-118-00730-3

1001 Algebra II Practice
Problems For Dummies
978-1-118-44662-1

Microsoft Office

Excel 2013 For Dummies
978-1-118-51012-4

Office 2013 All-in-One
For Dummies
978-1-118-51636-2

PowerPoint 2013
For Dummies
978-1-118-50253-2

Word 2013 For Dummies
978-1-118-49123-2

Music

Blues Harmonica
For Dummies
978-1-118-25269-7

Guitar For Dummies,
3rd Edition
978-1-118-11554-1

iPod & iTunes
For Dummies, 10th Edition
978-1-118-50864-0

Programming

Beginning Programming
with C For Dummies
978-1-118-73763-7

Excel VBA Programming
For Dummies, 3rd Edition
978-1-118-49037-2

Java For Dummies,
6th Edition
978-1-118-40780-6

Religion & Inspiration

The Bible For Dummies
978-0-7645-5296-0

Buddhism For Dummies,
2nd Edition
978-1-118-02379-2

Catholicism For Dummies,
2nd Edition
978-1-118-07778-8

Self-Help & Relationships

Beating Sugar Addiction
For Dummies
978-1-118-54645-1

Meditation For Dummies,
3rd Edition
978-1-118-29144-3

Seniors

Laptops For Seniors
For Dummies, 3rd Edition
978-1-118-71105-7

Computers For Seniors
For Dummies, 3rd Edition
978-1-118-11553-4

iPad For Seniors
For Dummies, 6th Edition
978-1-118-72826-0

Social Security
For Dummies
978-1-118-20573-0

Smartphones & Tablets

Android Phones
For Dummies, 2nd Edition
978-1-118-72030-1

Nexus Tablets
For Dummies
978-1-118-77243-0

Samsung Galaxy S 4
For Dummies
978-1-118-64222-1

Samsung Galaxy Tabs
For Dummies
978-1-118-77294-2

Test Prep

ACT For Dummies,
5th Edition
978-1-118-01259-8

ASVAB For Dummies,
3rd Edition
978-0-470-63760-9

GRE For Dummies,
7th Edition
978-0-470-88921-3

Officer Candidate Tests
For Dummies
978-0-470-59876-4

Physician's Assistant Exam
For Dummies
978-1-118-11556-5

Series 7 Exam For Dummies
978-0-470-09932-2

Windows 8

Windows 8.1 All-in-One
For Dummies
978-1-118-82087-2

Windows 8.1 For Dummies
978-1-118-82121-3

Windows 8.1 For Dummies,
Book + DVD Bundle
978-1-118-82107-7

Available in print and e-book formats.

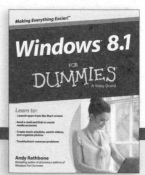

Available wherever books are sold. **For more information or to order direct visit www.dummies.com**